Teacher's Edition 

Phillip K. Trocki

Modern Curriculum Press

Acknowledgments

EXECUTIVE EDITOR Wendy Whitnah

PROJECT EDITOR Diane Dzamtovski

EDITORIAL DEVELOPMENT
DESIGN AND PRODUCTION The Hampton-Brown Company

ILLUSTRATORS Anthony Accardo, Peter Bianco, Joe Boddy, Mike Eagle, Ralph Hayashida, Meryl Henderson, Jane McCreary, Masami Miyamoto, Rik Olson, Doug Roy, Rod Thomas, John Sandford, Mike Schnorr, Joyce Zarins.

PHOTO CREDITS 8, Carol Palmer/Andrew Brilliant-Carol Palmer Photography; 18, Obremski/Image Bank; 24, Steve Takatsuno/The Picture Cube; 34, Ellis Herwig/The Picture Cube; 56, Mary Messenger/Mary Messenger Photography; 80, David Garvey/Image Bank; 82, Stewart M. Green/Tom Stack & Associates; 90, David M. Doody/Tom Stack & Associates; 96, Andrew Brilliant/Andrew Brilliant-Carol Palmer Photography; 112, Mary Messenger/Mary MessengerPhotography; 114, Carol Palmer/Andrew Brilliant-Carol Palmer Photography; 118, Mikki Ansin/The Picture Cube; 128, Al Lowry/Photo Researchers; 130, Jaye R. Phillips/The Picture Cube; 138, National Aeronautics & Space Administration (NASA); 142, Andrew Brilliant/Andrew Brilliant-Carol Palmer Photography.

COVER DESIGN The Hampton-Brown Company
COVER PHOTO Melchior DiGiacomo/Image Bank

Typefaces for the cursive type in this book were provided by Zaner-Bloser, Inc., Columbus, Ohio, copyright, 1993.

ISBN 0-8136-2846-6
Printed in the United States of America
16 17 18 19 20 V088 17 16 15 14 13

1-800-321-3106
www.pearsonlearning.com

Table of Contents

Integration of Spelling with Writing

Spelling Workout provides for the integration of writing, and spelling. In each lesson, students are asked to *write* about a topic related to the Bonus Words using various forms, such as poems, reports, advertisements, editorials, and letters.

The study of spelling should not be limited to a specific time in the school day. Use opportunities throughout the day to reinforce and maintain spelling skills by integrating spelling with other curriculum areas. Point out spelling words in books, texts, and the student's own writing. Encourage students to write. Students practice spelling through writing. Provide opportunities for writing with a purpose.

Across the Curriculum with Spelling Words

Each lesson of *Spelling Workout* contains a list of Bonus Words. These words were drawn from many subject areas including science, social studies, health, language arts, music, and art. Other Bonus Words feature terms related to recent changes in technology such as *biodegradable*, *videotape*, and *modem*.

Instructional Design

Spelling Workout takes a solid phonetic and structural analysis approach to encoding. In each list of twenty words, all relate to the organizing principle or relationship that is the focus of the lesson. Of those List Words, at least half are words that the student should be familiar with at that particular grade level. The remaining words introduce new vocabulary with emphasis on meaning, usage, and etymology.

Lessons have been organized as efficiently as possible with the degree of spelling difficulty in mind, and with as much diversity as possible. In addition to lessons based on phonetic and structural analysis, lessons containing hurdle words, content words, and words adopted from other languages have been included in order to vary the focus from lesson to lesson.

Research-Based Teaching Strategies

Spelling Workout utilizes a test-study-test method of teaching spelling. The student first takes a pretest of words that have not yet been introduced. Under the direction of the teacher, the student then corrects the test, rewriting correctly any word that has been missed. This approach not only provides an opportunity to determine how many words a student can already spell but also allows students to analyze spelling mistakes. In the process students also discover patterns that make it easier to spell List Words.

High-Utility List Words

Word lists for each lesson have been chosen with the following criteria in mind:

- Frequently misspelled words
- Application to the student's academic experiences
- Introduction of new or unfamiliar vocabulary
- Visible structural similarity (consonant and vowel patterns)
- Relationship groupings (prefixes, roots, subject areas, etc.)

Word Lists have been compiled from the following:

Columbia University, N.Y. Bureau of Publications. *Spelling Difficulties in 3,876 Words*

Dolch. *2,000 Commonest Words for Spelling*

Florida Department of Education. *Lists For Assessment of Spelling*

Fry, Fountokidis and Polk. *The New Reading Teacher's Book of Lists*

Green. *The New Iowa Spelling Scale*

Hanna. *Phoneme-Grapheme Correspondence as Cues to Spelling Improvement*

Smith and Ingersoll. *Written Vocabulary of Elementary School Pupils, Ages 6-14*

S.C. Dept. of Education. *South Carolina Word List,* Grades 1-12

Thomas. *Canadian Word Lists and Instructional Techniques*

University of Iowa. *The List of 1,000 Words Most Commonly Misspelled*

A format that results in success

Spelling Workout furnishes an intensive review of spelling skills previously taught and introduces the students to more sophisticated words and concepts. Lesson emphasis is on spelling strategies, developing vocabulary, practicing correct word usage, and understanding word derivations.

- *Game Plan provides a lesson focus.*
- *Word lists were selected on the basis of meaning, usage, and origin.*
- *Warm Up activites center on vocabulary development, dictionary skills, and word analysis.*

Words from Geography

LESSON **19**

Game Plan

Every subject you study in school has its own specific vocabulary. Words such as isthmus, meridian, and axis are words you often encounter when you study geography.

All the List Words are from geography. Memorize and practice spelling these words.

1. acre
2. dialect
3. foliage
4. isthmus
5. precipitation
6. aerial
7. ecological
8. horizontal
9. meridian
10. resources
11. axis
12. expedition
13. hurricane
14. ethnic
15. reservoir
16. bayou
17. fertile
18. irrigate
19. plateau
20. vicinity

Warm Up

Vocabulary Development

Write the List Word that matches each definition.

1. relating to a group with a common cultural heritage ________
2. a narrow strip of land with water on either side ________
3. a place where water is stored ________
4. a broad stretch of high level land ________
5. a form of a language used by a certain group ________
6. producing much fruit or crops ________
7. a measure of land ________
8. a long journey or voyage ________
9. a marshy body of water ________
10. to water by means of canals or ditches ________
11. opposite of vertical ________
12. snow, hail, sleet, rain ________

Dictionary Skills

Write the List Word that matches each sound spelling.

1. (və sin´ ə tē) ________
2. (fō´ lē ij) ________
3. (ak´ sis) ________
4. (mə rid´ ē ən) ________
5. (ek ə läj´ i k'l) ________
6. (hur´ ə kān´) ________
7. (er´ ē əl) ________
8. (rē´ sôrs ez) ________

77

- *DID YOU KNOW? exposes students to word origins and word histories while increasing vocabulary. An etymology is found in each lesson.*

Words from Geography — Lesson 19

Practice

Did you know?

Acre meant "field" in Old English. It is related to *ager*, the Latin word for field, and to the word *agriculture*.

Word Analysis

Write the List Word that contains the same root word as the word given.

1. precipitate ________
2. reservation ________
3. defoliate ________
4. irrigation ________
5. horizon ________
6. aerialist ________
7. resourceful ________
8. expedite ________
9. ecology ________
10. dialogue ________

Analogies

Write a List Word to complete each analogy.

1. Desert is to sand as forest is to ________.
2. Canal is to water as ________ is to land.
3. Grain is to silo as rainfall is to ________.
4. Wet is to dry as ________ is to drought.
5. Gallon is to liquid as ________ is to land.
6. Terrestrial is to land as ________ is to sky.
7. Breeze is to ________ as snow flurry is to blizzard.
8. Swamp is to ________ as tornado is to twister.
9. Fertilize is to plant food as ________ is to water.
10. Explorer is to ________ as sailor is to voyage.

Classification

Write a List Word to complete each series.

1. neighborhood, environment, ________
2. vertical, diagonal, ________
3. language, accent, ________
4. tornado, cyclone, ________
5. rainfall, snowfall, ________
6. productive, fruitful, ________
7. rotation, earth, ________
8. longitude, latitude, ________

78

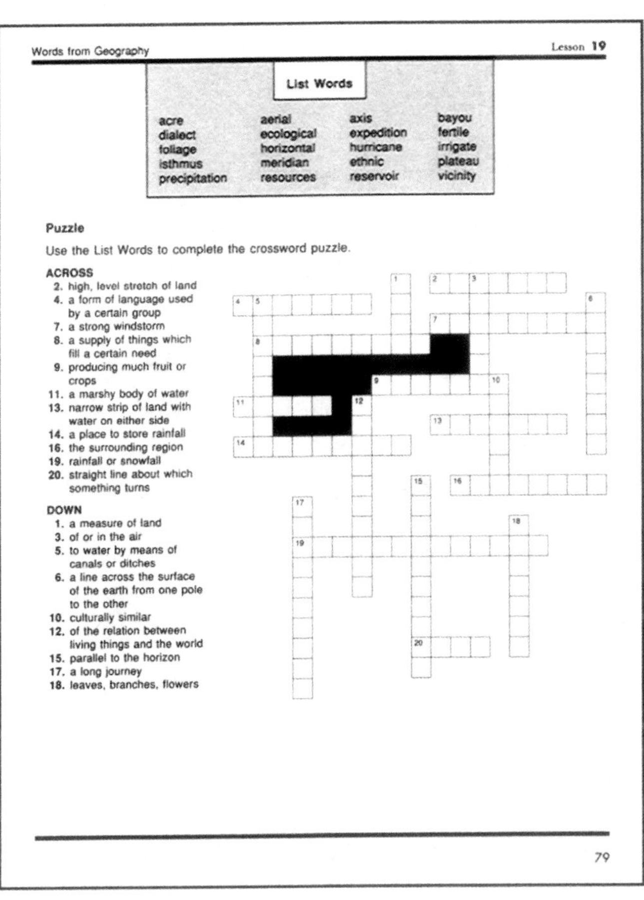

Words from Geography — Lesson 19

List Words

acre	aerial	axis	bayou
dialect	ecological	expedition	fertile
foliage	horizontal	hurricane	irrigate
isthmus	meridian	ethnic	plateau
precipitation	resources	reservoir	vicinity

Puzzle

Use the List Words to complete the crossword puzzle.

ACROSS

2. high, level stretch of land
4. a form of language used by a certain group
7. a strong windstorm
8. a supply of things which fill a certain need
9. producing much fruit or crops
11. a marshy body of water
13. narrow strip of land with water on either side
14. a place to store rainfall
16. the surrounding region
19. rainfall or snowfall
20. straight line about which something turns

DOWN

1. a measure of land
3. of or in the air
5. to water by means of canals or ditches
6. a line across the surface of the earth from one pole to the other
10. culturally similar
12. of the relation between living things and the world
15. parallel to the horizon
17. a long journey
18. leaves, branches, flowers

79

- *Many opportunities are provided to practice List Words.*

Words from Geography — Lesson 19

Proofreading

Use the proofreading marks to correct the mistakes in the article below. Then write the misspelled List Words on the lines.

Proofreading Marks
spelling mistake — small letter — capital letter — new paragraph

The Republic of panama is located at the narrowest point of the istmus that joins the Continents of North and south America. This is also the site of the Panama canal, which links the Atlantic and the pacific oceans. Panama has a tropical climate with foleage that includes a variety of flowers. Its rezources include copper and petroleum products. Its food crops include Bananas and sugarcane, which grow well in the fertil soil. Many different ethnik groups live in the visinity, including Indian groups, Africans, french, Spanish, and Chinese.

1. isthmus
2. foliage
3. resources
4. fertile
5. ethnic
6. vicinity

Challenges

Express Yourself

Imagine that you could visit any foreign country in the world. Think about the reasons why you would like to visit a particular country and what you would like to learn during your visit. Write five questions that you would like answered on your trip. Then use a geography book or encyclopedia to answer the questions you wrote. After proofreading and revising your questions and answers, share them with a group. Discuss additional questions they have about your country.

Bonus Words: Countries

Venezuela	Nicaragua	Libya	Thailand	Belgium
Argentina	Ethiopia	Afghanistan	Switzerland	Philippines

Write each Bonus Word under the continent in which it is located.

Asia
1. ______
2. ______
3. ______

Europe
4. ______
5. ______

South America
6. ______
7. ______

Africa
8. ______
9. ______

North America
10. ______

80

- ***Proofreading*** builds proofreading skills and encourages students to check their own writing.
- *Express Yourself provides opportunities for students to write spelling words in meaningful ways.*
- *Bonus Words are drawn from various curriculum areas.*

Classroom Management

Spelling Workout is designed as a flexible instructional program. The following plans are two ways the program can be taught.

The 5-day Plan
Day 1 - Pretest/Game Plan/Warm Up
Day 2 and 3 - Practice
Day 4 - Challenges
Day 5 - Final Test

The 3-day Plan
Day 1 - Pretest/Game Plan/Warm Up
Day 2 - Practice/Challenges
Day 3 - Final Test

Testing

Testing is accomplished in several ways. A pretest is administered before beginning the Game Plan and a final test at the end of each lesson. Dictation sentences for each pretest and final test are provided.

Research suggests that students benefit from correcting their own pretests. After the pretest has been administered, have students self-correct their tests in the following manner. As you read each letter of the word, ask students to point to each letter and circle any incorrect letters. Then have students rewrite each word correctly.

Dictation sentences for Bonus Words are also furnished for teachers desiring to include these words on weekly tests.

Tests for Instant Replay Lessons are provided as black line masters in the back of the Teacher's Edition. These tests provide not only an evaluation tool for teachers but also added practice in taking standardized tests for students.

Individualizing Instruction

Bonus Words are included in every lesson as a challenge for better spellers and to provide extension and enrichment for all students.

Review pages called Instant Replay Lessons reinforce correct spelling of difficult words from previous lessons.

The Instant Replay Lessons also provide for individual needs. Each has space for students to add words from previous lessons which they found especially difficult.

Students may wish to record their test scores on the reproducible individual Student Record Chart provided in the Teacher's Edition.

Dictionary

In the back of each student book is a comprehensive dictionary with definitions of all List Words and Bonus Words. Students will have this resource at their fingertips for any assignment.

A complete program that integrates spelling and writing

Spelling Through Writing

Using an integrated language arts approach, *Spelling Workout* helps students acquire spelling proficiency through activities that build vocabulary, reinforce key language skills, develop oral language, encourage reading, and stimulate writing.

LEVELS

	A	B	C	D	E	F	G	H
Poetry	•	•	•	•	•	•	•	•
Narrative Writings	•	•	•	•	•	•	•	•
Descriptive Writings	•	•	•	•	•	•	•	•
Expository Writings	•	•	•	•	•	•	•	•
Notes/Letters	•	•	•		•	•	•	•
Riddles/Jokes	•		•					
Recipes	•	•	•			•	•	
Newspaper Articles		•	•	•	•	•		•
Conversations/ Dialogues				•	•	•		•
Menus						•	•	
Questionaires					•	•	•	•
Logs/Journals			•	•	•	•	•	
Advertisements		•	•	•	•	•	•	•
Reports					•	•	•	•
Literary Devices							•	•
Scripts					•	•	•	•
Speeches						•		•

Latin Roots — Lesson **31**

Proofreading

Use the proofreading marks to correct the mistakes in the poem below. Then write the misspelled List Words on the lines.

Proofreading Marks
spelling mistake — add space
capital letter — small letter

an echo is like a sound ilushion,
which may create a little confusion.
When it bounces like a bouncing ball,
its source may eloode those Hearing its call.

now a mirage is as temperal as a Rainbow,
making far-away scenes look vivud you know.
But when trying toreach that illuzive place,
you'll see it vanish like bubbles In space.

1. ______
2. ______
3. ______
4. ______
5. ______

Challenges

Express Yourself

A **simile** compares two things using the words like or as.

The waterfall was as spectacular as fireworks.
Her vitality is like a babbling brook, forever in motion.

Write three similes. Try to include the adjectives: versatile, illusive, introverted, vivid, emaciated, earnest, and impractical. After proofreading and revising your similes, read them aloud to a group. Ask them if your comparisons make sense.

Bonus Words: Ecology
sanctuary, wildlife, preservation, uninhabited, conservation, photosynthesis, chlorophyll, biodegradable, oxidation, germinate

Write a Bonus Word to match each clue.

1. not lived in ______
2. green plant pigment ______
3. will disintegrate ______
4. process by which a plant uses light to make food ______
5. safe place ______
6. sprout ______
7. plants and animals ______
8. combining of oxygen with other substances ______

Write the Bonus Words that are synonyms for protection.

9. ______ 10. ______

128

- ***Proofreading** practice builds proofreading proficiency and encourages students to check their own writing.*
- *Students have many opportunities to express themselves through writing using a variety of styles and techniques.*
- *Activities emphasize word meaning.*

The Teacher's Edition — Everything You Need!

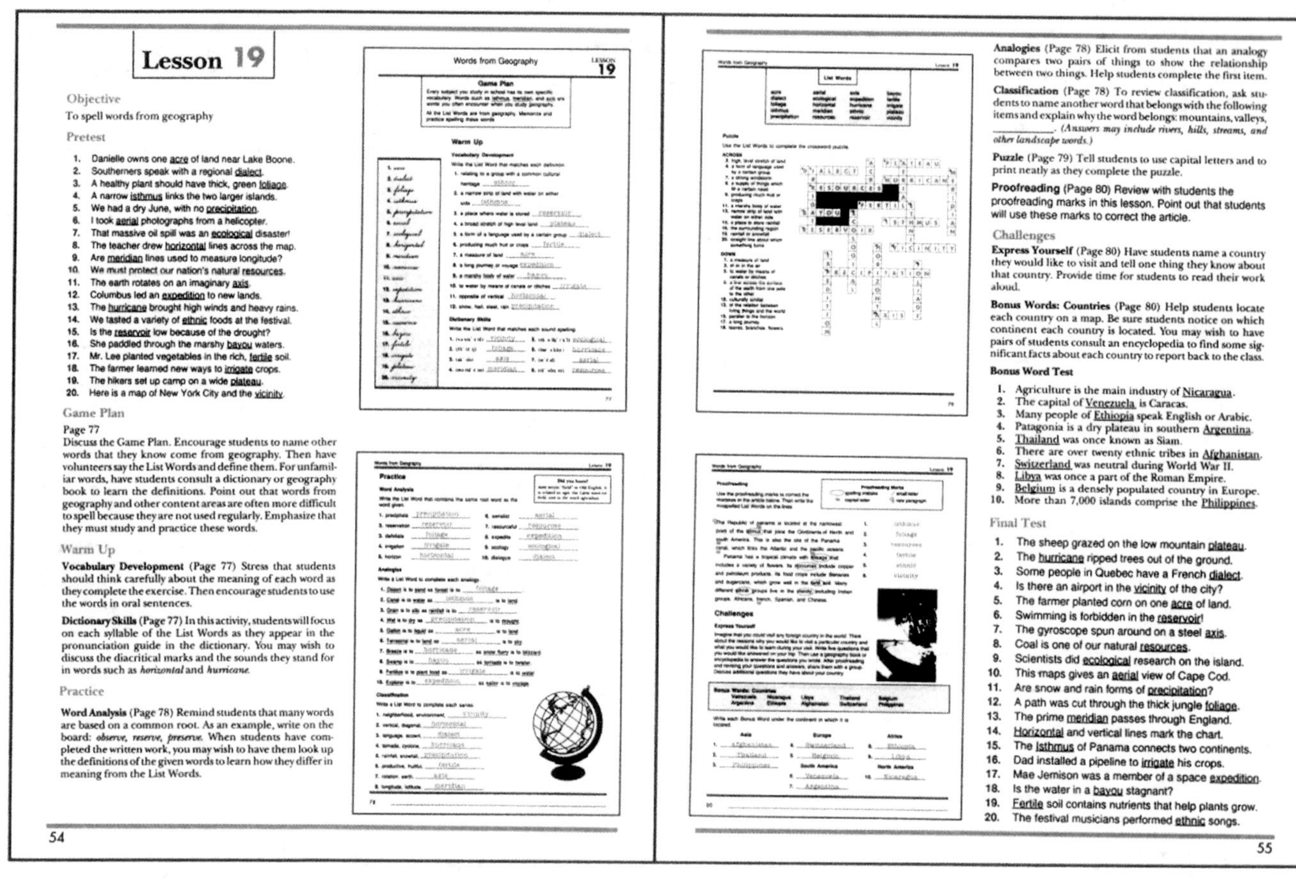

Lesson 19

Objective

To spell words from geography

Pretest

1. Danielle owns one acre of land near Lake Boone.
2. Southerners speak with a regional dialect.
3. A healthy plant should have thick, green foliage.
4. A narrow isthmus links the two larger islands.
5. We had a dry June, with no precipitation.
6. I took aerial photographs from a helicopter.
7. That massive oil spill was an ecological disaster!
8. The teacher drew horizontal lines across the map.
9. Are meridian lines used to measure longitude?
10. We must protect our nation's natural resources.
11. The earth rotates on an imaginary axis.
12. Columbus led an expedition to new lands.
13. The hurricane brought high winds and heavy rains.
14. We tasted a variety of ethnic foods at the festival.
15. Is the reservoir low because of the drought?
16. She paddled through the marshy bayou waters.
17. Mr. Lee planted vegetables in the rich, fertile soil.
18. The farmer learned new ways to irrigate crops.
19. The hikers set up camp on a wide plateau.
20. Here is a map of New York City and the vicinity.

Game Plan

Page 77
Discuss the Game Plan. Encourage students to name other words that they know come from geography. Then have volunteers say the List Words and define them. For unfamiliar words, have students consult a dictionary or geography book to learn the definitions. Point out that words from geography and other content areas are often more difficult to spell because they are not used regularly. Emphasize that they must study and practice these words.

Warm Up

Vocabulary Development (Page 77) Stress that students should think carefully about the meaning of each word as they complete the exercise. Then encourage students to use the words in oral sentences.

Dictionary Skills (Page 77) In this activity, students will focus on each syllable of the List Words as they appear in the pronunciation guide in the dictionary. You may wish to discuss the diacritical marks and the sounds they stand for in words such as *horizontal* and *hurricane*.

Practice

Word Analysis (Page 78) Remind students that many words are based on a common root. As an example, write on the board: *observe, reserve, preserve*. When students have completed the written work, you may wish to have them look up the definitions of the given words to learn how they differ in meaning from the List Words.

54

Analogies (Page 78) Elicit from students that an analogy compares two pairs of things to show the relationship between two things. Help students complete the first item.

Classification (Page 78) To review classification, ask students to name another word that belongs with the following items and explain why the word belongs: mountains, valleys, ________. *(Answers may include rivers, hills, streams, and other landscape words.)*

Puzzle (Page 79) Tell students to use capital letters and to print neatly as they complete the puzzle.

Proofreading (Page 80) Review with students the proofreading marks in this lesson. Point out that students will use these marks to correct the article.

Challenges

Express Yourself (Page 80) Have students name a country they would like to visit and tell one thing they know about that country. Provide time for students to read their work aloud.

Bonus Words: Countries (Page 80) Help students locate each country on a map. Be sure students notice on which continent each country is located. You may wish to have pairs of students consult an encyclopedia to find some significant facts about each country to report back to the class.

Bonus Word Test

1. Agriculture is the main industry of Nicaragua.
2. The capital of Venezuela is Caracas.
3. Many people of Ethiopia speak English or Arabic.
4. Patagonia is a dry plateau in southern Argentina.
5. Thailand was once known as Siam.
6. There are over twenty ethnic tribes in Afghanistan.
7. Switzerland was neutral during World War II.
8. Libya was once a part of the Roman Empire.
9. Belgium is a densely populated country in Europe.
10. More than 7,000 islands comprise the Philippines.

Final Test

1. The sheep grazed on the low mountain plateau.
2. The hurricane ripped trees out of the ground.
3. Some people in Quebec have a French dialect.
4. Is there an airport in the vicinity of the city?
5. The farmer planted corn on one acre of land.
6. Swimming is forbidden in the reservoir!
7. The gyroscope spun around on a steel axis.
8. Coal is one of our natural resources.
9. Scientists did ecological research on the island.
10. This maps gives an aerial view of Cape Cod.
11. Are snow and rain forms of precipitation?
12. A path was cut through the thick jungle foliage.
13. The prime meridian passes through England.
14. Horizontal and vertical lines mark the chart.
15. The Isthmus of Panama connects two continents.
16. Dad installed a pipeline to irrigate his crops.
17. Mae Jemison was a member of a space expedition.
18. Is the water in a bayou stagnant?
19. Fertile soil contains nutrients that help plants grow.
20. The festival musicians performed ethnic songs.

55

- The goals of each lesson are clearly stated.
- A pretest is administered before the start of each lesson. Dictation sentences are provided.
- Start-up activities offer suggestions for introducing the spelling principles.
- Concise teaching notes give ideas for motivating students.
- Thought-provoking questions stimulate classroom discussion and writing. Important background information is given as it relates to the content of the Bonus Words.
- Dictation sentences are provided for testing both the List Words and the Bonus Words.

- *Reproducible study sheets of Instant Replay Lesson words are included in the Teacher's Edition to help prepare students for test taking.*

- *A reproducible two-page standardized test is supplied for assessment purposes after each Instant Replay Lesson.*

Instant Replay Word List

Lesson 6

abdomen	testimony
amateur	capacity
allegiance	bulletin
actual	villain
bachelor	peninsula
advancement	microphone
alien	competition
anniversary	complicated
association	opponent
approximately	anticipation
exaggerate	patriotic
recollection	continuous
sterilize	commercial
lenient	conclusion
embarrass	ominous
tedious	amusement
medium	circumference
estimate	culture
hostess	industrious
environment	linoleum
cinnamon	unity
circular	premium
prohibit	smudge
isolate	subtle
illustration	vacuum

90

Instant Replay Word List

Lesson 12

appendage	recitation
appendix	lotion
apparatus	proportion
appropriate	revolution
appraise	occupation
assault	boulevard
appreciation	camouflage
apprentice	courteous
assurance	lacquer
apparel	pursuit
accelerate	lieutenant
accurate	
acquire	
attraction	
attitude	
accent	
affix	
accomplice	
accommodate	
accustomed	
complexion	
expression	
occasion	
suspicion	
civilization	

Instant Replay Test

Side A

LESSON **6**

Read each set of words. Fill in the circle next to the word that is spelled correctly.

1.	ⓐ envirement ⓑ enviroment	ⓒ enviremint ⓓ environment
2.	ⓐ onimous ⓑ omminous	ⓒ ominus ⓓ ominous
3.	ⓐ allegience ⓑ allegance	ⓒ allegiance ⓓ alegiance
4.	ⓐ cinamon ⓑ cinnamon	ⓒ cinnoman ⓓ cinnamen
5.	ⓐ commercial ⓑ comercial	ⓒ comertial ⓓ commertial
6.	ⓐ cuntinuos ⓑ continuos	ⓒ continous ⓓ continuous
7.	ⓐ tedious ⓑ tideous	ⓒ tedeous ⓓ tidious
8.	ⓐ abdoman ⓑ abdomen	ⓒ abdemen ⓓ abdamen
9.	ⓐ circumfrance ⓑ circumference	ⓒ circumferance ⓓ circumfrence
10.	ⓐ ilustration ⓑ illustrateion	ⓒ illustration ⓓ illustrasion
11.	ⓐ exxagerate ⓑ exaggarate	ⓒ exaggerrate ⓓ exaggerate
12.	ⓐ testemony ⓑ testimoney	ⓒ testimony ⓓ testamoney
13.	ⓐ amateur ⓑ ammature	ⓒ amachure ⓓ amatuer

Name ______________________ 93

Spelling Enrichment

Group Practice

Crossword Relay First draw a large grid on the board. Then divide the class into several teams. Teams compete against each other to form separate crossword puzzles on the board. Individuals on each team take turns racing against members of the other teams to join list words until all possibilities have been exhausted. A list word may appear on each crossword puzzle only once. The winning team is the team whose crossword puzzle contains the greatest number of correctly spelled list words or the team who finishes first.

Proofreading Relay Write two columns of misspelled list words on the board. Although the errors can differ, be sure that each list has the same number of errors. Divide the class into two teams and assign each team to a different column. Teams then compete against each other to correct their assigned lists by team members taking turns erasing and replacing an appropriate letter. Each member may correct only one letter per turn. The team that is first to correct its entire word list wins.

Detective Call on a student to be a detective. The detective must choose a spelling word from the list and think of a structural clue, definition, or synonym that will help classmates identify it. The detective then states the clue using the format, "I spy a word that..." Students are called on to guess and spell the mystery word. Whoever answers correctly gets to take a turn being the detective.

Spelling Tic-Tac-Toe Draw a tic-tac-toe square on the board. Divide the class into *X* and *O* teams. Take turns dictating spelling words to members of each team. If the word is spelled correctly, allow the team member to place an *X* or *O* on the square. The first team to place three *X*s or *O*s in a row wins.

Words of Fortune Have students put their heads down while you write a spelling word on the board in large letters. Then cover each letter with a sheet of sturdy paper. The paper can be fastened to the board with a magnet. Call on a student to guess any letter of the alphabet they think may be hidden. If that particular letter is hidden, then reveal the letter in every place where it appears in the word by removing the paper.

The student continues to guess letters until an incorrect guess is made or the word is revealed. In the event that an incorrect guess is made, a different student continues the game. Continue the game until every list word has been hidden and then revealed.

Applied Spelling

Journal Allow time each day for students to write into a journal. A spiral bound notebook can be used for this purpose. Encourage students to express their feelings about events that are happening in their lives at home or at school. Or they could write abo... started, you ma... use "invented"...

You may wish... comments that... example, a stud... bazball todae."... my favorite gam... This method al... sentence structu... negative way.

Letter to the Te... write a note to... suggest topics o... to suggest a top... The teacher sh... letter that provi... sentence structu...

Daily Edit E... board that cont... punctuation. H... Provide time lat... errors on the b...

Word Locker ... or staple togeth... (provided on pa... record of words... be added to so... sections for eac... use a dictionary or ask the teacher to help them spell the words with which they are having trouble. Periodically, allow the students to work in pairs to test each other on a set of words taken from their personal word list.

Acrostic Poems Have students write a word from the spelling list vertically. Then instruct them to join a word horizontally to each letter of the list word. The horizontal words must begin with the letters in the list word. They also should be words that describe or relate feelings about the list word. Encourage students to refer to a dictionary for help in finding appropriate words. Here is a sample acrostic poem:

Zebras
Otters
Ostriches

Nursery Rhyme Exchange Provide students with copies of a familiar nursery rhyme. Discuss how some of the words can be exchanged for other words that have similar meanings. Ask the students to rewrite the nursery rhyme exchanging some of the words. You may want to encourage the students to try this technique with nursery rhymes of their choice. Be sure to give students the opportunity to read their rhymes to the class.

110

- *Suggested games and group activities make spelling more fun.*

Meeting the Needs of Your ESL Students

Spelling Strategies for Your ESL Students

You may want to try some of these suggestions to help you promote successful language learning for ESL students.

- Prompt use of spelling words by showing pictures or objects that relate to the topic of each selection. Invite students to discuss the picture or object.
- Demonstrate actions or act out words. Encourage students to do the same.
- Read each selection aloud before asking students to read it independently.
- Define words in context and allow students to offer their own meanings of words.
- Make the meanings of words concrete by naming objects or pictures, role-playing, or pantomiming.

Spelling is the relationship between sounds and letters. Learning to spell words in English is an interesting challenge for English First Language speakers as well as English as a Second Language speakers. You may want to adapt some of the following activities to accommodate the needs of your students—both native and non-English speakers.

Rhymes and Songs

Use rhymes, songs, poems, or chants to introduce new letter sounds and spelling words. Repeat the rhyme or song several times during the day or week, having students listen to you first, then repeat back to you line by line. To enhance learning for visual learners in your classroom and provide opportunities for pointing out letter combinations and their sounds, you may want to write the rhyme, song, poem, or chant on the board. As you examine the words, students can easily see similarities and differences among them. Encourage volunteers to select and recite a rhyme or sing a song for the class. Students may enjoy some of the selections in *Miss Mary Mack and Other Children's Street Rhymes* by Joanna Cole and Stephanie Calmenson or *And the Green Grass Grew All Around* by Alvin Schwartz.

Student Dictation

To take advantage of individual students' known vocabulary, suggest that students build their own sentences incorporating the List Words. For example:

Mary ran.
Mary ran away.
Mary ran away quickly.

Sentence building can expand students' knowledge how to spell words and of how to notice language patterns, learn descriptive words, and so on.

Words in Context

Using words in context sentences will aid students' mastery of new vocabulary.

- Say several sentences using the List Words in context and have students repeat after you. Encourage more proficient students to make up sentences using List Words that you suggest.
- Write cloze sentences on the board and have students help you complete them with the List Words.

Point out the spelling patterns in the words, using colored chalk to underline or circle the elements.

Oral Drills

Use oral drills to help students make associations among sounds and the letters that represent them. You might use oral drills at listening stations to reinforce the language, allowing ESL students to list to the drills at their own pace.

Spelling Aloud Say each List Word and have students repeat the word. Next, write it on the board as you name each letter, then say the word again as you track the letters and sound by sweeping your hand under the word. Call attention to spelling changes for words to which endings or suffixes were added. For words with more than one syllable, emphasize each syllable as you write, encouraging students to clap out the syllables. Ask volunteers to repeat the procedure.

Variant Spellings For a group of words that contai the same vowel sound, but variant spellings, write a example on the board, say the word, and then prese other words in that word family *(cake: rake, bake, lake).* Point out the sound and the letter(s) that stan for the sound. Then add words to the list that have th same vowel sound *(play, say, day).* Say pairs of wor *(cake, play)* as you point to them, and identify the vowel sound and the different letters that represent the sound (long *a: a_e, ay).* Ask volunteers to selec different pair of words and repeat the procedure.

Vary this activity by drawing a chart on the board tha shows the variant spellings for a sound. Invite studer to add words under the correct spelling pattern. Provide a list of words for students to choose from tc help those ESL students with limited vocabularies.

tegorizing To help students discriminate among nsonant sounds and spellings, have them help you tegorize words with single consonant sounds and nsonant blends or digraphs. For example, ask idents to close their eyes so that they may focus lely on the sounds in the words, and then onounce *smart, smile, spend,* and *special.* Next, onounce the words as you write them on the board. ter spelling each word, create two columns—one for n, one for *sp.* Have volunteers pronounce each ord, decide which column it fits under, and write the ord in the correct column. Encourage students to d to the columns any other words they know that ve those consonant blends.

focus on initial, medial, or final consonant sounds, int out the position of the consonant blends or graphs in the List Words. Have students find and t the words under columns labeled *Beginning, iddle, End.*

pe Recording Encourage students to work with a rtner or their group to practice their spelling words. a tape recorder is available, students can practice at eir own pace by taking turns recording the words, aying back the tape, and writing each word they ear. Students can then help each other check their elling against their *Spelling Workout* books. oserve as needed to be sure students are spelling e words correctly.

omparing/Contrasting To help students focus on ord parts, write List Words with prefixes or suffixes the board and have volunteers circle, underline, or aw a line between the prefix or suffix and its root ord. Review the meaning of each root word, then vite students to work with their group to write two ntences: one using just the root word; the other ing the root word with its prefix or suffix. For ample: *My favorite mystery was* due *at the library onday afternoon. By Tuesday afternoon the book as* overdue! Or, *You can* depend *on Jen to arrive for ftball practice on time. She is* dependable. Have udents contrast the two sentences, encouraging em to tell how the prefix or suffix changed the eaning of the root word.

uestions/Answers Write List Words on the board nd ask pairs of students to brainstorm questions or nswers about the words, such as "Which word ames more than one? How do you know?" (foxes, *an s was added at the end)* or, "Which word tells that omething belongs to the children? How do you now?" *(*children's *is spelled with an* 's*)*

Games

You may want to invite students to participate in these activities.

Picture Clues Students can work with a partner to draw pictures or cut pictures out of magazines that represent the List Words, then trade papers and label each other's pictures. Encourage students to check each other's spelling against their *Spelling Workout* books.

Or, you can present magazine cutouts or items that picture the List Words. As you display each picture or item, say the word clearly and then write it on the board as you spell it aloud. Non-English speakers may wish to know the translation of the word in their native language so that they can mentally connect the new word with a familiar one. Students may also find similarities in the spellings of the words.

Letter Cards Have students create letter cards for vowels, vowel digraphs, consonants, consonant blends and digraphs, and so on. Then say a List Word and have students show the card that has the letters representing the sound for the vowels or consonants in that word as they repeat and spell the word after you. Students can use their cards independently as they work with their group.

Charades/Pantomime Students can use gestures and actions to act out the List Words. To receive credit for a correctly guessed word, players must spell the word correctly. Such activities can be played in pairs so that beginning English speakers will not feel pressured. If necessary, translate the words into students' native languages so that they understand the meanings of the words before attempting to act them out.

Change or No Change Have students make flash cards for root words and endings. One student holds up a root word; another holds up an ending. The class says "Change" or "No Change" to describe what happens when the root word and ending are combined. Encourage students to spell the word with its ending added.

Scope and Sequence for MCP Spelling Workout

Skills	Level A	Level B	Level C	Level D	Level E	Level F	Level G	Level H
Consonants	1-12	1-2	1-2	1	1	1,7,9	RC	RC
Short Vowels	14-18	3-5	4	2	RC	RC	RC	RC
Long Vowels	20-23	7-11	5,7	3	RC	RC	RC	RC
Consonant Blends/ Clusters	26-28	13-14	8-9 29	5,7	RC	RC	RC	RC
y as a Vowel	29-30	15-16	10-11	RC	RC	RC	RC	RC
Consonant Digraphs - **th, ch, sh, wh, ck**	32-33	28-29 32	27-28 31	9	RC	RC	RC	RC
Vowel Digraphs		25-26 33	21-22 25	19-22	7-10	11 13-16 19	25	RC
R-Controlled Vowels		19-20	13-14	8	RC	RC	RC	RC
Diphthongs	24	27	26	22-23	11	16-17	RC	RC
Silent Consonants			23	10	4	4-5	RC	RC
Hard and Soft **c** and **g**		32	3	4	2	2	RC	RC
Plurals			19-20	25-27 29	33-34	33	RC	RC
Prefixes		34	32-33	31-32	13-17	20-23 25	7-8	7-11 19-20
Suffixes	34-35	21-23	15-17	13-17	25-29 31-32	26-29 31-32	9 13-14 16, 26	5, 25-27
Contractions		17	34	28	23	RC	RC	RC
Possessives				28-29	23	RC	RC	RC
Compound Words				33	19	RC	RC	RC
Synonyms/ Antonyms				34	RC	RC	RC	RC
Homonyms		35	35	35	RC	RC	RC	RC

Skills	Level A	Level B	Level C	Level D	Level E	Level F	Level G	Level H
el or **le**		31	RC	RC	RC	RC	RC	RC
Spellings of /**f**/- **f, ff, ph, gh**				11	3	3	RC	RC
Syllables					20-22	RC	RC	RC
Commonly Misspelled Words					35	34	17,35	17,29 35
Abbreviations						35	RC	RC
Latin Roots							11,15 31	13-16
Words with French or Spanish Derivations							10,29	RC
Words of Latin/French/ Greek Origin								21-23 28
Latin Prefixes							33	RC
List Words related to specific curriculum areas							19-23 28,32	31-34
Vocabulary Development	•	•	•	•	•	•	•	•
Dictionary	•	•	•	•	•	•	•	•
Proofreading	•	•	•	•	•	•	•	•
Writing	•	•	•	•	•	•	•	•
Literature Selections	•	•	•	•	•	•		
Content- related Bonus Words	•	•	•	•	•	•	•	•
Review Tests in Standardized Format	•	•	•	•	•	•	•	•

Numbers in chart indicate lesson numbers
RC = reinforced in other contexts
• = found throughout level

Lesson 1

Objective

To spell words with the letter *a*

Pretest

1. Your abdomen is in the middle of your body.
2. The farmer fed the animals corn and alfalfa.
3. New foods taste alien the first time you try them.
4. Is your brother still a bachelor at thirty?
5. What a sweet and juicy tangerine!
6. The store can make a print from that transparency.
7. Each morning, we pledge allegiance to the flag.
8. Friday is my brother's fifth wedding anniversary.
9. Draw a circle six inches in diameter.
10. Write down your estimate and then the actual cost.
11. This job offers opportunities for advancement.
12. Juan is an amateur skater, not a professional.
13. We belong to a business association.
14. Proofread your manuscript for any spelling errors.
15. Which adhesive works best with vinyl wallpaper?
16. What kind of fabric is that dress made from?
17. You have no basis for your opinion, except rumor.
18. My mother is taking a course in astronomy.
19. The tenant will vacate the apartment on Friday.
20. Your drive will take approximately six hours.

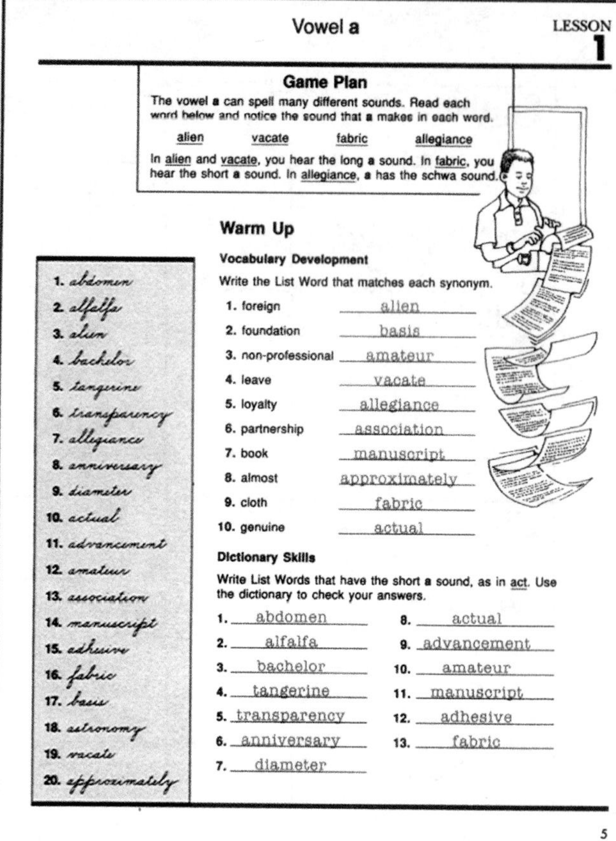

Vowel a

LESSON 1

Game Plan

The vowel a can spell many different sounds. Read each word below and notice the sound that a makes in each word.

alien vacate fabric allegiance

In alien and vacate, you hear the long a sound. In fabric, you hear the short a sound. In allegiance, a has the schwa sound.

1. abdomen
2. alfalfa
3. alien
4. bachelor
5. tangerine
6. transparency
7. allegiance
8. anniversary
9. diameter
10. actual
11. advancement
12. amateur
13. association
14. manuscript
15. adhesive
16. fabric
17. basis
18. astronomy
19. vacate
20. approximately

Warm Up

Vocabulary Development

Write the List Word that matches each synonym.

1. foreign alien
2. foundation basis
3. non-professional amateur
4. leave vacate
5. loyalty allegiance
6. partnership association
7. book manuscript
8. almost approximately
9. cloth fabric
10. genuine actual

Dictionary Skills

Write List Words that have the short a sound, as in act. Use the dictionary to check your answers.

1. abdomen
2. alfalfa
3. bachelor
4. tangerine
5. transparency
6. anniversary
7. diameter
8. actual
9. advancement
10. amateur
11. manuscript
12. adhesive
13. fabric

5

Game Plan

Page 5

Use these words to discuss the different sounds *a* can spell: *card, careful, among, start.* After each word, have students find List Words in which *a* has the same sound. Point out that in some words, such as *allegiance, a* may sound like a different vowel entirely. Then make sure that students understand the meanings of List Words, having them refer to dictionaries when necessary.

Warm Up

Vocabulary Development (Page 5) Write the words *big* and *large* on the chalkboard and ask how they are alike. (*They have the same meaning.*) Point out that such words are synonyms, and have volunteers suggest other synonyms. Students should then be able to complete the exercise.

Dictionary Skills (Page 5) Ask students if the word *fat* has the long *a* sound or the short *a* sound. (*short*) Write the word on the board and explain that the dictionary respelling looks just like the word, because the vowel has the short sound. Ask volunteers to name several List Words that also contain the short *a* sound.

Practice

Word Analysis (Page 6) Point out to students that many words contain unusual letter combinations or roots. Remembering these can help people remember how words are spelled. Point out, for example, that the first three letters in *alfalfa* are repeated. Then discuss other spelling patterns that students notice in List Words.

Vowel a Lesson 1

Practice

Word Analysis

Write the List Words containing the elements given below.

double consonants (**ll**, **nn**, **pp**, **ss**)

1. allegiance
2. anniversary
3. approximately
4. association

the same root as each word given

5. annual anniversary
6. astronomer astronomy
7. vacation vacate
8. transparent transparency
9. diametrical diameter
10. basic basis

Did you know?

Bachelor comes from a Latin word for a young nobleman who was trying to become a knight during the Middle Ages. Such a young man was unmarried.

Proofreading

Use the proofreading marks to correct the mistakes in the sentences. Then write the misspelled words correctly on the lines.

Proofreading Marks

spelling mistake ≡ capital letter

⊙ ? ! add period, question mark, or exclamation mark

add apostrophe

1. Geraldo, who was a batchelor, was studying astronomy at star College. bachelor
2. he was still an amature, but he really wanted to be a professional. amateur
3. A scientists allegience should be to the advancement of science. allegiance
4. Where is that manuescript about the transparency of alpha waves? manuscript
5. At noon, geraldo stopped and ate an alfalffa sprout sandwich. alfalfa
6. He also had a tangerine, accidently dropping part of it. accidentally
7. approximatly an hour later, Geraldo returned to his work. approximately
8. He saw a large orange object in the sky, about a mile in dimater. diameter
9. The earth was about to be wiped out by an allien orange planet! alien
10. He knew the schools associasion of astronomers should be called. association
11. Was the advancment of science at stake? advancement
12. A teacher asked geraldo what the bassis was for his discovery. basis
13. Ms. chu, the teacher, found the actuall cause of all the fuss. actual
14. The orange-colored planet was a piece of tangerene on the telescope. tangerine
15. Geraldos reputation in astronemy was bruised, but not ruined. astronomy

6

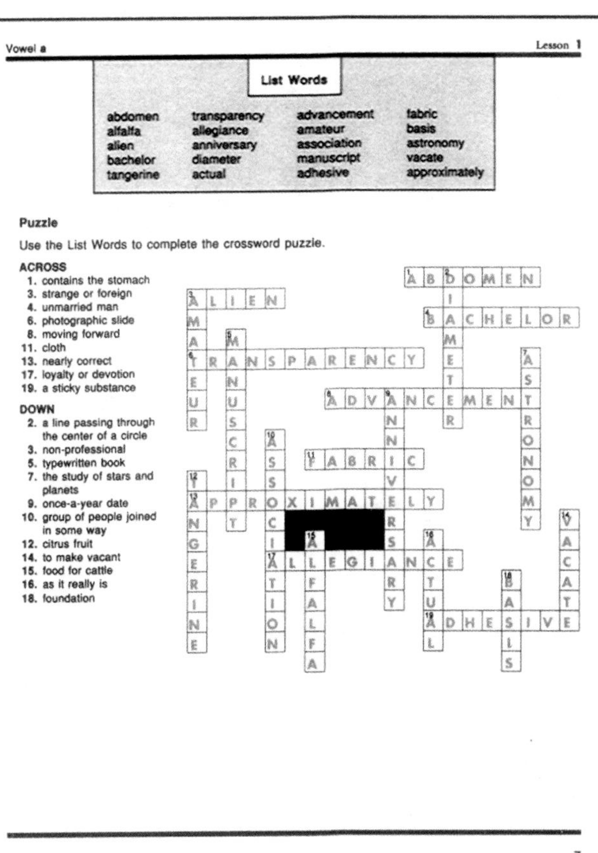

Vowel a — Lesson 1

List Words

abdomen	transparency	advancement	fabric
alfalfa	allegiance	amateur	basis
alien	anniversary	association	astronomy
bachelor	diameter	manuscript	vacate
tangerine	actual	adhesive	approximately

Puzzle

Use the List Words to complete the crossword puzzle.

ACROSS
1. contains the stomach
3. strange or foreign
4. unmarried man
6. photographic slide
8. moving forward
11. cloth
13. nearly correct
17. loyalty or devotion
19. a sticky substance

DOWN
2. a line passing through the center of a circle
3. non-professional
5. typewritten book
7. the study of stars and planets
9. once-a-year date
10. group of people joined in some way
12. citrus fruit
14. to make vacant
15. food for cattle
16. as it really is
18. foundation

7

Vowel a — Lesson 1

Test Yourself

In each pair of List Words, underline the misspelled word and write it correctly on the line.

1. adhesive, allien ___alien___
2. basis, amature ___amateur___
3. fabrick, alfalfa ___fabric___
4. transparancy, abdomen ___transparency___
5. bacheler, tangerine ___bachelor___
6. diameter, actuall ___actual___
7. aniversary, manuscript ___anniversary___
8. advancment, vacate ___advancement___
9. allegance, astronomy ___allegiance___
10. association, aproximately ___approximately___

Challenges

Express Yourself

Sometimes food recipes in magazines at the grocery check-out counter can sound pretty silly, like "Magical Meatless Meat Loaf" and "Chili con Carrots." Imagine that you have been hired to create one of these recipes. Write your own recipe. Include a list of ingredients and a description of how to make your special dish. Don't forget to give it an interesting title! Be sure to proofread and revise your recipe. Then trade recipes with your classmates. Maybe you can arrange for a taste-testing session for your new concoction!

Bonus Words: Home Economics

utensils	luncheon	buffet	blanch	marinate
beverage	perishable	casserole	microwave	garnish

Write the Bonus Word that matches each clue given.

1. scald or boil	blanch	6. baking dish	casserole
2. something to drink	beverage	7. midday meal	luncheon
3. decorate	garnish	8. soak in liquid	marinate
4. can spoil	perishable	9. kind of oven	microwave
5. tools	utensils	10. place to set out food	buffet

8

Proofreading (Page 6) Write *moms name is joan* on the board and use it to demonstrate the proofreading marks for spelling mistakes, capital letters, end punctuation, and missing apostrophes. Then point out that each sentence has several mistakes in it.

Puzzle (Page 7) Discuss crossword puzzle strategies with students. Remind them to print neatly and to first fill in all the answers that they know. These will help them figure out the other answers.

Test Yourself (Page 8) Explain that the self test will help students know whether they have mastered the spelling of List Words in this lesson. After the test, have students check their answers against List Words on page 7.

Challenges

Express Yourself (Page 8) Have students form groups to brainstorm ridiculous recipes and their names. Then have students write their recipes independently.

Bonus Words: Home Economics (Page 8) Point out that all Bonus Words are used in Home Economics. Through discussion and dictionary use, help students understand the words' meanings. Then have them complete the Bonus Word activity.

Bonus Word Test

1. Store perishable foods carefully.
2. Make sure that all your utensils are clean.
3. Potatoes will bake quickly in a microwave oven.
4. Parsley makes a pretty garnish for fish.
5. Don't drink an ice cold beverage when you are hot.
6. Put all the ingredients into an uncovered casserole.
7. Eat a light luncheon before you leave on your hike.
8. I like how you've arranged everything on the buffet.
9. Tough meat will be more tender if you marinate it.
10. First blanch the almonds in boiling water.

Final Test

1. The editor reviewed the manuscript that Jill wrote.
2. A liter is approximately the same size as a quart.
3. Jan made a dress from the fabric that she bought.
4. On the basis of these facts, I'll agree with you.
5. Is a bachelor an unmarried man?
6. Vacate the premises now!
7. The teacher showed a transparency of Africa.
8. A circle's diameter is twice its radius.
9. My favorite fruit is a tangerine.
10. Are those plants with the purple flowers alfalfa?
11. The actual cost was less than I had imagined.
12. The amateur golfer out scored the professional.
13. An ant's largest body segment is its abdomen.
14. My astronomy club is building a telescope.
15. The adhesive held the lamp together.
16. We joined an association of nature photographers.
17. Did your parents go to dinner on their anniversary?
18. Marco swore allegiance to his new country.
19. The new school was very alien to Greta.
20. I'm proud of my sister's professional advancement.

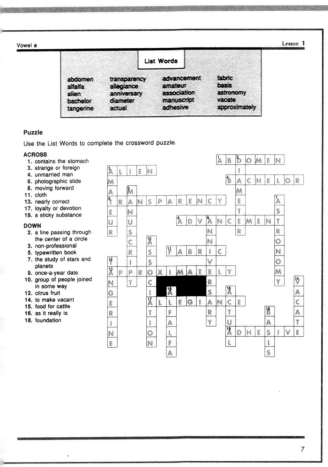

Lesson 2

Objective

To spell words with the vowel *e*

Pretest

1. Who will serve as our delegate at the convention?
2. Acid rain can harm the environment.
3. The hostess served a buffet luncheon.
4. Painting a long fence can become tedious.
5. Those artifacts are sacred to the Hawaiian people.
6. I absolutely despise spicy foods!
7. The ballerina was the epitome of grace.
8. Open-minded people have leeway in their ideas.
9. The rocks along the shore will erode in time.
10. Sterilize the jars before you fill them with pickles.
11. The king will appear at the embassy party tonight.
12. I estimate that 80,000 people were in the stadium.
13. The sympathetic judge was lenient in his ruling.
14. In my recollection, 1987 was a wonderful year.
15. Dr. Lee was asked to testify as an expert witness.
16. Is your sister a senior at Wittenberg University?
17. I can't exaggerate the importance of seat belts.
18. These gloves come in small, medium, and large.
19. A loyal dog would never betray its owner.
20. Please don't embarrass me by asking me to sing.

Game Plan

Page 9

Use these words for further examples of the sounds that the vowel *e* often stands for: /ē/: *freedom, theme, beat*; /e/: *head, pencil*; /i/: *actress*; /ə/: *towel, spotted*; /—/ [*silent e*]: *phone, discharge*. Have students name other examples. Then apply the discussion to List Words. Work with students to define each word, and call on volunteers to use each one in an oral sentence.

Warm Up

Vocabulary Development (Page 9) Before the exercise, have students name List Words to match these definitions: *to overstate (exaggerate); a female host (hostess).*

Dictionary Skills (Page 9) Use examples from a dictionary to review sound-spellings. Then have students look up the sound-spellings of the List Words *delegate, lenient,* and *sacred,* and write them on the chalkboard.

Practice

Word Analysis (Page 10) Have students analyze List Words on page 9 to find the letter components and syllabications required by the exercise.

Classification (Page 10) To review classification skills, write on the board: *guess, predict,* ________. Have students select a List Word to complete the group. (*estimate*)

Word Application (Page 10) Urge students to use context clues to find the List Word that best fits in each sentence. Students may enjoy making up similar context-clue sentences for the remaining List Words and issuing them as challenges to their classmates.

Vowel e — LESSON 2

Game Plan

The vowel **e** stands for many different sounds.

long e	/ē/	tree	teach
short e	/e/	bed	empty
short i	/i/	hostess	sacred
schwa	/ə/	spoken	parent
silent e		plate	partridge

1. *delegate* 2. *environment* 3. *hostess* 4. *tedious* 5. *sacred* 6. *despise* 7. *epitome* 8. *leeway* 9. *erode* 10. *sterilize* 11. *embassy* 12. *estimate* 13. *lenient* 14. *recollection* 15. *testify* 16. *senior* 17. *exaggerate* 18. *medium* 19. *betray* 20. *embarrass*

Warm Up

Vocabulary Development

Write the List Word that matches each definition.

1. dislike strongly despise
2. boring tedious
3. to make something free of germs sterilize
4. to wear away erode
5. a representative delegate
6. our world around us environment
7. one who shows all the qualities of something epitome
8. gentle or merciful lenient
9. something that is considered holy sacred
10. something remembered recollection

Dictionary Skills

Write the List Word that matches each sound spelling.

1. (im ber´ əs) embarrass
2. (mē´ dē əm) medium
3. (sēn´ yər) senior
4. (es´ tə māt) estimate
5. (hōs´ tis) hostess
6. (ig zaj´ ə rāt) exaggerate
7. (bi trā´) betray
8. (tes´ tə fī) testify
9. (em´ bə sē) embassy
10. (lē´ wā) leeway

9

Vowel e — Lesson 2

Practice

Did you know?
Exaggerate comes from a Latin word meaning "to heap up." Heaping something up into a tall pile tends to make it look larger.

Word Analysis

Write List Words to answer the following questions.

Which words contain silent **e**?

1. delegate 2. despise 3. erode 4. sterilize 5. estimate 6. exaggerate

Which words contain these double consonants?

7. rr embarrass 8. gg exaggerate 9. ll recollection

Which words contain the double consonants **ss**?

10. hostess 11. embassy 12. embarrass

Which words contain four syllables?

13. environment 14. epitome 15. recollection 16. exaggerate

Classification

Write a List Word to complete each series.

1. tiresome, long, tedious
2. small, medium, large
3. sophomore, junior, senior
4. holy, blessed, sacred
5. margin, allowance, leeway
6. deceive, desert, betray
7. declare, affirm, testify
8. mild, merciful, lenient
9. rot, decay, erode
10. rinse, wash, sterilize

Word Application

Write a List Word to complete each sentence.

1. Great Britain has an office, or embassy, located in Washington, D.C.
2. Peeling a whole bag of potatoes can be a long and tedious job.
3. To figure out the approximate number of people in a theater is to make an estimate.
4. If you exaggerate, you make something much bigger, funnier, or stranger than it really is.
5. Dentists sterilize their instruments to prevent germs from spreading among their patients.
6. Your class might elect a delegate to represent you at student council meetings.
7. People sometimes blush when situations embarrass them.

10

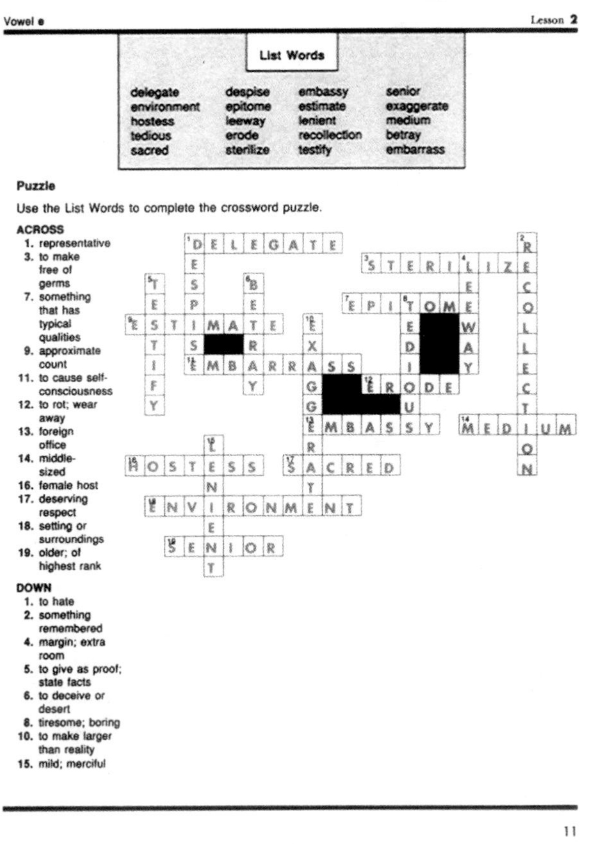

Vowel e — Lesson 2

List Words

delegate	despise	embassy	senior
environment	epitome	estimate	exaggerate
hostess	leeway	lenient	medium
tedious	erode	recollection	betray
sacred	sterilize	testify	embarrass

Puzzle

Use the List Words to complete the crossword puzzle.

ACROSS
1. representative
3. to make free of germs
7. something that has typical qualities
9. approximate count
11. to cause self-consciousness
12. to rot; wear away
13. foreign office
14. middle-sized
16. female host
17. deserving respect
18. setting or surroundings
19. older; of highest rank

DOWN
1. to hate
2. something remembered
4. margin; extra room
5. to give as proof; state facts
6. to deceive or desert
8. tiresome; boring
10. to make larger than reality
15. mild; merciful

11

Vowel e — Lesson 2

Proofreading

Use the proofreading marks to correct the mistakes in the letter to the editor. Then write the misspelled List Words on the lines.

Proofreading Marks
spelling mistake — add space
small letter — delete word

I do not exaggarate when I say that the the recycling program in our Community is one of the bestin the region. As a deligate to the Roseville Council, I estemate that each family in our area recycles a a meadium amount of materials every week. Hauling away additional pounds of materials must be tedius for our waste collectors, but Everyone's positive attitude, effort, and hardwork demonstrates that if we work together we can all do something to save our envirment!

1. exaggerate
2. delegate
3. estimate
4. medium
5. tedious
6. environment

Challenges

Express Yourself

Acid Rain Threatens Forests

Industrial Wastes Pollute Rivers

Vehicle Exhaust Fumes Harm Air Quality

Oil Spills In Ocean Damage Fish Populations

These headlines mention environmental issues affecting our air, land, and water. Research one of these topics or another environmental problem. Then write a two-paragraph plan that the government should follow in order to better manage the problem. After proofreading and revising your paragraphs, compare and discuss the plan with others.

Bonus Words: Social Studies

lobbyist	conservative	amendment	sovereign	coalition
diplomatic	federal	arbitrate	proponent	assembly

Write Bonus Words to answer the questions.

Which two nouns mean group?

1. coalition 2. assembly

Which two nouns mean one who supports a certain position?

3. lobbyist 4. proponent

Write the Bonus Word that matches each definition clue.

5. not liberal conservative
6. national federal
7. supreme or royal sovereign
8. tactful or fair diplomatic
9. to settle a dispute arbitrate
10. a revision or addition amendment

12

Puzzle (Page 11) If necessary, review the process for solving crossword puzzles before students begin work, explaining the relationship between the numbers preceding the clues and those in the puzzle grid.

Proofreading (Page 12) Write *David went too the the Store.* on the board and use it to demonstrate the proofreading marks in this lesson.

Challenges

Express Yourself (Page 12) To prepare students, display and discuss actual news stories and editorials on environmental issues. Point out that news stories contain facts, whereas editorials contain opinions supported by facts and reasons. Discuss topic ideas with students and urge them to jot down notes to use as they write their editorials. When they have finished writing, provide time for volunteers to read their work aloud. Students may enjoy submitting their editorials to the school newspaper for possible publication.

Bonus Words: Social Studies (Page 12) Call on volunteers to look up Bonus Words in a dictionary and read the definitions aloud. Have other students use the words in oral sentences. Relate the words to the writing project topics, as well as, current social studies readings and recent news.

Bonus Word Test

1. The king is sovereign ruler.
2. Mr. Garcia will arbitrate the labor dispute.
3. My uncle is a lobbyist for the dairy industry.
4. Susan hopes to work in the diplomatic corps.
5. The conservative politicians worked for tax reform.
6. A federal law mandates equal job opportunities.
7. An amendment gives voting rights to women.
8. Senator Ames is a leading proponent for lower taxes.
9. The president will address the assembly at noon.
10. Members of the coalition spoke for world peace.

Final Test

1. We visited the sacred burial ground of an old tribe.
2. Sarita will testify in court tomorrow morning.
3. The chemist will sterilize the jars in boiling water.
4. Stop or you will embarrass me!
5. Your recollection of the story differs from mine.
6. Sea water will cause the embankment to erode.
7. Joan enjoyed the lecture, but Jeff found it tedious.
8. Traitors are people who betray their countries.
9. Is Jim's brother a senior in high school?
10. The foreign minister arrives at the embassy today.
11. The committee sent a delegate to the conference.
12. Homeowners despise termites.
13. Everyone benefits from a safe environment.
14. I estimate that the Jets will win about ten games.
15. I exaggerate when I say I could eat a horse.
16. The judge was the epitome of wisdom and justice.
17. In bad weather, give other cars plenty of leeway.
18. After dinner, the hostess introduced the speaker.
19. The sweater labeled medium was actually small.
20. Is a trainer lenient with a dog that bites?

Lesson 3

Objective
To spell words with the vowel *i*

Pretest

1. Is that fence too low to be a real barrier?
2. Add a little cinnamon to the applesauce.
3. The error was due to an accident, not ignorance.
4. This project will involve the entire class.
5. The mechanic will align the car's wheels.
6. This is a real bristle brush, not a plastic one.
7. In the corner of the room was a circular staircase.
8. The writer wanted an illustration for each chapter.
9. Try to isolate anyone who has a bad cold.
10. The judge and jury heard each person's testimony.
11. The latest bulletin gave the most recent news.
12. My club does not prohibit anyone from joining.
13. Our car insurance paid for the repairs.
14. The mayor wore a white orchid on her jacket.
15. Do you get bored when you are idle too long?
16. This pitcher has a two-quart capacity.
17. That's a strange cure for hiccups!
18. The contestants all wore formal attire.
19. Is a peninsula surrounded by water on all sides?
20. In the play, Manuel played the villain.

Game Plan
Page 13
Use these words to discuss the different sounds the letter *i* can spell: *icicle, again, vanity, scarier, first.* After each word, have students find List Words in which *i* has the same sound. Point out that in words such as *barrier, i* may sound like a different vowel entirely. Encourage students to find other words in which *i* has an unexpected spelling. Make sure that students understand the meanings of List Words, having them refer to dictionaries when necessary.

Warm Up
Vocabulary Development (Page 13)
Write *not busy* on the chalkboard and ask which List Word matches it. (*idle*) Then have students complete the exercise independently.

Dictionary Skills (Page 13) Write *illustration* on the board as one word and also divided into syllables: *il/lus/tra/tion.* Discuss the rules of syllabication, giving other examples when necessary. You may wish to do the first two items with students to be sure they understand the concept.

Practice
Word Analysis (Page 14) Remind students that some words contain distinctive word parts or spellings, which can help people remember how words are spelled. Point out, for example, that the *t* in *bristle* is silent. Discuss other spelling patterns in List Words.

Vowel i — LESSON 3

Game Plan
The vowel I can spell many different sounds. Notice the sound that I makes in each word below.

attire involve bulletin barrier

You hear the long I sound in attire and the short I sound in involve. In bulletin and barrier, the letter I makes completely different sounds.

Warm Up

1. barrier
2. cinnamon
3. ignorance
4. involve
5. align
6. bristle
7. circular
8. illustration
9. isolate
10. testimony
11. bulletin
12. prohibit
13. insurance
14. orchid
15. idle
16. capacity
17. hiccups
18. attire
19. peninsula
20. villain

Vocabulary Development
Write the List Word that matches each synonym or definition.

1. part of a brush ___bristle___
2. clothing ___attire___
3. a beautiful flower ___orchid___
4. round ___circular___
5. a stretch of land into water ___peninsula___
6. a light brown spice ___cinnamon___
7. fence or barricade ___barrier___
8. bring into agreement ___align___
9. drawing ___illustration___
10. an evil character ___villain___

Dictionary Skills
When dividing words into syllables, we usually divide where the natural sound break occurs, as in cir/cu/lar. Quite often we divide between two consonants, as in fol/low or col/lec/tion.
Rewrite each of the following words to show how they are divided into syllables.

1. hiccups	hic/cups	6. involve	in/volve
2. ignorance	ig/no/rance	7. capacity	ca/pac/i/ty
3. bulletin	bul/le/tin	8. isolate	i/so/late
4. idle	i/dle	9. insurance	in/sur/ance
5. prohibit	pro/hib/it	10. testimony	tes/ti/mo/ny

13

Vowel I — Lesson 3

Practice

Word Analysis
Write the List Words containing the elements given below.

the prefix in or il

1. ___involve___
2. ___illustration___
3. ___insurance___

the long I sound

4. ___align___
5. ___isolate___
6. ___idle___
7. ___attire___

double consonants

8. ___barrier___
9. ___cinnamon___
10. ___illustration___
11. ___bulletin___
12. ___hiccups___
13. ___attire___
14. ___villain___

Did you know?
Peninsula comes from Latin words that mean "almost an island." A *peninsula* would be an island if it were completely surrounded by water.

Word Application
Write a List Word to complete each sentence.

1. That witness's ___testimony___ convinced the jury.
2. Get the paint off every ___bristle___ on the paintbrush.
3. Florida is a ___peninsula___ that extends into the Atlantic Ocean.
4. Every ___illustration___ was drawn with great care.
5. Most states require that drivers buy auto ___insurance___.
6. My hardworking parents are almost never ___idle___.
7. Our ___ignorance___ of local customs led to many misunderstandings.
8. A planet's orbit is not completely ___circular___ in shape.

14

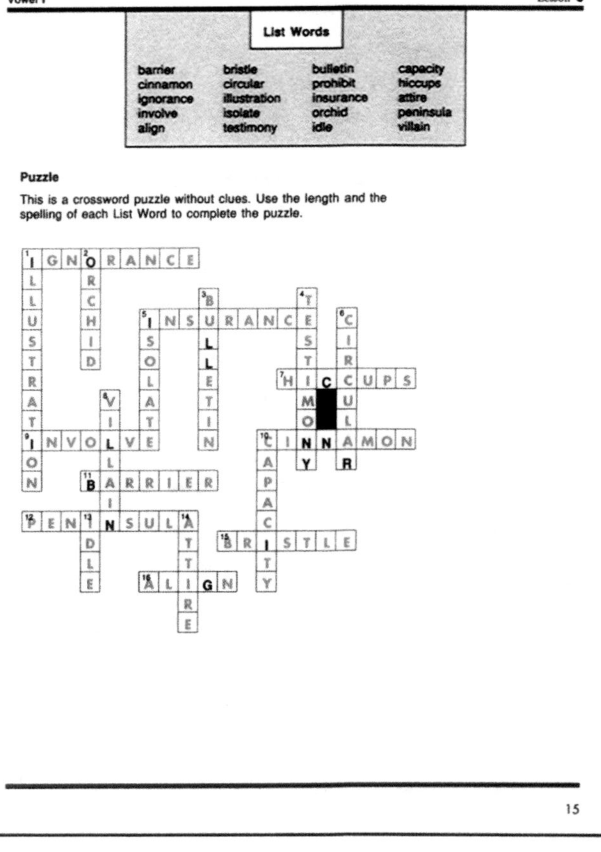

Vowel I — Lesson 3

List Words

barrier	bristle	bulletin	capacity
cinnamon	circular	prohibit	hiccups
ignorance	illustration	insurance	attire
involve	isolate	orchid	peninsula
align	testimony	idle	villain

Puzzle

This is a crossword puzzle without clues. Use the length and the spelling of each List Word to complete the puzzle.

15

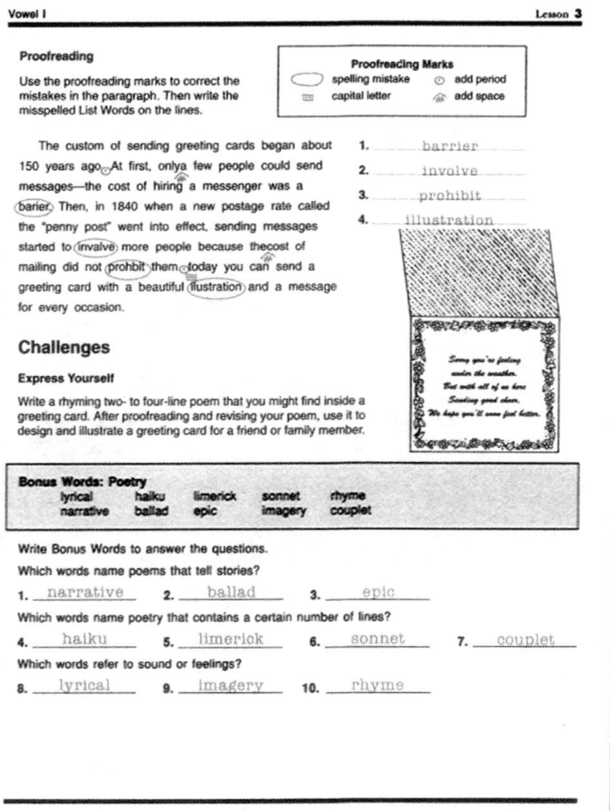

Vowel I — Lesson 3

Proofreading

Use the proofreading marks to correct the mistakes in the paragraph. Then write the misspelled List Words on the lines.

Proofreading Marks
spelling mistake — add period
capital letter — add space

The custom of sending greeting cards began about 150 years ago At first, onlya few people could send messages—the cost of hiring a messenger was a barier Then, in 1840 when a new postage rate called the "penny post" went into effect, sending messages started to invalve more people because thecost of mailing did not prohbit them today you can send a greeting card with a beautiful llustration and a message for every occasion.

1. barrier
2. involve
3. prohibit
4. illustration

Challenges

Express Yourself

Write a rhyming two- to four-line poem that you might find inside a greeting card. After proofreading and revising your poem, use it to design and illustrate a greeting card for a friend or family member.

Bonus Words: Poetry

lyrical, haiku, limerick, sonnet, rhyme, narrative, ballad, epic, imagery, couplet

Write Bonus Words to answer the questions.

Which words name poems that tell stories?

1. narrative 2. ballad 3. epic

Which words name poetry that contains a certain number of lines?

4. haiku 5. limerick 6. sonnet 7. couplet

Which words refer to sound or feelings?

8. lyrical 9. imagery 10. rhyme

16

Word Application (Page 14) Remind students that the answers they choose must be spelled correctly and must make sense in the sentence. Later, you may wish to have students discuss the clues that help them know which answers are correct.

Puzzle (Page 15) Discuss how students might complete the crossword puzzle. Remind them to print neatly, and suggest that they first fill in known answers, rather than proceeding in some other order.

Proofreading (Page 16) Write *Todayis irma's berthday* on the board and use it to demonstrate the proofreading marks in this lesson. Point out that students will use these marks to correct the paragraph.

Challenges

Express Yourself (Page 16) Have students discuss various types of greeting cards and messages. After they have written their poems, they may wish to illustrate them and use them as actual cards to be sent.

Bonus Words: Poetry (Page 16) Point out that all Bonus Words are related to poetry. If possible, try to find poems or words that exemplify each term, using poetry anthologies as sources. Help students understand each word's meaning, and then have them complete the Bonus Word activity.

Bonus Word Test

1. Try to find a word that will rhyme with my name.
2. That limerick is very silly!
3. We read a lyrical poem about nature's beauties.
4. The haiku is a Japanese verse form.
5. Those two lines form a famous couplet.
6. An epic poem is often about a national hero.
7. The poet's imagery creates pictures in your mind.
8. A narrative poem tells some kind of story.
9. A ballad might be a poem or a song.
10. This sonnet was written by William Shakespeare.

Final Test

1. At the end of the story, the villain is punished.
2. Will the new law prohibit left turns at that corner?
3. The house on the peninsula has ocean views.
4. You should always wear warm attire in the winter.
5. I love the smell of cinnamon!
6. Every parent should have life insurance.
7. Jan's hiccups vanished after she held her breath.
8. This plan will involve the entire teaching staff.
9. Although he appeared idle, Tuan was thinking.
10. First, align the window with its frame.
11. My ignorance was obvious when I failed the test.
12. This baking pan has a two-quart capacity.
13. The barrier keeps the dog out of the living room.
14. Try to isolate the sick birds from the healthy ones.
15. Don't wash a bristle brush in water.
16. In what climate will an orchid grow best?
17. A clerk wrote down every word of testimony.
18. This illustration shows the floor plan of the house.
19. The shape of the room is circular, not square.
20. Did the weather bulletin predict rain today?

Lesson 4

Objective

To spell words with the vowel *o*

Pretest

1. Was Ramón nervous in anticipation of his speech?
2. A blockade across the harbor kept ships out.
3. The finest racers signed up for the competition.
4. This continuous rainfall will flood the streets!
5. Saluting the flag is a patriotic gesture.
6. At the armory museum, we saw suits of armor.
7. The funds were given by a generous donor.
8. I saw that actor in a commercial for cereal.
9. At the conclusion of the play, they find the gold.
10. The company's policy is to satisfy its customers.
11. Speak into the microphone so we can hear you.
12. The cereal's advertising slogan is "Vote for Oats!"
13. Gail worked to solve the complicated problem.
14. The secretary took copious notes of the meeting.
15. The prospector was searching for gold.
16. Photographers need models who are photogenic.
17. The controls of a plane are in the cockpit.
18. Is the continent of Australia a large island?
19. Dark, ominous clouds preceded the thunderstorm.
20. Who will be Jason's opponent in the tennis match?

Game Plan

Page 17

Discuss the Game Plan. Use these words for further examples of the common sounds of the vowel *o*: /ō/: *total, road;* /ô/: *pork, court;* /ä/: *lock, hospital;* /u/: *tongue, son;* /o͝o/: *hook, hood;* /o͞o/: *soon, broom;* /ou/ *loud, out;* /ə/: *actor, committee.* Then apply the discussion to List Words. Work with students to define each word.

Warm Up

Vocabulary Development (Page 17)

Before the exercise, call on volunteers to identify List Words that match these definitions: *someone who gives (donor); a large land mass (continent).*

Dictionary Skills (Page 17) Review syllabication by having students tell the syllable count in *anticipation (5), photogenic (4),* and *patriotic (4).*

Practice

Word Analysis (Page 18) Review root words by having students name them in *unnoticed (notice), recover (cover),* and *composition (compose).*

Analogies (Page 18) Review analogies by writing on the chalkboard: *movie, television, radio.* Then read this incomplete analogy aloud and have students select the word that best completes it: *Vision is to books as hearing is to* ________ *(radio).*

Word Application (Page 18) Urge students to use context clues to find the missing word in each sentence.

Vowel o — LESSON **4**

Game Plan

The vowel **o** stands for many different sounds.
Here are some of the most common **o** sounds.

/ō/ phone	hostess		/o͝o/ book	wolf
/ô/ horn	orchestra		/o͞o/ spool	room
/ä/ block	prospect		/ou/ shout	crowd
/u/ sponge	ton		/ə/ continue	armory

1. anticipation
2. blockade
3. competition
4. continuous
5. patriotic
6. armory
7. donor
8. commercial
9. conclusion
10. policy
11. microphone
12. slogan
13. complicated
14. copious
15. prospector
16. photogenic
17. cockpit
18. continent
19. ominous
20. opponent

Warm Up

Vocabulary Development

Write the List Word that matches each definition.

1. proud of one's country ___patriotic___
2. very threatening ___ominous___
3. without a stop or break ___continuous___
4. a contest or rivalry ___competition___
5. the act of looking forward to something ___anticipation___
6. the end ___conclusion___
7. difficult to understand ___complicated___
8. a device for augmenting voices ___microphone___
9. attractive in photographs ___photogenic___
10. a place to store weapons ___armory___

Dictionary Skills

Write the List Words that contain two syllables.

1. ___blockade___ 3. ___slogan___
2. ___donor___ 4. ___cockpit___

Write the List Words that contain three syllables.

5. ___armory___ 10. ___copious___
6. ___commercial___ 11. ___prospector___
7. ___conclusion___ 12. ___continent___
8. ___policy___ 13. ___ominous___
9. ___microphone___ 14. ___opponent___

17

Vowel o — Lesson **4**

Practice

Word Analysis

Write the List Word that contains the same root as the word given.

1. commerce ___commercial___ 8. oppose ___opponent___
2. conclude ___conclusion___ 9. compete ___competition___
3. telephone ___microphone___ 10. photograph ___photogenic___
4. anticipate ___anticipation___ 11. complicate ___complicated___
5. armor ___armory___ 12. block ___blockade___
6. continue ___continuous___ 13. donate ___donor___
7. prospect ___prospect___ 14. patriot ___patriotic___

Did you know?

Slogan comes from a Gaelic word used by Scottish Highland and Irish clans as a battle cry or to call the clan together. Now the word *slogan* has little to do with war, but it is used to get people to rally around a political party or leader.

Analogies

Write a List Word to complete each analogy.

1. Pilot is to ___cockpit___ as rider is to saddle.
2. Boston is to city as Asia is to ___continent___.
3. Bricks are to wall as words are to ___slogan___.
4. Simple is to ___complicated___ as easy is to difficult.
5. "Go!" is to beginning as "Stop!" is to ___conclusion___.
6. Miner is to ___prospector___ as detective is to investigator.
7. Receiver is to take as ___donor___ is to give.
8. Funny is to humorous as threatening is to ___ominous___.
9. Recollection is to yesterday as ___anticipation___ is to tomorrow.

Word Application

Write a List Word to complete each sentence.

1. I hope that you play better than your ___opponent___ in your tennis match.
2. Janet's school pictures came out beautifully because she is extremely ___photogenic___.
3. The tape recording was difficult to hear because the ___microphone___ had not been working well.
4. The school has a firm ___policy___ regarding unexcused absences.
5. Tools for a ___prospector___ in the 1849 California Gold Rush included pickaxes.

18

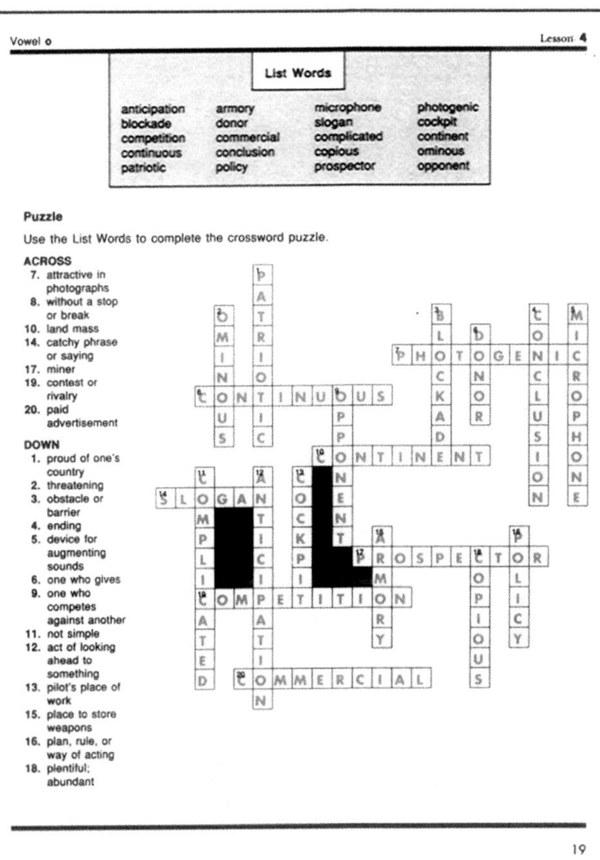

Vowel o — Lesson 4

List Words

anticipation	armory	microphone	photogenic
blockade	donor	slogan	cockpit
competition	commercial	complicated	continent
continuous	conclusion	copious	ominous
patriotic	policy	prospector	opponent

Puzzle

Use the List Words to complete the crossword puzzle.

ACROSS

7. attractive in photographs
8. without a stop or break
10. land mass
14. catchy phrase or saying
17. miner
19. contest or rivalry
20. paid advertisement

DOWN

1. proud of one's country
2. threatening
3. obstacle or barrier
4. ending
5. device for augmenting sounds
6. one who gives
9. one who competes against another
11. not simple
12. act of looking ahead to something
13. pilot's place of work
15. place to store weapons
16. plan, rule, or way of acting
18. plentiful; abundant

19

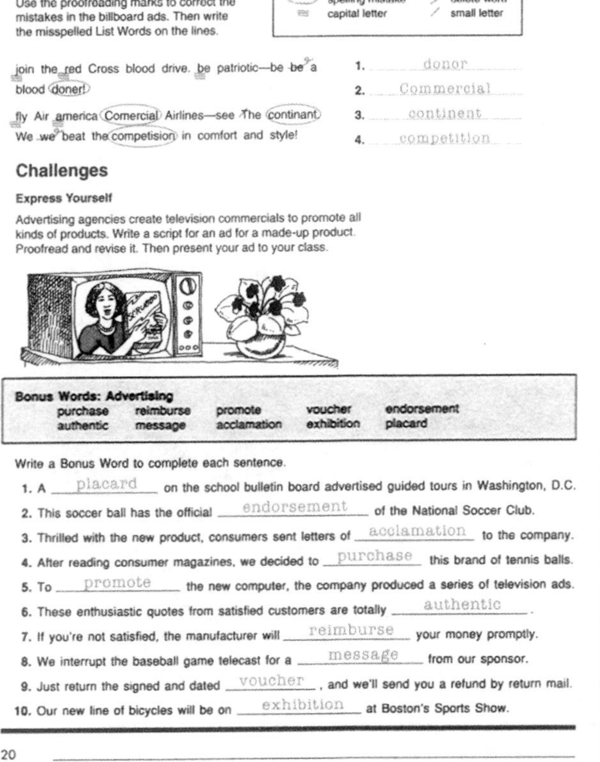

Vowel o — Lesson 4

Proofreading

Use the proofreading marks to correct the mistakes in the billboard ads. Then write the misspelled List Words on the lines.

Proofreading Marks: spelling mistake; delete word; capital letter; small letter

join the red Cross blood drive. be patriotic—be be a blood doner!

fly Air america Comercial Airlines—see The continant

We we beat the competision in comfort and style!

1. donor
2. Commercial
3. continent
4. competition

Challenges

Express Yourself

Advertising agencies create television commercials to promote all kinds of products. Write a script for an ad for a made-up product. Proofread and revise it. Then present your ad to your class.

Bonus Words: Advertising

purchase	reimburse	promote	voucher	endorsement
authentic	message	acclamation	exhibition	placard

Write a Bonus Word to complete each sentence.

1. A placard on the school bulletin board advertised guided tours in Washington, D.C.
2. This soccer ball has the official endorsement of the National Soccer Club.
3. Thrilled with the new product, consumers sent letters of acclamation to the company.
4. After reading consumer magazines, we decided to purchase this brand of tennis balls.
5. To promote the new computer, the company produced a series of television ads.
6. These enthusiastic quotes from satisfied customers are totally authentic.
7. If you're not satisfied, the manufacturer will reimburse your money promptly.
8. We interrupt the baseball game telecast for a message from our sponsor.
9. Just return the signed and dated voucher, and we'll send you a refund by return mail.
10. Our new line of bicycles will be on exhibition at Boston's Sports Show.

20

Puzzle (Page 19) If necessary, review the process for solving crossword puzzles before students begin work, explaining the relationship between the numbers preceding the clues and those in the puzzle grid.

Proofreading (Page 20) Show examples on the board to illustrate the proofreading marks in this lesson.

Challenges

Express Yourself (Page 20) Discuss the components of the sample page of script, pointing out the tag lines and stage directions. Have students describe television advertisements that they feel are particularly effective, and have them support their opinions with reasons. Brainstorm "fantastic" products that might be popular to consumers, such as robots that do homework assignments or automatic cars that can be programmed to travel to a particular place. Urge students to jot down notes before they begin to write. When they have finished writing, provide time for oral presentations of the ads.

Bonus Words: Advertising (Page 20) Discuss Bonus Words, having students define those that are familiar and calling on volunteers to read dictionary definitions for those that are not. Relate the words to the writing project and students' experiences as consumers.

Bonus Word Test

1. I saw an exhibition of new computers.
2. The athlete was paid for his endorsement.
3. We decided to purchase a new carpet for the hall.
4. I will reimburse you if you're not satisfied.
5. Listen to a message from our sponsor.
6. The play was greeted by critical acclamation.
7. The clerk gave me a voucher marked "Paid in full."
8. This advertising placard was designed by my uncle.
9. The company uses radio ads to promote its product.
10. The claims in ads are not always authentic facts.

Final Test

1. The band played a medley of patriotic marches.
2. The prospector examined the rocks for gold.
3. The politician will debate her opponent on TV.
4. The restaurant's policy is to accept credit cards.
5. I went to bed early in anticipation of a busy day.
6. Shields and swords were on display at the armory.
7. A fashion model must be photogenic.
8. When making a tape, speak into the microphone.
9. A dam was built to blockade the river.
10. A donor provided funds for the new gymnasium.
11. The pilot and navigator sit in the cockpit.
12. My campaign slogan is "Kate's Great!"
13. The cat food commercial featured dancing cats.
14. Did you find the computer manual complicated?
15. Asia is the largest continent.
16. The school has a poetry writing competition.
17. The continuous noise was making me nervous.
18. George took copious notes during the lecture.
19. The picnic was cancelled due to ominous clouds.
20. Will this question mark the conclusion of the test?

Lesson 5

Objective

To spell words with the vowel *u*

Pretest

1. Kindness is her most outstanding attribute.
2. Will new students be given a map of the campus?
3. The actor showed only subtle changes in emotion.
4. What a beautiful lullaby that is!
5. Like many medicines, this serum saves lives.
6. One radioactive element is called uranium.
7. The horses ran the circumference of the corral.
8. I want to plant a geranium near the front door.
9. You will find nail scissors in the manicure kit.
10. The smudge on Kim's shirt wouldn't come off.
11. One of your chores is to vacuum the carpet.
12. Our chorus sounds good because of its unity.
13. One industrious worker can paint the wall in a day.
14. Will regular exercise improve muscular strength?
15. Pigment is the substance that gives paint its color.
16. For amusement, we can play a game.
17. You can learn about a country's culture by visiting.
18. The linoleum covered an old wooden floor.
19. You will have to pay a premium for front-row seats.
20. Wear your suspenders instead of a belt.

Game Plan

Page 21
Discuss the different sounds the letter *u* can spell, using these words as examples: *blush, flute, focus.* After each word, have students find List Words in which *u* has the same sound. Point out that in words such as *tutor, u* may sound like a different vowel entirely. Make sure that students understand the meanings of List Words, having them refer to dictionaries when necessary. You may wish to have them use the words in oral sentences.

Warm Up

Vocabulary Development (Page 21) Write *level* and *flat* on the chalkboard, explaining that they are synonyms. Then have students give other examples of synonym pairs.

Dictionary Skills (Page 21) Write *industrious* on the board as one word and also divided into syllables: *in/dus/tri/ous.* Discuss the rules of syllabication, giving other examples if necessary. You may wish to do the first two items with students before having them complete the activity independently.

Practice

Word Analysis (Page 22) Discuss with students different ways they remember word spellings. Point out, for example, that the words *unity* and *unify* are spelled alike except for one letter. Have students give examples of spelling patterns they have noticed.

Vowel u — LESSON 5

Game Plan

The vowel u can spell many different sounds. Listen for the sound of u in each word below.

smudge attribute campus

You hear the sound of short u in smudge and the sound of long u in attribute. In campus, the letter u stands for the schwa sound.

1. attribute
2. campus
3. subtle
4. lullaby
5. serum
6. uranium
7. circumference
8. geranium
9. manicure
10. smudge
11. vacuum
12. unity
13. industrious
14. muscular
15. substance
16. amusement
17. culture
18. linoleum
19. premium
20. suspenders

Warm Up

Vocabulary Development

Write the List Word that matches each synonym.

1. flooring linoleum
2. schoolyard campus
3. smear smudge
4. flower geranium
5. medicine serum
6. hardworking industrious
7. strong muscular
8. characteristic attribute
9. perimeter circumference
10. void vacuum

Dictionary Skills

Rewrite each of the following List Words to show how they are divided into syllables.

1. lullaby lull/a/by
2. uranium u/ra/ni/um
3. premium pre/mi/um
4. suspenders sus/pen/ders
5. culture cul/ture
6. campus cam/pus
7. manicure man/i/cure
8. substance sub/stance
9. unity u/ni/ty
10. amusement a/muse/ment
11. subtle sub/tle
12. attribute at/trib/ute

21

Vowel u — Lesson 5

Practice

Word Analysis

Write the List Words containing the elements given below.

the ending lum

1. uranium
2. geranium
3. premium

double letters

4. attribute
5. lullaby
6. vacuum

short u or schwa

7. campus
8. subtle
9. lullaby
10. serum
11. uranium
12. circumference
13. geranium
14. smudge
15. industrious
16. muscular
17. substance
18. linoleum
19. premium
20. suspenders

Did you know?

Subtle comes from a Latin word meaning "closely woven," used to describe delicate fabrics. *Subtle* first meant "delicate" but later came to mean "made with skill." Something *subtle* then is "finely woven" or "delicate and skillful."

Classification

Write a List Word to complete each series.

1. sweep, dust, vacuum
2. flooring, tile, linoleum
3. medicine, cure, serum
4. perimeter, circle, circumference
5. singleness, harmony, unity
6. belts, ties, suspenders
7. haircut, pedicure, manicure
8. song, melody, lullaby
9. entertainment, laughter, amusement
10. radium, plutonium, uranium

22

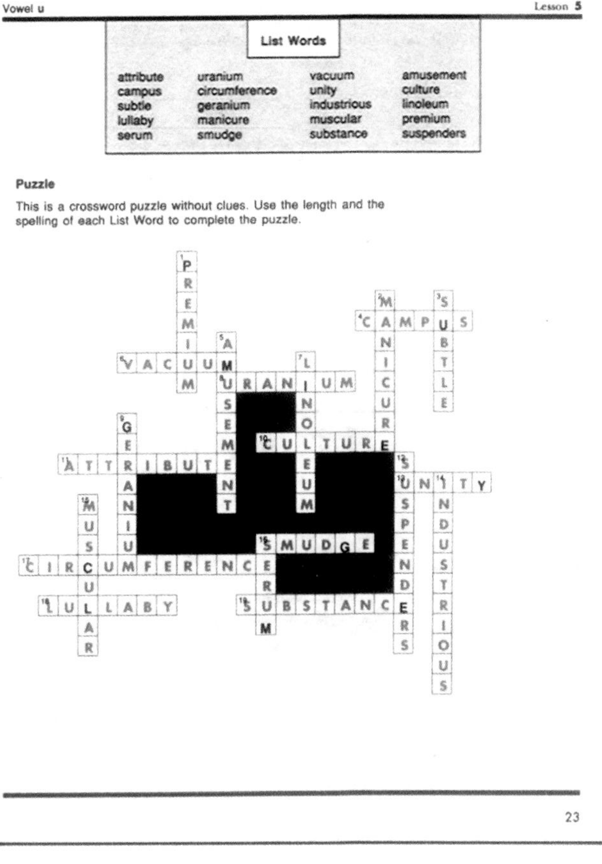
Vowel u — Lesson 5

List Words

attribute	uranium	vacuum	amusement
campus	circumference	unity	culture
subtle	geranium	industrious	linoleum
lullaby	manicure	muscular	premium
serum	smudge	substance	suspenders

Puzzle

This is a crossword puzzle without clues. Use the length and the spelling of each List Word to complete the puzzle.

23

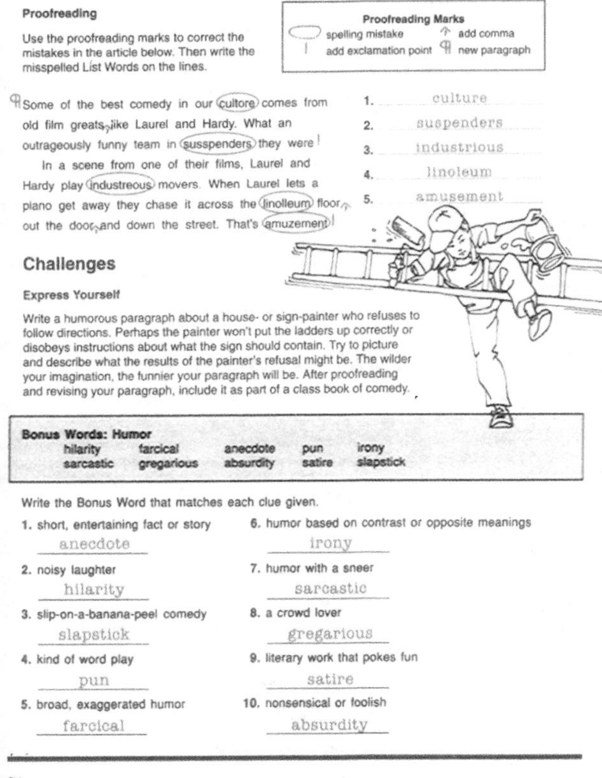
Vowel u — Lesson 5

Proofreading

Use the proofreading marks to correct the mistakes in the article below. Then write the misspelled List Words on the lines.

Proofreading Marks: spelling mistake; add comma; add exclamation point; new paragraph

Some of the best comedy in our cultore comes from old film greats like Laurel and Hardy. What an outrageously funny team in susspenders they were In a scene from one of their films, Laurel and Hardy play industreous movers. When Laurel lets a piano get away they chase it across the linolleum floor out the door and down the street. That's amuzement

1. culture
2. suspenders
3. industrious
4. linoleum
5. amusement

Challenges

Express Yourself

Write a humorous paragraph about a house- or sign-painter who refuses to follow directions. Perhaps the painter won't put the ladders up correctly or disobeys instructions about what the sign should contain. Try to picture and describe what the results of the painter's refusal might be. The wilder your imagination, the funnier your paragraph will be. After proofreading and revising your paragraph, include it as part of a class book of comedy.

Bonus Words: Humor

hilarity	farcical	anecdote	pun	irony
sarcastic	gregarious	absurdity	satire	slapstick

Write the Bonus Word that matches each clue given.

1. short, entertaining fact or story — anecdote
2. noisy laughter — hilarity
3. slip-on-a-banana-peel comedy — slapstick
4. kind of word play — pun
5. broad, exaggerated humor — farcical
6. humor based on contrast or opposite meanings — irony
7. humor with a sneer — sarcastic
8. a crowd lover — gregarious
9. literary work that pokes fun — satire
10. nonsensical or foolish — absurdity

24

Classification (Page 22) Ask students what List Word would belong with the words *rose* and *daisy*. (*geranium*) Discuss why this answer is correct, and different ways words in a series might be related. Help students work through the first item.

Puzzle (Page 23) Discuss how students can use the bold-faced letters, the length of List Words, and List Words they fill in first to help them complete the puzzle. Remind them to print neatly, first filling in all the answers about which they are sure.

Proofreading (Page 24) Write *Watch out yeled Nancy.* on the board and use it to show the proofreading marks for spelling mistakes and exclamation point. Also illustrate the add comma and indent paragraph marks.

Challenges

Express Yourself (Page 24) As a group, have students discuss various scenarios for their paragraphs. Encourage a variety of responses. Then have students write their paragraphs independently.

Bonus Words—Humor (Page 24) Point out that all Bonus Words are related to humor. Try to have students suggest situations or examples to clarify the meanings of words. Through discussion and dictionary use, help students understand each word's meaning. Then have them complete the Bonus Word activity.

Bonus Word Test

1. A pun depends on a word's multiple meanings.
2. A joke is one type of anecdote.
3. The hilarity was caused by the comedy.
4. The farcical uniforms barely resembled real ones.
5. Irony depends on the audience knowing the truth.
6. Most slapstick comedy has lots of physical action.
7. That sarcastic tone of voice sounds unkind.
8. A gregarious person is rarely alone.
9. We laughed at the absurdity of a fish in each shoe.
10. The play is a satire about the politics of the time.

Final Test

1. The lullaby soon put the baby to sleep.
2. A manicure will improve your fingernails.
3. Look how muscular that horse is!
4. The bank is offering a premium to new investors.
5. I noticed the suspenders under his jacket.
6. The substance can be a gas or a solid.
7. You can see the smudge that the eraser left.
8. That serum will save thousands of lives!
9. List each attribute that a candidate should have.
10. Uranium is named in honor of the planet Uranus.
11. That artist uses only subtle colors in her works.
12. Sue's classroom is all the way across the campus.
13. Did you measure the circumference of the circle?
14. Can a geranium be grown indoors and outdoors?
15. Beavers are very industrious animals.
16. A vacuum is a completely empty space.
17. Team unity is more important than the score.
18. An old linoleum floor requires waxing to shine.
19. Every country has its own distinctive culture.
20. Dave likes to skate for amusement.

Lesson 6

Objective

To review spelling patterns of words from Lessons 1–5

Game Plan

Page 25

Tell students that in this lesson they will review the spelling patterns of words they studied in Lessons 1–5. Read and discuss the Game Plan with students, having them name each vowel and the sounds it stands for in the example words. Have students give other examples of words containing similar sounds.

Practice

Lesson 1 (Page 25) Write these words on the board: *alfalfa, basis, car, ago* and use them to discuss the sounds that the vowel *a* can stand for. Then have students identify the sound *a* stands for in each List Word. Point out the additional write-on lines and encourage students to add two words from Lesson 1 that they found especially difficult, or select and assign certain words that seem difficult for everyone. (Repeat this procedure for each lesson review in the Replay.)

Lesson 2 (Page 26) Use these words to review the sounds that *e* can stand for: *epitome, senior, plated, token, erode.* Then have students identify the sounds *e* stands for in the List Words. Have students identify other words which contain these sounds.

Lesson 3 (Page 26) Write *circus, orchid, prohibit, high* on the board. Use the words to review different sounds that the vowel *i* can stand for. Then have students identify the same sounds in their List Words. You may wish to work through the first item with the students, asking why *capacity* is the correct answer. (*It makes sense in the sentence.*)

Lesson 4 (Page 27) Use these words to review different sounds that the vowel o can stand for: *flock, corn, stone, son, hook, pool, found, conspire.* Then have the students identify the sounds that o stands for in their List Words. To extend, students could provide clues for words from Lessons 1–3 as well.

Lesson 5 (Page 27) Write the words *uranium, put, sure,* and *custom* on the board. Use them to discuss the sounds that *u* can stand for. Before students attempt the puzzle, elicit from students the steps involved.

Mixed Practice (Page 28) Have volunteers describe what guide words are and what they do. Then discuss how students might proceed with this exercise. You might suggest that they use scrap paper to first write the words that fit between each pair of guide words, sequence them, and then copy them.

Test Yourself (Page 28) Point out to students that this test will help them know if they have mastered the words in Lessons 1-5. Have a volunteer restate the directions and tell which word in the first item should be marked. (*unitty*)

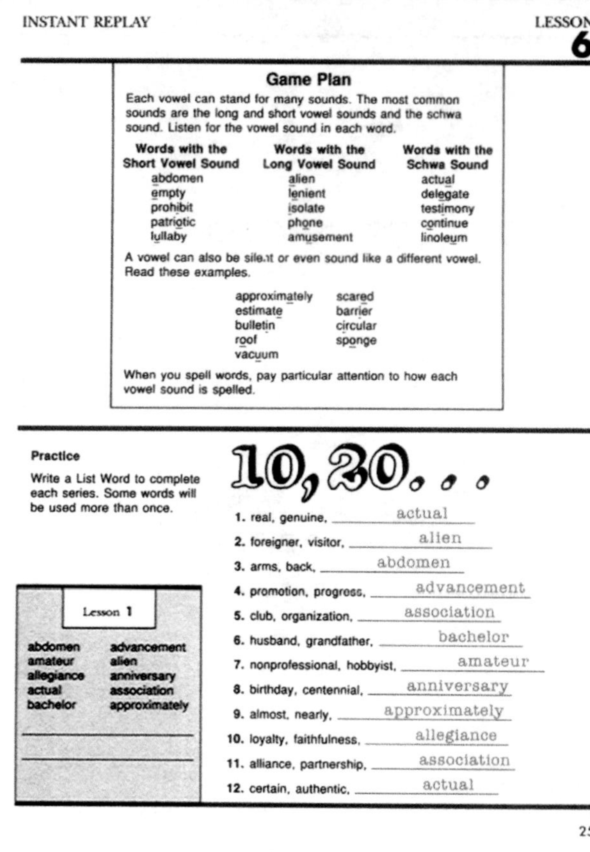

INSTANT REPLAY LESSON 6

Game Plan

Each vowel can stand for many sounds. The most common sounds are the long and short vowel sounds and the schwa sound. Listen for the vowel sound in each word.

Words with the Short Vowel Sound	Words with the Long Vowel Sound	Words with the Schwa Sound
abdomen	alien	actual
empty	lenient	delegate
prohibit	isolate	testimony
patriotic	phone	continue
lullaby	amusement	linoleum

A vowel can also be silent or even sound like a different vowel. Read these examples.

approximately	scared
estimate	barrier
bulletin	circular
roof	sponge
vacuum	

When you spell words, pay particular attention to how each vowel sound is spelled.

Practice

Write a List Word to complete each series. Some words will be used more than once.

10, 20, . . .

1. real, genuine, actual
2. foreigner, visitor, alien
3. arms, back, abdomen
4. promotion, progress, advancement
5. club, organization, association
6. husband, grandfather, bachelor
7. nonprofessional, hobbyist, amateur
8. birthday, centennial, anniversary
9. almost, nearly, approximately
10. loyalty, faithfulness, allegiance
11. alliance, partnership, association
12. certain, authentic, actual

Lesson 1

abdomen	advancement
amateur	alien
allegiance	anniversary
actual	association
bachelor	approximately

25

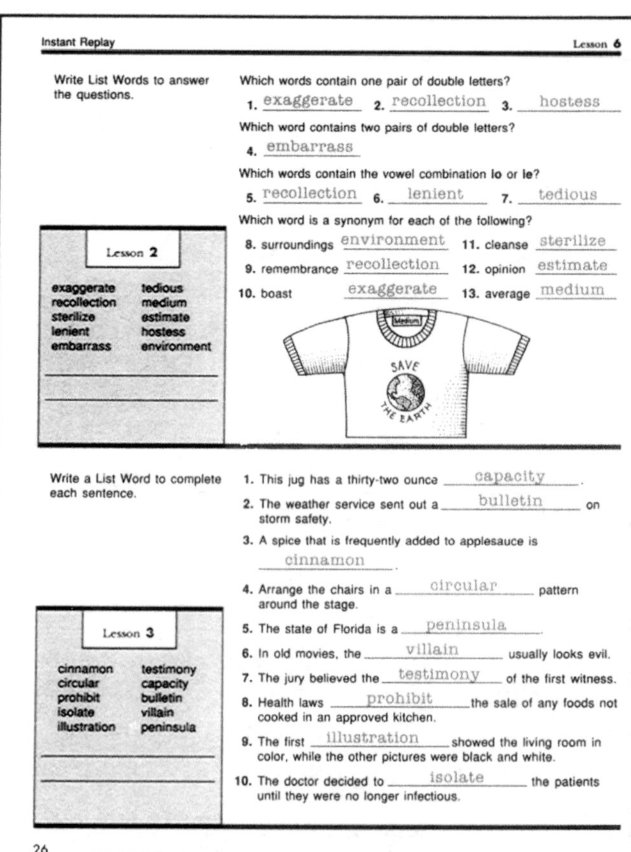

Instant Replay Lesson 6

Write List Words to answer the questions.

Which words contain one pair of double letters?
1. exaggerate 2. recollection 3. hostess

Which word contains two pairs of double letters?
4. embarrass

Which words contain the vowel combination io or ie?
5. recollection 6. lenient 7. tedious

Which word is a synonym for each of the following?
8. surroundings environment
9. remembrance recollection
10. boast exaggerate
11. cleanse sterilize
12. opinion estimate
13. average medium

Lesson 2

exaggerate	tedious
recollection	medium
sterilize	estimate
lenient	hostess
embarrass	environment

Write a List Word to complete each sentence.

1. This jug has a thirty-two ounce capacity.
2. The weather service sent out a bulletin on storm safety.
3. A spice that is frequently added to applesauce is cinnamon.
4. Arrange the chairs in a circular pattern around the stage.
5. The state of Florida is a peninsula.
6. In old movies, the villain usually looks evil.
7. The jury believed the testimony of the first witness.
8. Health laws prohibit the sale of any foods not cooked in an approved kitchen.
9. The first illustration showed the living room in color, while the other pictures were black and white.
10. The doctor decided to isolate the patients until they were no longer infectious.

Lesson 3

cinnamon	testimony
circular	capacity
prohibit	bulletin
isolate	villain
illustration	peninsula

26

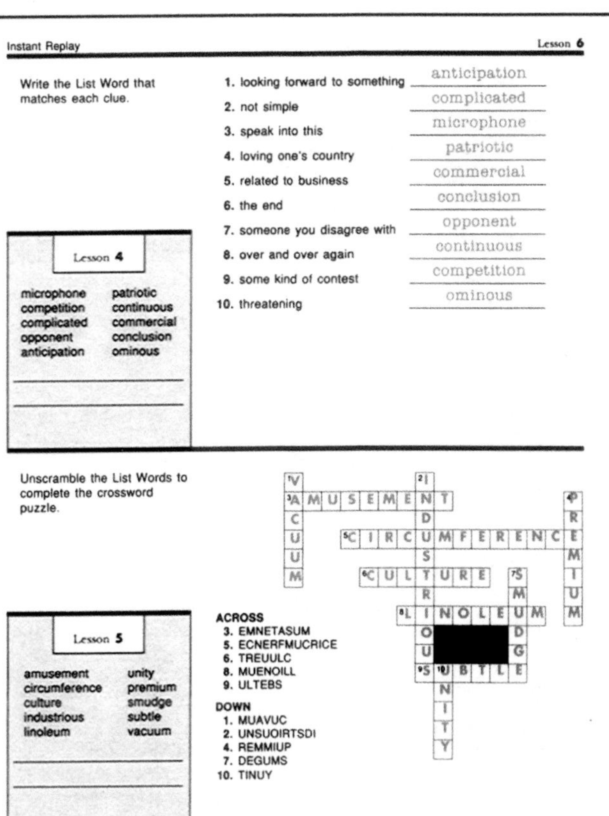

Instant Replay — Lesson 6

Write the List Word that matches each clue.

1. looking forward to something — anticipation
2. not simple — complicated
3. speak into this — microphone
4. loving one's country — patriotic
5. related to business — commercial
6. the end — conclusion
7. someone you disagree with — opponent
8. over and over again — continuous
9. some kind of contest — competition
10. threatening — ominous

Lesson 4

microphone, patriotic, competition, continuous, complicated, commercial, opponent, conclusion, anticipation, ominous

Unscramble the List Words to complete the crossword puzzle.

ACROSS
3. EMNETASUM
5. ECNERFMUCRICE
6. TREUULC
8. MUENOILL
9. ULTEBS

DOWN
1. MUAVUC
2. UNSUOIRTSDI
4. REMMIUP
7. DEGUMS
10. TINUY

Lesson 5

amusement, unity, circumference, premium, culture, smudge, industrious, subtle, linoleum, vacuum

27

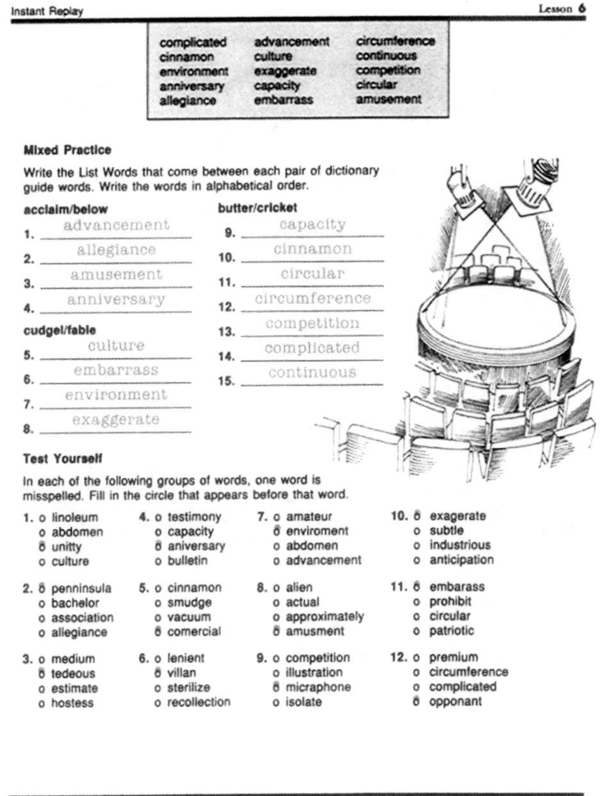

Instant Replay — Lesson 6

complicated, cinnamon, environment, anniversary, allegiance, advancement, culture, exaggerate, capacity, embarrass, circumference, continuous, competition, circular, amusement

Mixed Practice

Write the List Words that come between each pair of dictionary guide words. Write the words in alphabetical order.

acclaim/below
1. advancement
2. allegiance
3. amusement
4. anniversary

cudgel/fable
5. culture
6. embarrass
7. environment
8. exaggerate

butter/cricket
9. capacity
10. cinnamon
11. circular
12. circumference
13. competition
14. complicated
15. continuous

Test Yourself

In each of the following groups of words, one word is misspelled. Fill in the circle that appears before that word.

1. o linoleum, o abdomen, ● unitty, o culture
2. ● penninsula, o bachelor, o association, o allegiance
3. o medium, ● tedeous, o estimate, o hostess
4. o testimony, o capacity, ● aniversary, o bulletin
5. o cinnamon, o smudge, o vacuum, ● comercial
6. o lenient, ● villan, o sterilize, o recollection
7. o amateur, ● enviroment, o abdomen, o advancement
8. o alien, o actual, o approximately, ● amusment
9. o competition, o illustration, ● micraphone, o isolate
10. ● exagerate, o subtle, o industrious, o anticipation
11. ● embarass, o prohibit, o circular, o patriotic
12. o premium, o circumference, o complicated, ● opponant

28

Final Replay Test

1. Sara is an amateur chef, not a professional.
2. The settlers felt homesick in the alien land.
3. This party is to celebrate our wedding anniversary.
4. The actual cost was a bit more than the estimate.
5. Each shelf is approximately two feet long.
6. Stop! Please don't embarrass me.
7. Carol had a recollection of buying shoes that day.
8. Dr. Farnum asked the nurse to sterilize the tools.
9. Is the punishment for a first offense lenient?
10. My little brother may exaggerate, but he won't lie.
11. One person's testimony changed the trial.
12. Is the capacity of this box large enough?
13. Don't miss the emergency weather bulletin!
14. The real villain was not who readers expected.
15. Jon's cottage is out on the end of a peninsula.
16. What ominous black clouds those are!
17. We all applauded at the conclusion of the speech.
18. What a hilarious cereal commercial!
19. A continuous stream of visitors filled the halls.
20. Beneath the flag were portraits of patriotic people.
21. Our baseball team plays well because it has unity.
22. Are premium peaches the most expensive?
23. The smudge came out when the tie was cleaned.
24. There are subtle differences between the colors.
25. Is vacuum short for vacuum cleaner?
26. My uncle was a bachelor until he was thirty-five.
27. Is the Chamber of Commerce an association?
28. Citizens must promise allegiance to our country.
29. Ana's advancement in her profession was steady.
30. Dr. Tsao gently tapped the patient's abdomen.
31. I'll be glad when this tedious job is done.
32. Use a medium-sized hammer for this job.
33. Did the plumber give you an estimate of the cost?
34. Our hostess is the woman wearing the red skirt.
35. Help keep the environment clean!
36. Each illustration is a genuine work of art.
37. Try to isolate the dangerous virus from the others.
38. The club will prohibit guests from loitering.
39. This clock has a circular face, not a square one.
40. Did you put a dash of cinnamon in the apple pie?
41. Try to speak directly into the microphone.
42. That was a fierce competition between the teams!
43. Break a complicated problem into several steps.
44. My opponent refused to debate with me anymore.
45. Patrick cleaned the room in anticipation of guests.
46. Watch out! The linoleum floor was just waxed.
47. On Saturday, Dad took us to an amusement park.
48. Can you measure the circumference of a circle?
49. What an incredible culture the Romans had!
50. An industrious worker can finish this job quickly.

Lesson 7

Objective

To spell words beginning with *ap* or *as*

Pretest

1. A leg is an appendage to the body.
2. The crowd cheered to show their appreciation.
3. Jeremy is a cashier in a men's apparel shop.
4. Cocker spaniels have great appeal as pets.
5. Does the store offer a large assortment of shoes?
6. Vote "YES" to show your approval of the issue.
7. The realtor will appraise the value of the house.
8. Try to appease Rowena with a gracious apology.
9. The citizens paid for new firefighting apparatus.
10. Speak clearly to assert your opinion.
11. The crowd rose to their feet to applaud the singer.
12. What a delicious appetizer this is!
13. Granddad was an electrician's apprentice.
14. Abraham Lincoln was killed by an assassin.
15. Was the assault on the castle successful?
16. Are the charts in the appendix of the report?
17. A swimsuit is not appropriate dress for a prom.
18. We bought a new stove at the appliance store.
19. Mom gave us her assurance that she'd fix the car.
20. A good education is a valuable personal asset.

Game Plan

Page 29

Discuss the Game Plan. For further examples of words in which *ap* and *as* are prefixes, use: *appear, appoint, assign, associate.* For further examples of words in which they are not prefixes, use: *apple, appaloosa, asparagus, asphalt.* Have students check dictionaries to find the etymologies of List Words. Work with them to define each word.

Warm Up

Vocabulary Development (Page 29) Before the exercise, have students name List Words to match these definitions: *proper (appropriate); to quiet or satisfy (appease).*

Dictionary Skills (Page 29) If necessary, use these words to review alphabetization to the sixth letter: *transform, transaction, transport, transition.*

Practice

Word Analysis (Page 30) Before the first exercise, have students name the List Word that has the same root as *application (appliance).* To extend the second exercise, have students separate the words into syllables. Have them use dictionaries to check their work.

Word Application (Page 30) Urge students to use context clues to find the missing word in each sentence. To extend, have them make up similar sentences for the remaining List Words.

Classification (Page 30) Before the exercise, have students name the List Word that completes this series: *student, beginner, ________. (apprentice)*

Words Beginning with **ap, as** — LESSON 7

Game Plan

Sometimes the prefixes **ap** or **as** are added to Latin roots to form nouns or verbs. Both prefixes mean "motion toward, addition to, or nearness to." The prefix **ap** is added to roots beginning with **p**. The prefix **as** is added to roots beginning with **s**.

Latin Root	Meaning	English Word with Prefix	New Meaning
proprius	one's own	**appropriate** (v.)	to take for one's own use
serere	to claim	**assert** (v.)	to state or declare

Other words beginning with **ap** or **as** are derived directly from foreign roots. Appetizer comes from the French word appetit. Assault comes from the Latin word assaltus.

1. appendage
2. appreciation
3. apparel
4. appeal
5. assortment
6. approval
7. appraise
8. appease
9. apparatus
10. assert
11. applaud
12. appetizer
13. apprentice
14. assassin
15. assault
16. appendix
17. appropriate
18. appliance
19. assurance
20. asset

Warm Up

Vocabulary Development

Write the List Word that matches each synonym or definition.

1. clothes apparel
2. variety assortment
3. equipment apparatus
4. clap applaud
5. machine appliance
6. to evaluate appraise
7. student worker apprentice
8. gratitude or thanks appreciation
9. first course of meal appetizer
10. valuable possession asset

Dictionary Skills

Write the List Words that begin with **ap** in alphabetical order.

1. apparatus
2. apparel
3. appeal
4. appease
5. appendage
6. appendix
7. appetizer
8. applaud
9. appliance
10. appraise
11. appreciation
12. apprentice
13. appropriate
14. approval

Write the List Words that begin with **as** in alphabetical order.

15. assassin
16. assault
17. assert
18. asset
19. assortment
20. assurance

29

Words Beginning with **ap, as** — Lesson 7

Practice

Word Analysis

Write the List Word that contains the same root as the word given.

1. sort assortment
2. proper appropriate
3. praise appraise
4. apply appliance
5. peace appease
6. prove approve
7. sure assurance
8. appetite appetizer
9. appreciate appreciation
10. applause applaud

Write each List Word under the correct category.

Words of Two Syllables

1. appeal
2. appraise
3. appease
4. assert
5. applaud
6. assault
7. asset

Words of Three Syllables

8. appendage
9. apparel
10. assortment
11. approval
12. apprentice
13. assassin
14. appendix
15. appliance
16. assurance

Words of Four Syllables

17. apparatus
18. appetizer
19. appropriate

Words of Five Syllables

20. appreciation

Did you know?

When the director of a TV program wants a demonstration of approval from the audience, an applause sign is shown. In Roman times at the end of a play, the actors would turn to the audience and command *plaudite*, meaning "clap your hands." Today, when people **applaud**, we say the perfomers earned plaudits from the crowd.

Word Application

Write a List Word to complete each sentence.

1. The audience stood to applaud the president as he approached the podium.
2. Jake will learn carpentry by serving as an apprentice to a master carpenter.
3. If all the conditions are met, the committee will grant its approval to the project.
4. The flowers were given by Dr. Garcia as a token of her appreciation.

Classification

Write a List Word to complete each series.

1. table of contents, index, appendix
2. head, body, appendage
3. clothing, shoes, apparel
4. state, declare, assert
5. tools, equipment, apparatus
6. attack, battle, assault

30

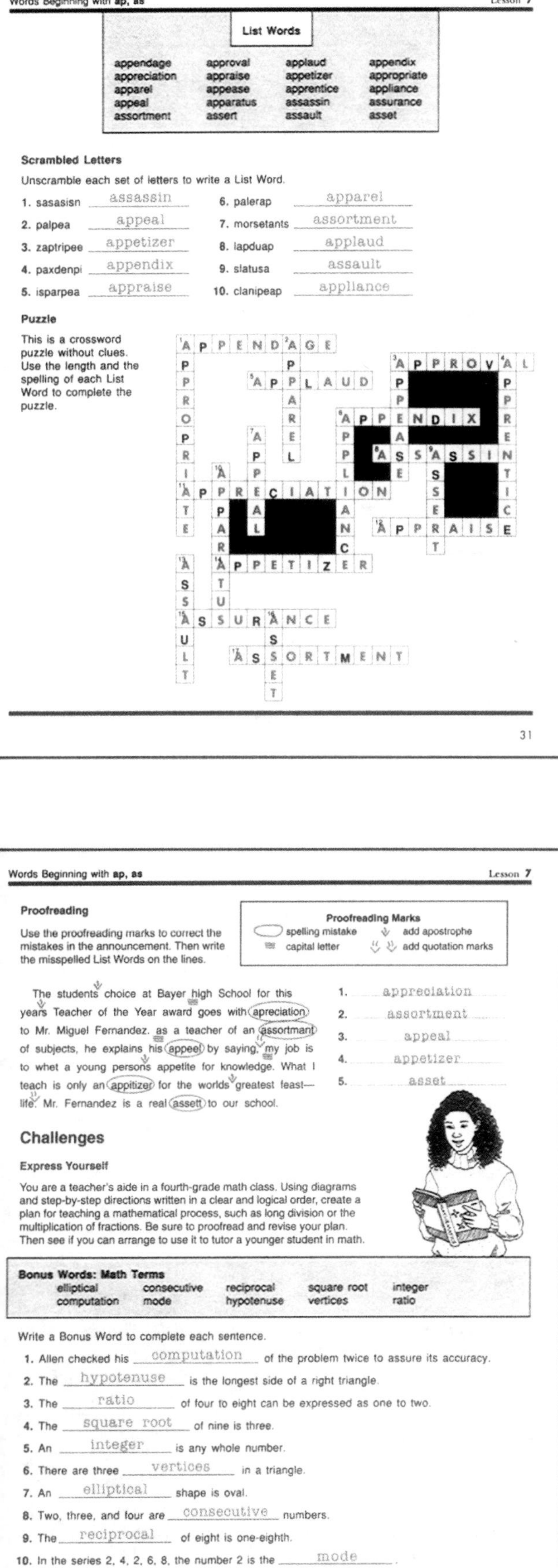

Words Beginning with **ap, as** Lesson 7

List Words

appendage	approval	applaud	appendix
appreciation	appraise	appetizer	appropriate
apparel	appease	apprentice	appliance
appeal	apparatus	assassin	assurance
assortment	assert	assault	asset

Scrambled Letters

Unscramble each set of letters to write a List Word.

1. sasasisn	assassin	6. palerap	apparel
2. palpea	appeal	7. morsetants	assortment
3. zaptripee	appetizer	8. lapduap	applaud
4. paxdenpi	appendix	9. slatusa	assault
5. isparpea	appraise	10. clanipeap	appliance

Puzzle

This is a crossword puzzle without clues. Use the length and the spelling of each List Word to complete the puzzle.

31

Words Beginning with **ap, as** Lesson 7

Proofreading

Use the proofreading marks to correct the mistakes in the announcement. Then write the misspelled List Words on the lines.

Proofreading Marks
spelling mistake — add apostrophe
capital letter — add quotation marks

The students choice at Bayer high School for this years Teacher of the Year award goes with apreciation to Mr. Miguel Fernandez. as a teacher of an assortmant of subjects, he explains his appeel by saying, my job is to whet a young persons appetite for knowledge. What I teach is only an appitizer for the worlds greatest feast—life. Mr. Fernandez is a real assett to our school.

1. appreciation
2. assortment
3. appeal
4. appetizer
5. asset

Challenges

Express Yourself

You are a teacher's aide in a fourth-grade math class. Using diagrams and step-by-step directions written in a clear and logical order, create a plan for teaching a mathematical process, such as long division or the multiplication of fractions. Be sure to proofread and revise your plan. Then see if you can arrange to use it to tutor a younger student in math.

Bonus Words: Math Terms

elliptical	consecutive	reciprocal	square root	integer
computation	mode	hypotenuse	vertices	ratio

Write a Bonus Word to complete each sentence.

1. Allen checked his computation of the problem twice to assure its accuracy.
2. The hypotenuse is the longest side of a right triangle.
3. The ratio of four to eight can be expressed as one to two.
4. The square root of nine is three.
5. An integer is any whole number.
6. There are three vertices in a triangle.
7. An elliptical shape is oval.
8. Two, three, and four are consecutive numbers.
9. The reciprocal of eight is one-eighth.
10. In the series 2, 4, 2, 6, 8, the number 2 is the mode.

32

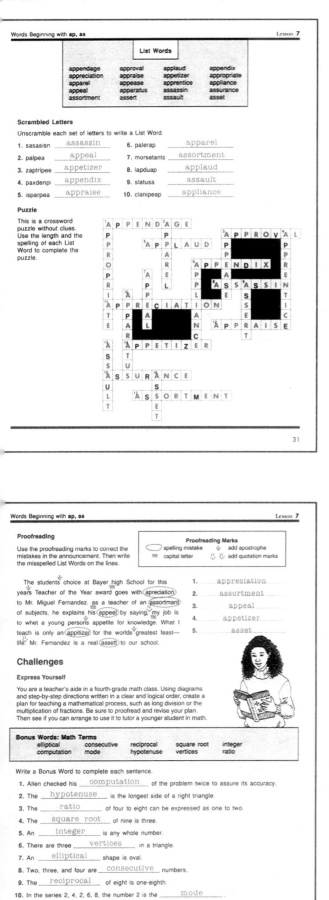

Scrambled Letters (Page 31) Before the exercise, have students unscramble these letters to find a List Word: *padgapeen. (appendage)*

Puzzle (Page 31) Urge students to count the number of spaces in each answer blank to help them solve the puzzle. Point out that each List Word appears once.

Proofreading (Page 32) Review the proofreading marks, emphasizing the apostrophe and quotation marks.

Challenges

Express Yourself (Page 32) Discuss the importance of clarity of language and a logical order of steps in the presentation of directions. Remind students that writers must keep their audiences in mind, pointing out that fourth-graders would require more explanation than would seventh-graders. If you wish, relate the project to a current math lesson, using it to have students review and summarize what they are currently learning. Provide time for volunteers to present their "lessons" to the class.

Bonus Words: Math Terms (Page 32) Use math books, encyclopedias, and diagrams to define and discuss Bonus Words. Relate them to the writing project and students' knowledge of mathematical terms and functions.

Bonus Word Test

1. The mode is a number that occurs most frequently.
2. The base of a cone can form an elliptical shape.
3. One, two, and three are consecutive numbers.
4. Finish your computation and circle your answer.
5. The square root of sixteen is four.
6. Every whole number is an integer.
7. Mark the vertices of the angles with red dots.
8. The ratio of 3 to 9 is equal to 1 to 3.
9. We will calculate the hypotenuse of a triangle.
10. The reciprocal of three is one-third.

Final Test

1. Gloria designs sportswear apparel.
2. What a wonderful assortment of cheeses!
3. The manager will appease the unhappy workers.
4. Take a bow as the people applaud your speech.
5. The detective looked for a motive for the assault.
6. Cold shrimp is a delicious and elegant appetizer.
7. Her greatest asset is her brilliant mind.
8. Did the movie appeal to the critics?
9. A jeweler will appraise Aunt Helen's emerald pin.
10. Will you help assemble my exercise apparatus?
11. Was President McKinley killed by an assassin?
12. Write an appropriate thank-you note for the gift.
13. Ben Franklin was an apprentice in a printer's shop.
14. I need your assurance that you'll clean your room.
15. An appendix is at the end of the resource book.
16. A dishwasher is an appliance that saves time.
17. I need their approval before I accept the job.
18. Assert yourself by speaking up at the meeting.
19. Blood circulates to the tip of each appendage.
20. In appreciation for your help, I made you a gift.

Lesson 8

Objective

To spell words with the prefixes *ac, af, at*

Pretest

1. Wow! Today's weather forecast was accurate.
2. Both parties finally reached an accord.
3. My mother is accustomed to taking a daily walk.
4. The wedding will be a private affair for family only.
5. The ambassador will send an attaché in his place.
6. My neighbor still speaks with a British accent.
7. Grandma Lopez will accompany us on our trip.
8. The bank will acquire two new branch offices.
9. Two agents had to affirm the truth of the report.
10. Certain music has no attraction for me.
11. Will the accomplice be punished for the crime?
12. This card gives you access to the library's books.
13. Will you affix mailing labels to the packages?
14. Be attentive and you will learn a great deal.
15. Jamal kept a positive attitude toward his work.
16. Can this car accommodate a large family?
17. Watch the ball accelerate down the steep slope.
18. The note was meant to be funny, not be an affront.
19. My niece has a strong attachment to one toy.
20. Friends are attune to one another's needs.

Game Plan

Page 33
After students have read the Game Plan, have them identify the prefix in each word and note when it produces a doubled consonant. Have students identify the List Word that does not contain a doubled letter. (*acquire*). Then help students learn the meanings of List Words, having them refer to dictionaries when necessary.

Warm Up

Vocabulary Development (Page 33)
Write *gain speed* on the chalkboard, and ask which List Word it defines. (*accelerate*) Have students give other definitions for List Words.

Dictionary Skills (Page 33) Review the symbols for sound-spellings that students have learned and discuss why they are useful. (*They teach a word's pronunciation.*) Point out the importance of applying the accent on the appropriate syllable.

Practice

Word Analysis (Page 34) Encourage the students to try to complete this exercise without referring to List Words on page 35.

Analogies (Page 34) Review how analogies compare words. Then work through the first item with students, discussing why *attaché* is the correct answer.

Classification (Page 34) Write *sheep, pig, horse* on the board and ask students why they belong together. (*All name animals.*) Have volunteers add other words to the series. Discuss their answers and the reasons for each.

Game Plan

The prefixes **ac**, **af**, and **at** are different forms of the prefix **ad**, which means toward, at, in addition to, or near. Each prefix is used before certain letters:
ac is used before **c** or **q**, as in accent and acquire
af is used before **f**, as in affix
at is used before **t**, as in attune

1. accurate
2. accord
3. accustomed
4. affair
5. attaché
6. accent
7. accompany
8. acquire
9. affirm
10. attraction
11. accomplice
12. access
13. affix
14. attentive
15. attitude
16. accommodate
17. accelerate
18. affront
19. attachment
20. attune

Warm Up

Vocabulary Development

Write the List Word that matches each definition.

1. an agreement ___accord___
2. insult to one's face ___affront___
3. stress given to a syllable ___accent___
4. partner in a crime ___accomplice___
5. to become the owner of something ___acquire___
6. go along with someone ___accompany___
7. fasten or stick onto ___affix___
8. way of approach ___access___
9. bring into harmony or agreement ___attune___
10. without mistakes or errors ___accurate___
11. person in the diplomatic corps ___attaché___
12. to answer "yes" ___affirm___

Dictionary Skills

Write the List Word that matches each sound-spelling.

1. (ə tach´ mənt)	attachment	7. (at ə shā´)	attaché
2. (ə trak´ shən)	attraction	8. (at´ ə to͞od)	attitude
3. (ə käm´ ə dāt)	accommodate	9. (ə furm´)	affirm
4. (ə kus´ təmd)	accustomed	10. (ə fer´)	affair
5. (ə käm´ plis)	accomplice	11. (ə ten´ tiv)	attentive
6. (ək sel´ ə rāt)	accelerate	12. (ak´ ses)	access

Practice

Word Analysis

Write the List Word formed by adding the appropriate prefix to each base given.

1. fair	affair	7. tache	attaché
2. cess	access	8. celerate	accelerate
3. traction	attraction	9. front	affront
4. customed	accustomed	10. company	accompany
5. curate	accurate		
6. fix	affix		

Did you know?

The root of the word **accommodate** comes from the Latin, *modus*, which means "measure." It later became a term that defined a manner of singing, particularly, "in tune." *Modus* later came to mean "a manner of doing anything." The prefixes, *ad*, meaning "to," and *com*, meaning "together" joined with *modus* to become *accommodate*, meaning "coming together in tune." Today, it is used to describe the manner of making things come together in a pleasant way.

Analogies

Write a List Word to complete each analogy.

1. Innaccurate is to incorrect as ___accurate___ is to correct.
2. Treaty is to pact as ___accord___ is to agreement.
3. Hurt is to offend as insult is to ___affront___.
4. Negate is to no as ___affirm___ is to yes.
5. Hate is to love as detachment is to ___attachment___.
6. Slow is to decelerate as fast is to ___accelerate___.
7. Staple is to join as glue is to ___affix___.
8. Lead is to guide as escort is to ___accompany___.

Classification

Write a List Word to complete each series.

1. entrance, opening, ___access___
2. alert, aware, ___attentive___
3. buy, purchase, ___acquire___
4. right, correct, ___accurate___
5. occurrence, gathering, ___affair___
6. opinion, disposition, ___attitude___
7. fascination, charm, ___attraction___
8. partner, helper, ___accomplice___

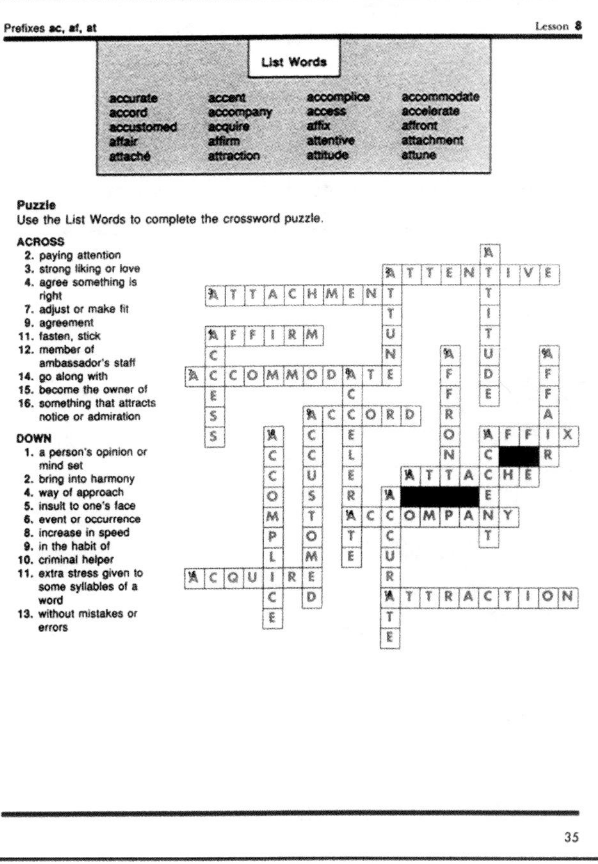

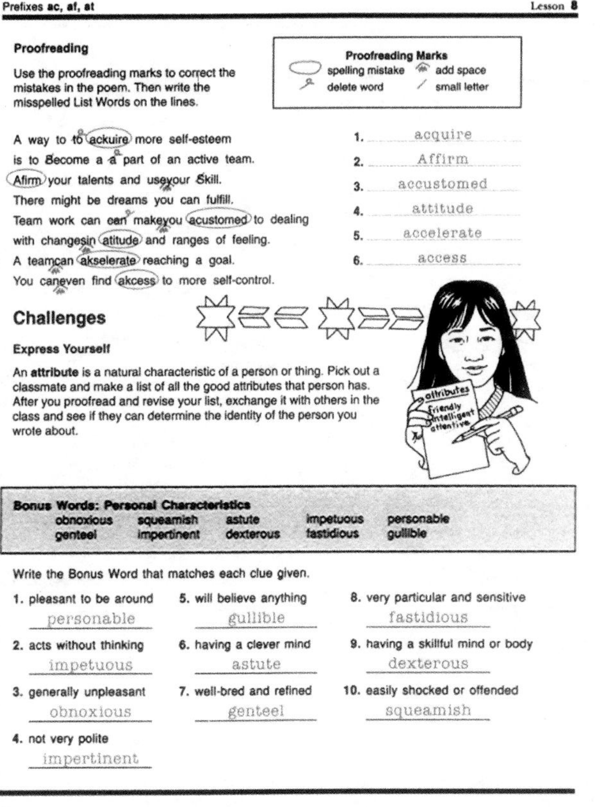

Puzzle (Page 35) Remind students that they have two clues to each answer: its definition and the number of letters it has. Students should be able to complete the puzzle independently.

Proofreading (Page 36) Use the sentence *His Nameis spelled wrong wrong.* to demonstrate the proofreading marks in this lesson.

Challenges

Express Yourself (Page 36) Have students work together to name as many positive attributes as they can. Help them think of such categories as personality, achievements, and ethical behavior.

Bonus Words: Personal Characteristics (Page 36) Explain that all Bonus Words name characteristics a person might have. Through discussion and dictionary use, help students understand the meaning of each word. To make sure they understand each word, you may wish to have them suggest actions people might take that would demonstrate each characteristic.

Bonus Word Test

1. An impertinent person often asks rude questions.
2. In grand society, people are genteel.
3. Everyone wanted the personable traveler to stay.
4. An impetuous person may later regret his action.
5. No one wants to spend time with obnoxious people.
6. A gullible person is easily fooled.
7. Few people can trick someone who is astute.
8. They are too squeamish to clean the fish.
9. That fastidious family does laundry daily.
10. For a dexterous person, juggling is simple.

Final Test

1. This room can accommodate a large crowd.
2. This car can accelerate quickly for passing.
3. That report is an affront to the mayor!
4. I have a strong attachment to my home town.
5. Try to attune yourself to the clients' wishes.
6. The news report said the driver was an accomplice.
7. Does this gate provide access to the field?
8. Will you please affix a name tag to each package?
9. Everyone was attentive to the announcer's words.
10. Our coach congratulated us on our good attitude.
11. People from Maine speak with a different accent.
12. Will the museum guide accompany us on the tour?
13. My town was able to acquire the land it needed.
14. The court will affirm my claim to the money.
15. Those rose gardens are a great tourist attraction.
16. Are you sure the figures in this list are accurate?
17. Did the jury reach an accord on the verdict?
18. My dog is accustomed to sleeping under my bed.
19. The party was an exciting affair with many guests.
20. Are you an attaché at the embassy?

Lesson 9

Objective

To spell words with the ending *ion*

Pretest

1. I feel great affection for my childhood home.
2. His bright expression proved that he was pleased.
3. I have a firm conviction about justice.
4. The doctor prescribed a lotion for my poison ivy.
5. Columbus disproved the notion the world is flat.
6. The stomach and liver aid digestion.
7. Mix an equal proportion of milk and water.
8. The doctor bandaged the lesion on Roberta's arm.
9. Did the detective's suspicion prove to be correct?
10. Did Juan use red velvet to cover the sofa cushion?
11. My mother's occupation is sports writer.
12. You may sunburn if you have a light complexion.
13. Computers brought about a revolution in office work.
14. Thank you for your devotion and hard work.
15. The exciting game created tension among the fans.
16. The Greek civilization inspired Western culture.
17. Is it your intention to become a doctor?
18. Cooperation among the staff will simplify the work.
19. On this happy occasion, I'd like to thank Uncle Al.
20. What an incredible recitation of the poem!

Game Plan

Page 37

Discuss the Game Plan and examples. For further examples of words with the *ation* or *ion* suffix, use *conversation, combination, radiation, circulation.* For additional words ending in *ion* that come from early root words, use *potion, position, legion.* Then discuss the structure, derivations, and meanings of List Words.

Warm Up

Vocabulary Development (Page 37) Before the exercise, have volunteers identify the List Words that match these short definitions: *relationship in size or volume (proportion); facial look (expression).*

Dictionary Skills (Page 37) Before the exercise, call on volunteers to define the function of guide words and point out examples in a dictionary.

Practice

Word Analysis (Page 38) Have students name words that have the same roots as these words: *beautiful (beauty, beautify); frightening (fright, frighten, frightful).*

Classification (Page 38) To review classification skills, have students select a List Word to complete this series: *speech, presentation, _______ (recitation).*

Word Application (Page 38) Urge students to use context clues to help them to decide upon the correct answers. To extend the exercise, have students create similar sentences for the exercise distractors.

Words Ending with **ion** — LESSON 9

Game Plan

Often, the suffixes **ion** or **ation** are added to verbs to make nouns that mean the act of.

Verb	Meaning	Plus Ending	New Meaning
recite	to repeat from memory	**recitation**	the act of repeating something from memory
digest	to break down food	**digestion**	the act of breaking down food

Many other nouns ending in **ion** have been derived from early root words. For example, the modern noun cushion comes from the Middle English word cuisshin, which in turn came from the Old French word coissin.

1. affection
2. expression
3. conviction
4. lotion
5. notion
6. digestion
7. proportion
8. lesion
9. suspicion
10. cushion
11. occupation
12. complexion
13. revolution
14. devotion
15. tension
16. civilization
17. intention
18. cooperation
19. occasion
20. recitation

Warm Up

Vocabulary Development

Write the List Word that matches each synonym or definition.

1. stress tension
2. wound lesion
3. job occupation
4. sudden uprising revolution
5. mistrust suspicion
6. pillow cushion
7. event occasion
8. plan or goal intention
9. joint effort cooperation
10. cream lotion

Dictionary Skills

Write the List Word that comes between each pair of dictionary guide words.

1. dew/digit digestion
2. rebel/rest recitation
3. addition/again affection
4. nose/noun notion
5. proper/propose proportion
6. common/control complexion
7. especially/eye expression
8. comply/cook conviction
9. center/clue civilization
10. desk/dice devotion

37

Words Ending with Ion — Lesson 9

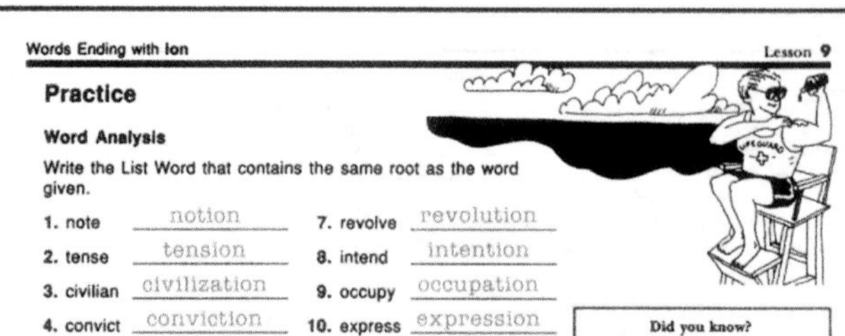

Practice

Word Analysis

Write the List Word that contains the same root as the word given.

1. note notion
2. tense tension
3. civilian civilization
4. convict conviction
5. recite recitation
6. operate cooperation
7. revolve revolution
8. intend intention
9. occupy occupation
10. express expression
11. devote devotion
12. suspect suspicion

Did you know?

Tension comes from the Latin word, *tendo,* which means "stretch" or "strain." There might be too much *tension* on a guitar string if it is stretched too tightly. People talk about nervous *tension* when they are under a lot of strain.

Classification

Write a List Word to complete each series.

1. relationship, ratio, proportion
2. position, career, occupation
3. coloring, skin type, complexion
4. culture, society, civilization
5. upholstery, slipcover, cushion
6. chewing, swallowing, digestion
7. event, happening, occasion
8. cut, scrape, lesion
9. cream, powder, lotion
10. aim, goal, intention

Word Application

Select a List Word from the choices in parentheses to complete each sentence. Write your answer on the line.

1. Al memorized a poem for recitation in class. (devotion, recitation)
2. Janet feels great affection for her pet chinchilla. (suspicion, affection)
3. Fran quoted the old expression, "Here today, gone tomorrow." (expression, occupation)
4. Poison ivy made Hannah's complexion red and rough for a few days. (digestion, complexion)
5. Jim shows his devotion to the club by working hard for it. (devotion, proportion)
6. The airplane caused a revolution in overseas transportation. (intention, revolution)
7. A diet rich in fiber will aid in the digestion of food. (lesion, digestion)
8. I was right in my suspicion that Gail left this gift for me. (suspicion, occasion)
9. Tension and worry can cause one to have a stiff back and a headache. (Tension, Cooperation)
10. I sent Kay flowers to mark the occasion of her anniversary. (recitation, occasion)

38

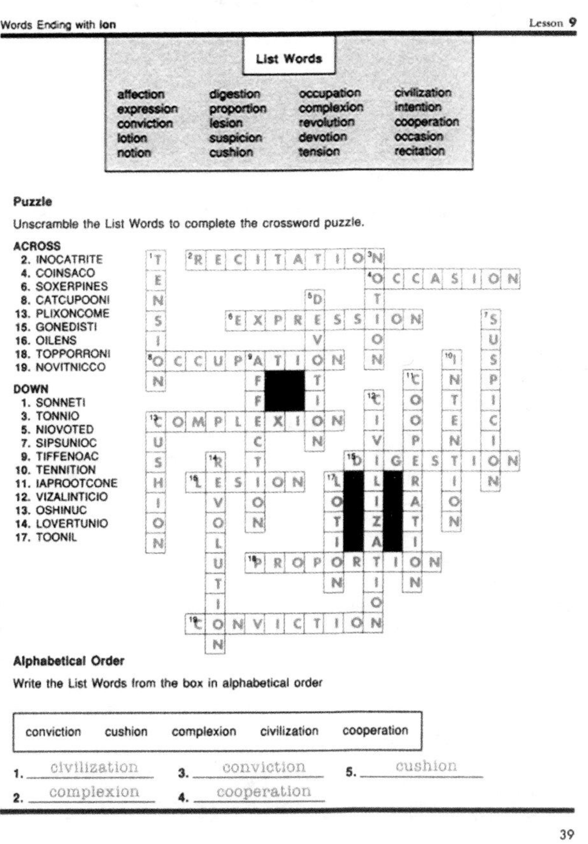

Words Ending with ion Lesson 9

List Words

affection digestion occupation civilization
expression proportion complexion intention
conviction lesion revolution cooperation
lotion suspicion devotion occasion
notion cushion tension recitation

Puzzle

Unscramble the List Words to complete the crossword puzzle.

ACROSS
2. INOCATRITE
4. COINSACO
6. SOXERPINES
8. CATCUPOONI
13. PLIXONCOME
15. GONEDISTI
16. OILENS
18. TOPPORRONI
19. NOVITNICCO

DOWN
1. SONNETI
3. TONNIO
5. NIOVOTED
7. SIPSUNIOC
9. TIFFENOAC
10. TENNITION
11. IAPROOTCONE
12. VIZALINTICIO
13. OSHINUC
14. LOVERTUNIO
17. TOONIL

Alphabetical Order

Write the List Words from the box in alphabetical order

conviction cushion complexion civilization cooperation

1. civilization
2. complexion
3. conviction
4. cooperation
5. cushion

39

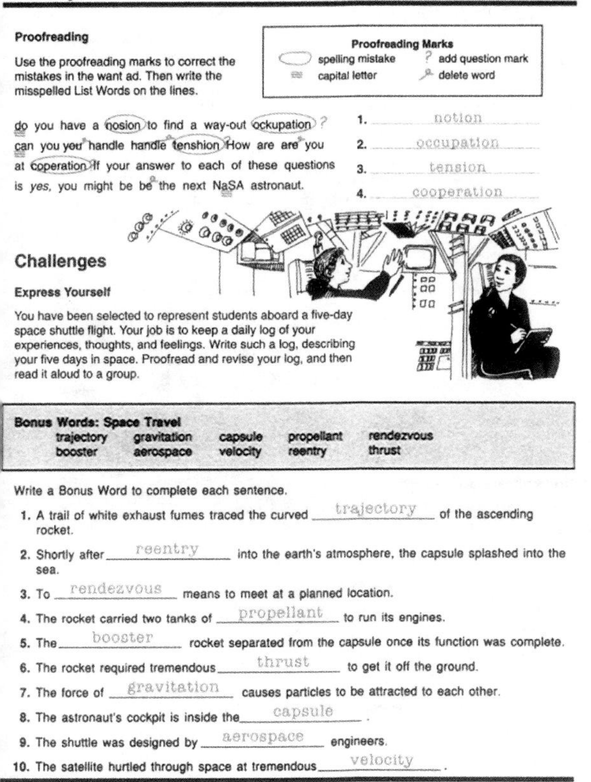

Words Ending with ion Lesson 9

Proofreading

Use the proofreading marks to correct the mistakes in the want ad. Then write the misspelled List Words on the lines.

Proofreading Marks: spelling mistake; add question mark; capital letter; delete word

do you have a nosion to find a way-out ockupation can you you handle handle tenshion How are are you at coperation If your answer to each of these questions is *yes*, you might be be the next NaSA astronaut.

1. notion
2. occupation
3. tension
4. cooperation

Challenges

Express Yourself

You have been selected to represent students aboard a five-day space shuttle flight. Your job is to keep a daily log of your experiences, thoughts, and feelings. Write such a log, describing your five days in space. Proofread and revise your log, and then read it aloud to a group.

Bonus Words: Space Travel

trajectory gravitation capsule propellant rendezvous
booster aerospace velocity reentry thrust

Write a Bonus Word to complete each sentence.

1. A trail of white exhaust fumes traced the curved trajectory of the ascending rocket.
2. Shortly after reentry into the earth's atmosphere, the capsule splashed into the sea.
3. To rendezvous means to meet at a planned location.
4. The rocket carried two tanks of propellant to run its engines.
5. The booster rocket separated from the capsule once its function was complete.
6. The rocket required tremendous thrust to get it off the ground.
7. The force of gravitation causes particles to be attracted to each other.
8. The astronaut's cockpit is inside the capsule.
9. The shuttle was designed by aerospace engineers.
10. The satellite hurtled through space at tremendous velocity.

40

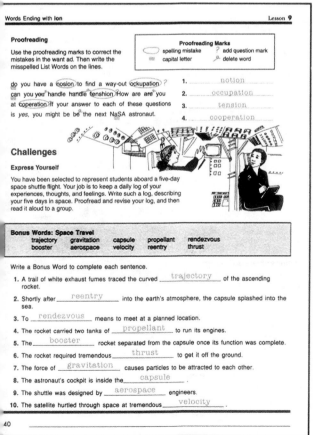

Puzzle (Page 39) Urge students to find clues not only in the scrambled letters, but also in the number of spaces in each answer and the letter clues found once some of the words have been entered in the grid.

Alphabetical Order (Page 39) To extend this exercise, have students add to their list of alphabetized words: *conclusion, competition, coalition, constitution.*

Proofreading (Page 40) Review the use of the delete mark and the other proofreading marks in this lesson.

Challenges

Express Yourself (Page 40) To help students prepare to write, read and discuss articles concerning the events on actual space shuttle missions—including rendezvous and repair missions with satellites, photography sessions, and various experiments. Have students suggest feelings they might have as assistants to the crews. When they have finished writing, provide time for presentation and discussion.

Bonus Words: Space Travel (Page 40) With dictionaries and diagrams or illustrations from an encyclopedia, define and discuss Bonus Words. Relate them to the writing project and accompanying discussion. Have students use each one in an oral sentence.

Bonus Word Test

1. The space shuttle will rendezvous with a satellite.
2. Angelo hopes to become an aerospace engineer.
3. Reentry into the atmosphere will occur soon.
4. A chimpanzee piloted an early space capsule.
5. A technician tested the booster rocket.
6. Rocket engines create the thrust for take-off.
7. The propellant is measured periodically.
8. Trajectory is the curved path of a rocket.
9. Velocity is another term for "rate of speed."
10. Gravitation creates magnetism.

Final Test

1. A parade marked the occasion of the hero's birth.
2. Speak clearly during your recitation of the essay.
3. A balanced diet maintains a healthy complexion.
4. Your cooperation made the project fun and simple.
5. Is it your intention to finish the report after dinner?
6. The pyramids are a legacy of an early civilization.
7. The revolution helped the colonists gain freedom.
8. Apply suntan lotion to protect your skin.
9. Do you enjoy your occupation as a journalist?
10. I have a suspicion that Alana planned a surprise.
11. The digestion of food creates energy.
12. What a silly notion that idea is!
13. My cat likes to take naps on that blue cushion.
14. Grandpa always greets me with affection.
15. Did you see the surprised expression on her face?
16. Proportion shows distance and dimension.
17. Cleanse the lesion thoroughly with warm water.
18. Express your ideas with confidence and conviction.
19. A writer with a deadline operates under tension.
20. She showed her devotion by working all weekend.

Lesson 10

Objective

To spell words with French derivations

Pretest

1. On what street is the boutique located?
2. The boulevard is lined with tall oak trees.
3. Mia works hard in her pursuit to be a musician.
4. What a moving speech the chaplain gave!
5. Mrs. Ishi will be a chaperone on the students' trip.
6. My father, who is a gourmet, writes a food column.
7. A courteous woman helped me to find the route.
8. Some rabbits turn white in winter for camouflage.
9. Will a coat of lacquer protect the table's surface?
10. Majestic cliffs line the coast of West Wales.
11. Jorgé wore a mask to the masquerade party.
12. Should I carry a passport when traveling abroad?
13. The runners felt fatigue after the race.
14. The tree appeared in silhouette in the photograph.
15. My family stayed in a suite at the Concord Hotel.
16. He recorded his daily calorie intake during his diet.
17. Through practice, Jill gained expertise as a skater.
18. My boss explained the daily routine of my job.
19. The chauffeur parked the limousine in the garage.
20. Is a lieutenant required to salute a major?

Game Plan

Page 41

Discuss the Game Plan. Work with students to find these words of French derivation in a college edition dictionary, and discuss the given etymologies: *restaurant, table, verb, vermin, plate, parasol, laissez faire, menu, bouquet.* Use the examples *laissez faire* and *bouquet* to stress the sounds that such endings as *ez* and *et* stand for in the French language, and thus in the English words that have been "borrowed" from the French. Then apply the discussion to List Words. Work with students to define each word.

Warm Up

Vocabulary Development (Page 41) Before the exercise, call on volunteers to identify the List Words that match these definitions: *to disguise (camouflage); a wide street (boulevard).*

Dictionary Skills (Page 41) Tell students to examine each etymology carefully to find clues as to the identity of each List Word.

Practice

Word Analysis (Page 42) Have students refer to List Words on page 43 to find each letter combination.

Word Application (Page 42) Before the exercise, have students use a List Word to replace the underlined word in: *To hide itself from predators, the copperhead snake blends with the colors of the forest floor. (camouflage)*

Words with French Derivations — LESSON **10**

Game Plan

The English language is enriched with words borrowed or derived from the French language.

English Word and Meaning	French Word and Meaning
bureau (chest of drawers)	**bureau** (writing table)
cab (hired car)	**cabriolet** (light carriage)

Study the List Words carefully. Words like gourmet and fatigue are not spelled the way they sound.

1. boutique
2. boulevard
3. pursuit
4. chaplain
5. chaperone
6. gourmet
7. courteous
8. camouflage
9. lacquer
10. majestic
11. masquerade
12. passport
13. fatigue
14. silhouette
15. suite
16. calorie
17. expertise
18. routine
19. chauffeur
20. lieutenant

Warm Up

Vocabulary Development

Write the List Word that matches each definition.

1. polite courteous
2. street boulevard
3. shop boutique
4. driver chauffeur
5. grand majestic
6. officer lieutenant
7. outline silhouette
8. trip escort chaperone
9. connected rooms suite
10. procedure routine
11. advanced skills expertise
12. religious leader chaplain
13. food expert gourmet
14. tiredness fatigue

Dictionary Skills

Write the List Word that matches each etymology.

1. French, camoufler; "to disguise" camouflage
2. Old French, chapelain; from Latin capella, "cape" chaplain
3. Old French, poursuite; "to follow" pursuit
4. French, from Latin calor, "heat" calorie
5. French, from Greek botica, "storeroom" boutique
6. Old French, lacre; "sealing wax" lacquer
7. Old French, boloart; "walkway" boulevard
8. Old French, majeste; "grandeur" majestic
9. French, mascarade; from Italian maschera, "mask" masquerade
10. Old French, passer, "to pass"; + port, "harbor" passport

41

Words with French Derivations — Lesson **10**

Practice

Did you know?

Chauffeur is a French word that comes from the French verb *chauffer,* meaning "to heat." Some early automobiles were driven by steam, and the driver had to stoke the furnace that heated the water. Such drivers were called *chauffeurs,* or stokers.

Word Analysis

Write List Words to answer the following questions.

Which words contain these double consonants?

1. ff chauffeur
2. ss passport
3. tt silhouette

Which words contain the letter combination **qu**?

4. boutique
5. lacquer
6. masquerade

Which words contain the letter combination **ou**?

7. boutique
8. boulevard
9. gourmet
10. courteous
11. camouflage
12. silhouette
13. routine

Which words contain the vowel combination **ui**?

14. pursuit
15. suite

Which word contains the vowel combination **ieu**?

16. lieutenant

Word Application

Replace the underlined word or words in each sentence with a List Word. Write the List Word on the line.

1. The hikers were almost overcome with tiredness. fatigue
2. Show your identification papers to a customs official when you enter Poland. passport
3. After painting the table, brush on a thin coat of varnish. lacquer
4. Hospital's religious services are planned by a minister, priest, or rabbi. chaplain
5. The parade will proceed down the main avenue. boulevard
6. We found the flight attendants to be polite and helpful. courteous
7. The club's next event will be a costume party. masquerade
8. The cookbook author is a person who appreciates fine food. gourmet
9. A tall mountain loomed on the other side of the river. majestic
10. James proved his skill as a bicyclist during the race. expertise

42

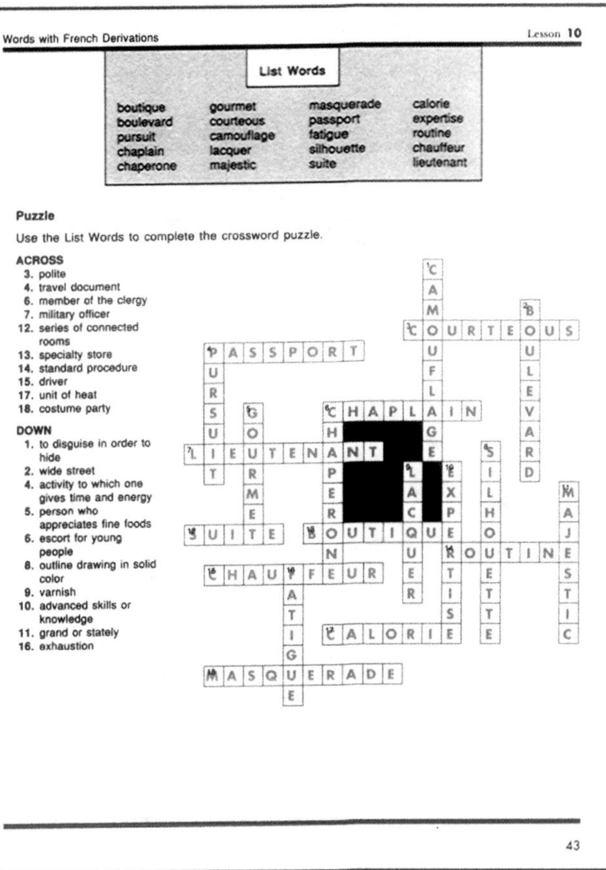

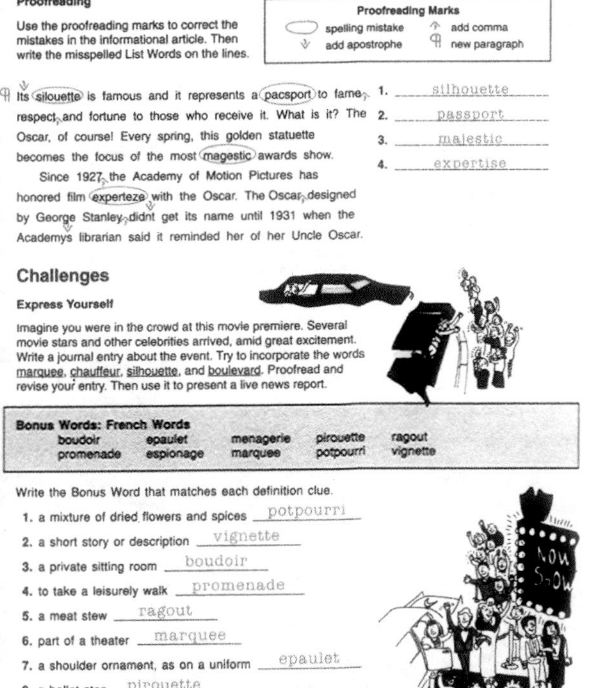

Puzzle (Page 43) If necessary, review the process for solving crossword puzzles before students begin work, explaining the relationship between the numbers preceding the clues and those in the puzzle grid.

Proofreading (Page 44) Write *Hugh Tina, and Lee wont be able to atend the meeting.* on the board and use it to illustrate the proofreading marks in this lesson.

Challenges

Express Yourself (Page 44) To help students prepare to write, discuss current movies that they have enjoyed. Have them suggest stars and other celebrities who might appear at the premieres of these movies. Ask them how they'd feel if they were in the crowd clustered at the theater entrance as the stars entered. Encourage them to jot down notes to use as they write their journal entries. When they have finished writing, provide time for them to share their work with partners.

Bonus Words: French Words (Page 44) Have students find the definitions and etymologies of Bonus Words in dictionaries. Have students use the words in oral sentences. Review what they have learned about the pronunciation of French words that have been "borrowed" by the English language.

Bonus Word Test

1. We saw a fierce Bengal tiger at the menagerie.
2. He wore a gold epaulet on each shoulder.
3. We selected new wallpaper for Joan's boudoir.
4. The vignette was written by Ernest Hemingway.
5. Please cut up two carrots for the ragout.
6. The attendant changed the theater marquee.
7. Partners promenade to begin the square dance.
8. The ballerina danced a graceful pirouette.
9. The movie describes the life of an espionage agent.
10. Fran used dried rose petals to make potpourri.

Final Test

1. After dinner, we strolled along the boulevard.
2. Does your passport include a current picture?
3. The expertise of the artist shows in her work.
4. Write a courteous note to acknowledge the gift.
5. A hot shower and a nap will cure your fatigue.
6. For camouflage, caterpillars blend with leaves.
7. People take vacations to escape daily routines.
8. Good luck in your pursuit of a career!
9. Did you know that my father is a gourmet cook?
10. The annual masquerade ball is on February 14.
11. Becky bought her new dress at a boutique.
12. Did you know that a calorie is a unit of heat?
13. Stir the lacquer thoroughly before using it.
14. My shadow made a perfect silhouette on the wall.
15. Uncle Hank has a part-time job as a chauffeur.
16. The chaplain will conduct a service at noon.
17. A suite is more expensive than a single room.
18. Our chaperone will meet us at the airport.
19. What a majestic sight the Grand Canyon is!
20. My mother served as a lieutenant in the army.

Lesson 11

Objective

To spell words with Latin roots

Pretest

1. Therapy helped him overcome his affliction.
2. He orders people around like a dictator.
3. Because she was persistent, she got a refund.
4. The lawyer advised her client to sign the contract.
5. Tom and Ramón resolved their conflict peacefully.
6. Your actions must cease and desist now!
7. Does the village church have a new minister?
8. Human bones consist of hard and soft tissue.
9. Lizzie fractured her ankle playing baseball.
10. The actress used clear diction as she spoke.
11. A a result of the impact, both cars were dented.
12. When will construction of the new school begin?
13. Please don't try to distract me while I'm studying.
14. Some people are resistant to change.
15. Kendra read a historical account of the Civil War.
16. The apartment was compact.
17. Dad pointed out the financial district of the city.
18. Will the leg cast restrict your movements?
19. This tight collar will constrict my breathing.
20. Lena was tactful when she told Al about his error.

Game Plan

Page 45

Help students find the Latin roots or Latin derivations of these words in the dictionary: *inflict, dictate, assist, attract, administer, fragment, compactor, structure, history, strictly, tactile.* Discuss how the meaning of each word is related to the meaning of the Latin root or Latin word. Apply the discussion to the List Words and help students to define each word.

Warm Up

Word Analysis (Page 45) Encourage students to refer to the List Words to determine the words with the same roots.

Vocabulary Development (Page 45) Before students begin written work, have them identify the List Words that are synonyms for the following words: *broken (fractured), tyrant (dictator), stop (desist).*

Practice

Classification (Page 46) To review classification, ask students to name the List Word that belongs in the following series and explain why the word belongs: tourniquet, blood, ______. (Constrict; a tourniquet will constrict the blood flow.)

Dictionary Skills (Page 46) Elicit from students the function of dictionary guide words. If necessary, remind students that all the words on a dictionary page are arranged alphabetically between the two guide words.

Latin Roots — LESSON 11

Game Plan

Many English words are formed with Latin roots.

Latin Root and Meaning	English Word and Meaning
dict, dic (say)	**diction** (manner of speaking)

Other English words are borrowed or derived from Latin words.

Latin Word and Meaning	English Word and Meaning
minister (Christian preacher)	**minister** (preacher)

All the List Words are based on Latin roots or Latin words. Study these words carefully and practice spelling them.

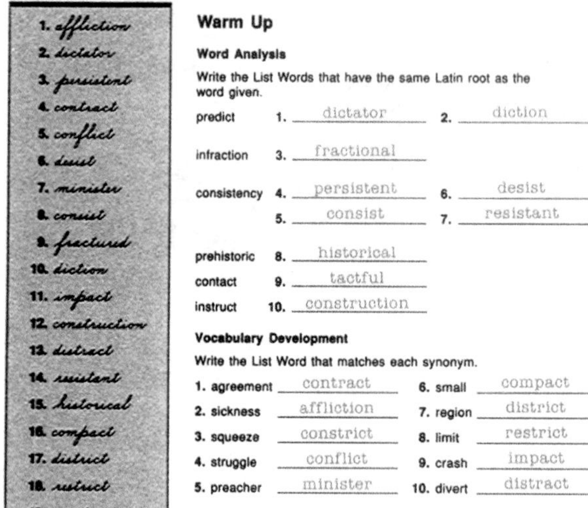

1. affliction
2. dictator
3. persistent
4. contract
5. conflict
6. desist
7. minister
8. consist
9. fractured
10. diction
11. impact
12. construction
13. distract
14. resistant
15. historical
16. compact
17. district
18. restrict
19. constrict
20. tactful

Warm Up

Word Analysis

Write the List Words that have the same Latin root as the word given.

predict 1. dictator 2. diction

infraction 3. fractional

consistency 4. persistent 5. consist 6. desist 7. resistant

prehistoric 8. historical

contact 9. tactful

instruct 10. construction

Vocabulary Development

Write the List Word that matches each synonym.

1. agreement contract
2. sickness affliction
3. squeeze constrict
4. struggle conflict
5. preacher minister
6. small compact
7. region district
8. limit restrict
9. crash impact
10. divert distract

45

Latin Roots — Lesson 11

Practice

Classification

Write a List Word to complete each series.

1. deacon, preacher, minister
2. village, town, district
3. illness, injury, affliction
4. small, packed, compact
5. polite, respectful, tactful
6. insistent, determined, persistent
7. crash, collision, impact
8. ancient, old, historical
9. agreement, pact, contract
10. stop, cease, desist
11. speech, pronunciation, diction
12. cracked, broken, fractured
13. opinions, disagreement, conflict
14. architect, building, construction
15. tyrant, oppressor, dictator

Did you know?

Contract is from the Latin *contractor.* It is formed from *con-*, meaning "together," and *tractus*, meaning "drawn." That is why we "draw up" a *contract.*

Dictionary Skills

Write the List Words that come between each pair of dictionary guide words. Write the words in alphabetical order.

aggravate/distress

1. compact
2. conflict
3. consist
4. constrict
5. construction
6. contract
7. desist
8. dictator
9. diction
10. distract

imagine/tasteful

11. impact
12. minister
13. persistent
14. resistant
15. restrict
16. tactful

46

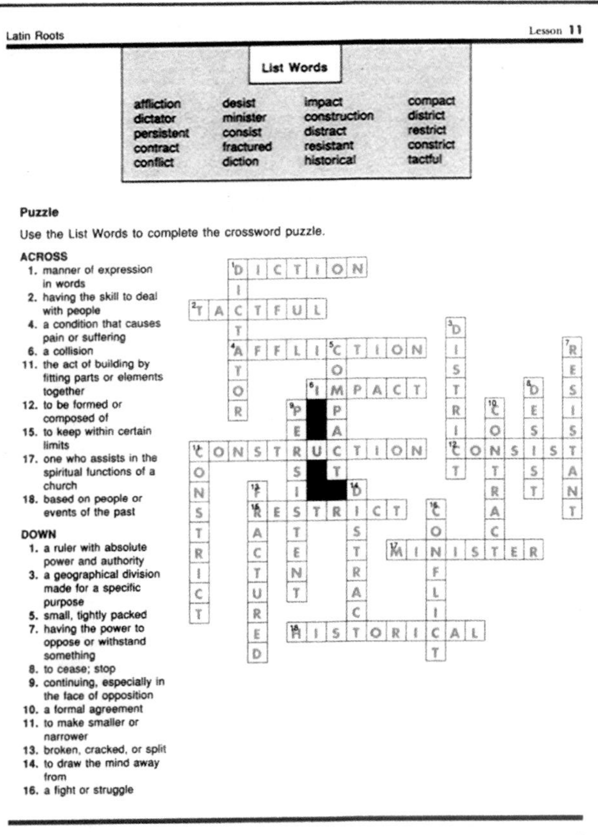

Latin Roots — Lesson 11

List Words

affliction	desist	impact	compact
dictator	minister	construction	district
persistent	consist	distract	restrict
contract	fractured	resistant	constrict
conflict	diction	historical	tactful

Puzzle

Use the List Words to complete the crossword puzzle.

ACROSS
1. manner of expression in words
2. having the skill to deal with people
4. a condition that causes pain or suffering
6. a collision
11. the act of building by fitting parts or elements together
12. to be formed or composed of
15. to keep within certain limits
17. one who assists in the spiritual functions of a church
18. based on people or events of the past

DOWN
1. a ruler with absolute power and authority
3. a geographical division made for a specific purpose
5. small, tightly packed
7. having the power to oppose or withstand something
8. to cease; stop
9. continuing, especially in the face of opposition
10. a formal agreement
11. to make smaller or narrower
13. broken, cracked, or split
14. to draw the mind away from
16. a fight or struggle

47

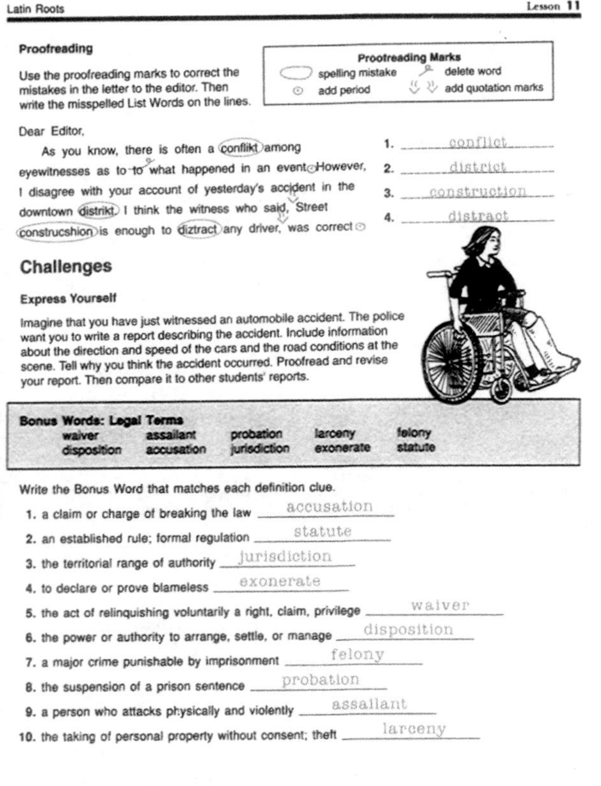

Latin Roots — Lesson 11

Proofreading

Use the proofreading marks to correct the mistakes in the letter to the editor. Then write the misspelled List Words on the lines.

Proofreading Marks: spelling mistake; add period; delete word; add quotation marks

Dear Editor,

As you know, there is often a conflikt among eyewitnesses as to to what happened in an event However, I disagree with your account of yesterday's accident in the downtown distrikt I think the witness who said, Street construcshion is enough to diztract any driver, was correct

1. conflict
2. district
3. construction
4. distract

Challenges

Express Yourself

Imagine that you have just witnessed an automobile accident. The police want you to write a report describing the accident. Include information about the direction and speed of the cars and the road conditions at the scene. Tell why you think the accident occurred. Proofread and revise your report. Then compare it to other students' reports.

Bonus Words: Legal Terms

waiver	assailant	probation	larceny	felony
disposition	accusation	jurisdiction	exonerate	statute

Write the Bonus Word that matches each definition clue.

1. a claim or charge of breaking the law accusation
2. an established rule; formal regulation statute
3. the territorial range of authority jurisdiction
4. to declare or prove blameless exonerate
5. the act of relinquishing voluntarily a right, claim, privilege waiver
6. the power or authority to arrange, settle, or manage disposition
7. a major crime punishable by imprisonment felony
8. the suspension of a prison sentence probation
9. a person who attacks physically and violently assailant
10. the taking of personal property without consent; theft larceny

48

Puzzle (Page 47) To review the process for completing a crossword puzzle, work with students to complete one item across and one item down.

Proofreading (Page 48) Write on the board: *The car was was going to fast, said Alex.* Have students help you correct the sentence using the proofreading marks. Point out that they will use these marks to correct the letter.

Challenges

Express Yourself (Page 48) To help students prepare to write, discuss the kinds of details that might be important to the investigation of an accident. As students suggest ideas, write them on the board. Encourage students to use these ideas as they write. Students may enjoy sharing their eyewitness accounts in small groups.

Bonus Words—Legal Terms (Page 48) Have students work in pairs to find the meanings of the Bonus Words in dictionaries. For words with more than one meaning, have students identify the meaning of the word that is related to law.

Bonus Word Test

1. A felony is a serious crime, punishable by law.
2. My client will not sign a waiver of her right.
3. This case is beyond the jurisdiction of the state.
4. The disposition of your case is in the jury's hands.
5. This statute allows stores to open on holidays.
6. The facts will exonerate my client of all guilt.
7. The assailant was quickly captured by the police.
8. He was released on probation for good behavior.
9. The defendant denied the accusation.
10. The police investigated a larceny at the store.

Final Test

1. The two teams had a conflict over the rules.
2. Speak with clear, precise diction to be understood.
3. This story is historical fiction set in the 1800s.
4. Kate was tactful when she spoke to her boss.
5. According to the contract, the job pays well.
6. The x-rays showed that the bone was fractured.
7. Is the carpet in the family room resistant to stains?
8. A tourniquet will help constrict the flow of blood.
9. He was persistent and would never stop trying.
10. How many members did the committee consist of?
11. The loud music may distract the bus driver.
12. The fence will restrict the puppy to the back yard.
13. The people feared the tyrannical dictator.
14. The minister spoke about the homeless.
15. Mr. Díaz will oversee construction of the house.
16. Three towns make up our school district.
17. Chicken pox is a common childhood affliction.
18. "Desist your noisy chatter now!" said the librarian.
19. Did the impact of the baseball crack the window?
20. The wood was piled in small, compact bundles.

Lesson 12

Objective

To review spelling rules and patterns from Lessons 7–11

Game Plan

Page 49

Read and discuss the Game Plan. Reinforce by asking students to name other words to illustrate the information summarized in each of the four sections. You may wish to have students turn back to the opening pages of Lessons 7–11 to review each Game Plan separately and to apply it to its full selection of List Words.

Practice

Lesson 7 (Page 49) Review the meanings of prefixes *ap* and *as* by discussing the Latin prefixes and roots in *appeal, approval, assert,* and *assortment.* Remind students that *ap* precedes roots beginning with *p,* and *as* precedes roots beginning with *s.* Then apply the discussion to the List Words, and have students use them in oral sentences. Point out the additional write-on lines to students and encourage them to add two words from Lesson 7 that they found especially difficult, or select and assign certain words that seemed to be difficult for everyone. (Repeat this procedure for each lesson review that follows in the Replay.) To extend the exercise, have students create similar context-clue sentences for the additional words.

Lesson 8 (Page 50) Review the meanings of prefixes *ac, af,* and *at* by discussing the Latin prefixes and roots in *accompany, affront,* and *attune.* Have students name the first letter or letters of roots that follow each prefix. Then review the List Words, having students use them in oral sentences. Have them write brief definitions for their additional words as well.

Lesson 9 (Page 50) To review the meanings of nouns with the suffixes *ion* and *ation,* discuss: *transportation, exploration, digestion, vacation.* Have students name the verb to which each suffix was added. Then repeat with the List Words.

Lesson 10 (Page 51) To review "spelling tricks" that may occur in words of French origin, discuss: *masquerade, suite, fatigue, croquet.* Then review the List Words. Point out that each sentence in the activity contains two List Words, but that only one is spelled correctly.

Lesson 11 (Page 51) To review words with Latin roots, have students look up the etymologies of: *constrict, diction, contract, conflict.* To extend the exercise, have students write sentences using their additional words, and then scramble all words in each sentence. Have them exchange their "coded messages" for solution.

Mixed Practice (Page 52) Review classification skills by writing these words on the board: *expertise, construction, cooperation.* Have students select one word to complete the series *superiority, ability* ____ . (*expertise*)

Test Yourself (Page 52) You may wish to write further test items on the board to include or to emphasize any words from Lessons 7-11 that students found particularly difficult.

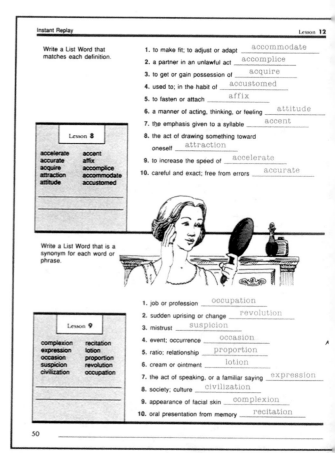

INSTANT REPLAY — LESSON 12

Game Plan

The prefixes **ap, as, ac, af,** and **at** often mean toward, at, in addition to, or near. The second letter in each of the prefixes **ap, as, af,** and **at** repeats the first letter in the root word.

ap + **prove** = approve **af** + **fair** = affair
as + **sure** = assure **at** + **tune** = attune

The prefix **ac** is added to roots that begin with **c** or **q**.

ac + **cent** = accent **ac** + **quire** = acquire

The suffixes **ion** and **ation** are often added to verbs to make nouns that mean the act of.

express + **ion** = expression **occupy** + **ation** = occupation

English words derived from French words can contain "spelling tricks." The usual French vowel and consonant spellings seem unusual to English-speaking people. For example, in French the ending **et** often stands for the long **a** sound, as in gourmet. The consonant digraph **ch** may stand for /**sh**/ sound, as in chaperone. Many English words have Latin roots. The English word compact, which means closely put together, comes from the Latin roots **com** (together) and **pangere** (to fasten). Other English words are borrowed or derived from Latin words. The word district comes from the Latin **districtus**. Both words mean territory.

Practice

Write a List Word to complete each sentence.

1. I gave Ned a gift to show my appreciation for his help.
2. Please help carry the camping apparatus to the truck.
3. As an apprentice, Jake learned from a master plumber.
4. The knights' assault on the castle ended in victory.
5. Several line graphs appear in the appendix of the book.
6. The manufacturers gave us their assurance that the product had been thoroughly tested.
7. I want to find an appropriate gift for someone who is going on a long trip.
8. If a starfish loses an appendage, it grows a new one.
9. Experts from the museum will appraise the old painting.
10. She won many awards for designing the apparel that was worn in several famous movies.

Lesson 7

appendage	assault
appendix	appreciation
apparatus	apprentice
appropriate	assurance
appraise	apparel

49

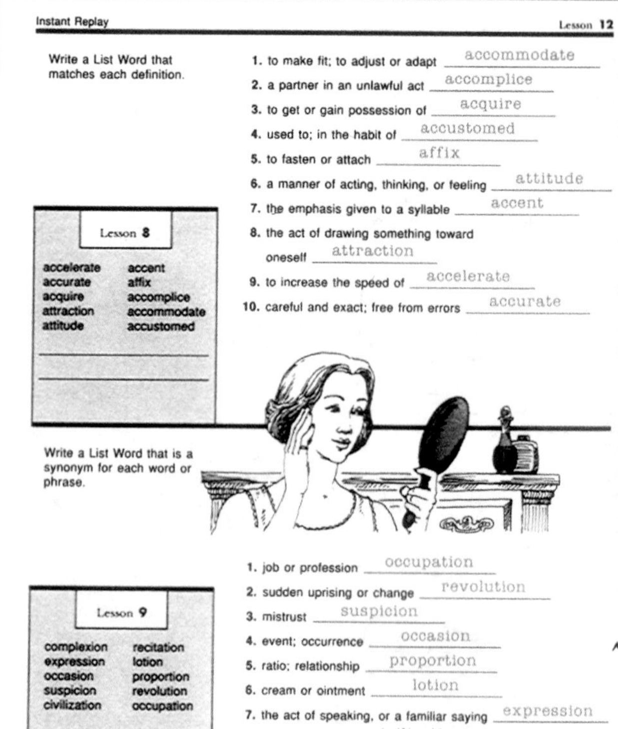

Instant Replay — Lesson 12

Write a List Word that matches each definition.

1. to make fit; to adjust or adapt accommodate
2. a partner in an unlawful act accomplice
3. to get or gain possession of acquire
4. used to; in the habit of accustomed
5. to fasten or attach affix
6. a manner of acting, thinking, or feeling attitude
7. the emphasis given to a syllable accent
8. the act of drawing something toward oneself attraction
9. to increase the speed of accelerate
10. careful and exact; free from errors accurate

Lesson 8

accelerate	accent
accurate	affix
acquire	accomplice
attraction	accommodate
attitude	accustomed

Write a List Word that is a synonym for each word or phrase.

1. job or profession occupation
2. sudden uprising or change revolution
3. mistrust suspicion
4. event; occurrence occasion
5. ratio; relationship proportion
6. cream or ointment lotion
7. the act of speaking, or a familiar saying expression
8. society; culture civilization
9. appearance of facial skin complexion
10. oral presentation from memory recitation

Lesson 9

complexion	recitation
expression	lotion
occasion	proportion
suspicion	revolution
civilization	occupation

50

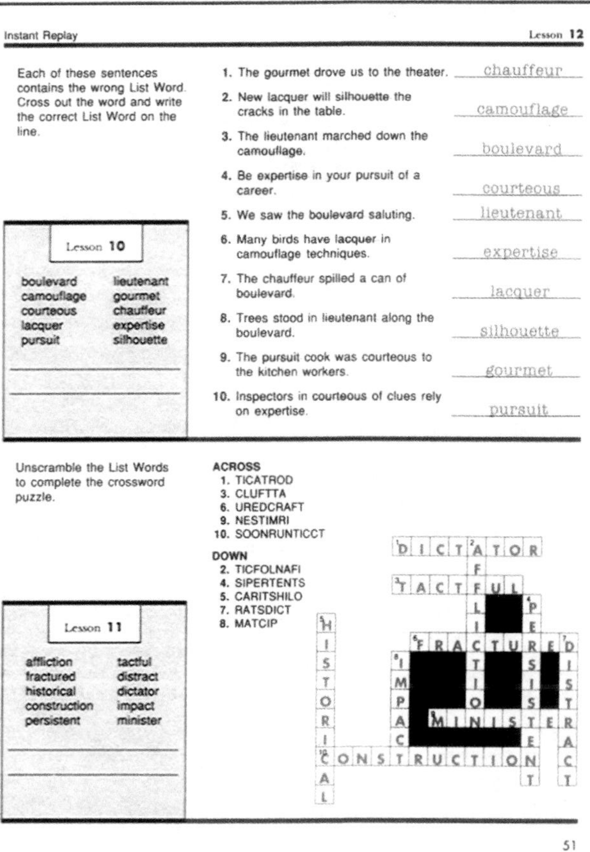
Instant Replay — Lesson 12

Each of these sentences contains the wrong List Word. Cross out the word and write the correct List Word on the line.

1. The gourmet drove us to the theater. chauffeur
2. New lacquer will silhouette the cracks in the table. camouflage
3. The lieutenant marched down the camouflage. boulevard
4. Be expertise in your pursuit of a career. courteous
5. We saw the boulevard saluting. lieutenant
6. Many birds have lacquer in camouflage techniques. expertise
7. The chauffeur spilled a can of boulevard. lacquer
8. Trees stood in lieutenant along the boulevard. silhouette
9. The pursuit cook was courteous to the kitchen workers. gourmet
10. Inspectors in courteous of clues rely on expertise. pursuit

Lesson 10

boulevard, lieutenant, camouflage, gourmet, courteous, chauffeur, lacquer, expertise, pursuit, silhouette

Unscramble the List Words to complete the crossword puzzle.

ACROSS
1. TICATROD
3. CLUFTTA
6. UREDCRAFT
9. NESTIMRI
10. SOONRUNTICCT

DOWN
2. TICFOLNAFI
4. SIPERTENTS
5. CARITSHILO
7. RATSDICT
8. MATCIP

Lesson 11

affliction, tactful, fractured, distract, historical, dictator, construction, impact, persistent, minister

51

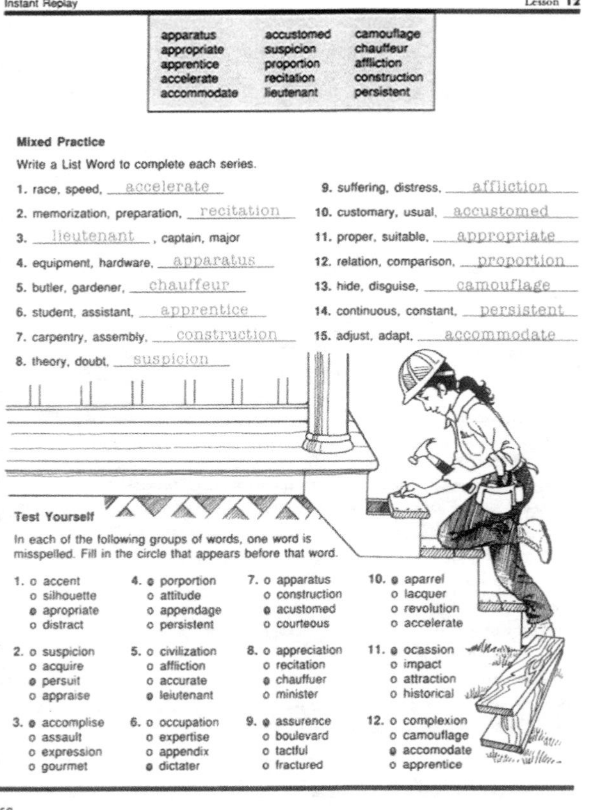
Instant Replay — Lesson 12

apparatus, appropriate, apprentice, accelerate, accommodate, accustomed, suspicion, proportion, recitation, lieutenant, camouflage, chauffeur, affliction, construction, persistent

Mixed Practice

Write a List Word to complete each series.

1. race, speed, accelerate
2. memorization, preparation, recitation
3. lieutenant, captain, major
4. equipment, hardware, apparatus
5. butler, gardener, chauffeur
6. student, assistant, apprentice
7. carpentry, assembly, construction
8. theory, doubt, suspicion
9. suffering, distress, affliction
10. customary, usual, accustomed
11. proper, suitable, appropriate
12. relation, comparison, proportion
13. hide, disguise, camouflage
14. continuous, constant, persistent
15. adjust, adapt, accommodate

Test Yourself

In each of the following groups of words, one word is misspelled. Fill in the circle that appears before that word.

1. o accent o silhouette ● apropriate o distract
2. o suspicion o acquire ● persuit o appraise
3. ● accomplise o assault o expression o gourmet
4. ● porportion o attitude o appendage o persistent
5. o civilization o affliction o accurate ● leiutenant
6. o occupation o expertise o appendix ● dictater
7. o apparatus o construction ● acustomed o courteous
8. o appreciation o recitation ● chauffuer o minister
9. ● assurence o boulevard o tactful o fractured
10. ● aparrel o lacquer o revolution o accelerate
11. ● ocassion o impact o attraction o historical
12. o complexion o camouflage ● accomodate o apprentice

52

Final Replay Test

1. A realtor will appraise the value of the house.
2. To show our appreciation, we cheered.
3. Use a hot iron to affix the name tag to your shirt.
4. Was the driver an accomplice to the crime?
5. A redhead usually has a very light complexion.
6. The law brought a revolution in health coverage.
7. Do you have a suspicion about who sent the note?
8. The cabinet showed great expertise in carpentry.
9. Did you use a clean brush to spread the lacquer?
10. The lieutenant was honored for his courage.
11. Glaucoma is an affliction affecting the eyes.
12. The impact of the rock smashed the window pane.
13. She was polite and tactful during the discussion.
14. Historical fiction blends facts with imagination.
15. The dull feathers of the bird provide camouflage.
16. In the film, the chauffeur was the criminal.
17. I'll meet you on the boulevard at noon.
18. Jim's recitation of the poem was dramatic.
19. This lotion may ease the itchiness of poison ivy.
20. His facial expression showed that he was surprised.
21. That boat can really accelerate!
22. The waiter tried to accommodate our every need.
23. I've grown accustomed to the noise of the city.
24. Make sure a fact is accurate before you quote it.
25. A lobster has a claw at the tip of each appendage.
26. The tale told of a dragon's assault on the village.
27. They opened a shop that sells formal apparel.
28. Footnotes are in an appendix at the end of a book.
29. Is this suit appropriate for the occasion?
30. Will the museum acquire a Mary Cassatt painting?
31. Ana's cheerful attitude makes her a great friend.
32. The four sides of a square are in equal proportion.
33. We studied the civilization of ancient Greece.
34. His thank-you note was prompt and courteous.
35. Use black paper to make the silhouette.
36. Tuan hopes to become a minister.
37. A government run by a dictator is oppressive.
38. I fractured one of my toes during the soccer game.
39. Will the loud music distract the workers?
40. We were delayed due to the highway construction.
41. What a terrible, persistent cough!
42. Julia Child is a famous gourmet cook.
43. The team was in pursuit of the state championship.
44. What a wonderful occasion to have a party!
45. I'd like to have an occupation as a travel agent.
46. The accent is on the first syllable in *kitten*.
47. Ted has an attraction to rural comforts.
48. She became an apprentice to a fine goldsmith.
49. Did the coach order new gymnastics apparatus?
50. Ken gave his assurance that he'd repay the loan.

Lesson 13

Objective

To spell words with the endings *ial, ious*

Pretest

1. The deceased sailor's burial was held at sea.
2. Please keep the information I told you confidential.
3. Cleanliness limits the spread of infectious diseases.
4. Zoe asked for all the material I had on Taiwan.
5. Do those windows make the room look spacious?
6. An ambitious person can go far in this company.
7. That 1938 hurricane was a ferocious storm!
8. Boris knows many influential people in government.
9. These are provincial regions and those are urban.
10. Each candidate made a gracious acceptance speech.
11. Arthur is too conscientious to leave early.
12. Ms. Kearn is knowledgeable about financial matters.
13. Did you capitalize the initial letter of each word?
14. We could not pry off the tenacious barnacles.
15. Will the judge wear ceremonial robes for the service?
16. Everyone was sorry to leave such a glorious beach.
17. Our voices created a harmonious melody.
18. The soldiers were stirred by the martial music.
19. When working, Jaina is unconscious of any noises.
20. An impartial person shows no favoritism.

Game Plan

Page 53
After students have read the Game Plan, have them identify words in which *i* takes the place of *y* and words in which it does not. Discuss the spelling patterns of the words and ways that students can remember them. Help students learn the meanings of the List Words, referring them to dictionaries when necessary.

Warm Up

Vocabulary Development (Page 53) Write *plain* and *fancy* on the chalkboard, explaining that they are antonyms. Before students complete the first part of the exercise, have them give other examples of antonym pairs. Students should be able to complete the second part of the exercise independently.

Practice

Word Analysis (Page 54) Write *the three red roses* on the chalkboard and use it to illustrate the difference between nouns and adjectives. Then have students complete the activity. When they have finished, ask volunteers which words had *A* and *N* beside them. (*initial, material*)

Word Application (Page 54) Work through the first item with students, asking them to tell why *financial* is the correct answer. (*It has to do with money.*)

Game Plan

Many words end with the letters **ial** and **ious**. Sometimes the ending is a suffix in which **i** takes the place of a dropped **y**, as in burial and harmonious. At other times, as in initial and ferocious, those letters are part of the word's spelling. Remembering what letters make up these endings will help you remember the spelling of many words.

Warm Up

1. burial
2. confidential
3. infectious
4. material
5. spacious
6. ambitious
7. ferocious
8. influential
9. provincial
10. gracious
11. conscientious
12. financial
13. initial
14. tenacious
15. ceremonial
16. glorious
17. harmonious
18. martial
19. unconscious
20. impartial

Vocabulary Development

Write the List Word that matches each antonym.

1. civilian ___martial___
2. gentle ___ferocious___
3. final ___initial___
4. crowded ___spacious___
5. rude ___gracious___
6. lazy ___conscientious___
7. prejudiced ___impartial___
8. disagreeing ___harmonious___
9. conscious ___unconscious___
10. open-minded ___provincial___

Write the List Word that matches each synonym or definition.

1. impressive, magnificent ___glorious___
2. having a drive for success ___ambitious___
3. ritual, relating to a religious event ___ceremonial___
4. steadfast, tough ___tenacious___
5. concerning money ___financial___
6. powerful, having influence ___influential___
7. having to do with matter or things ___material___
8. the act of placing something in the ground ___burial___
9. secret, private ___confidential___
10. catching, contagious ___infectious___

Practice

Word Analysis

Write each List Word under the correct category. If the word can be used as an adjective, write A after it. If the word can be used as a noun, write N. Two words can be used as both.

ial		ious	
1.	burial N	11.	infectious A
2.	confidential A	12.	spacious A
3.	material N, A	13.	ambitious A
4.	influential A	14.	ferocious A
5.	provincial A	15.	gracious A
6.	financial A	16.	conscientious A
7.	initial N, A	17.	tenacious A
8.	ceremonial A	18.	glorious A
9.	martial A	19.	harmonious A
10.	impartial A	20.	unconscious A

Did you know?

Martial is a word derived from one of the months on the Roman calendar, *March*. It is the month when fair weather returns, and when soldiers would go off to fight. March is the month dedicated to Mars, the Roman god of war. Today, the word *martial* is an adjective which describes war-like or military things.

Word Application

Replace the underlined word in each sentence with a List Word. Write the List Word on the line.

1. The firm's accountant will take care of any money matters. ___financial___
2. Laura was persistent in her struggle to help the needy. ___tenacious___
3. Information in the letter 's to be kept private. ___confidential___
4. The whole family gave the visitors a polite greeting. ___gracious___
5. The governor imposed military law on the town. ___martial___
6. Cassie did not realize that measles was a contagious disease. ___infectious___
7. Juan's first impression of the play was unfavorable. ___initial___
8. We were surprised at how roomy the apartment was. ___spacious___
9. Only family members will be permitted to attend the funeral. ___burial___
10. Please leave the building supplies at the side of the garage. ___material___
11. The savage storm caused widespread damage to the island. ___ferocious___
12. Urban politicians need to know that country attitudes may differ. ___provincial___

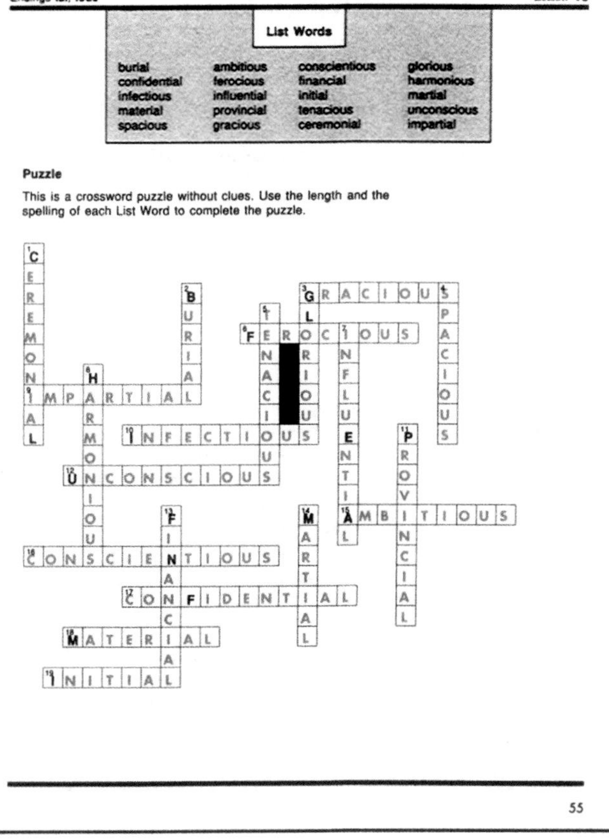

Endings ial, ious — Lesson 13

List Words

burial	ambitious	conscientious	glorious
confidential	ferocious	financial	harmonious
infectious	influential	initial	martial
material	provincial	tenacious	unconscious
spacious	gracious	ceremonial	impartial

Puzzle

This is a crossword puzzle without clues. Use the length and the spelling of each List Word to complete the puzzle.

55

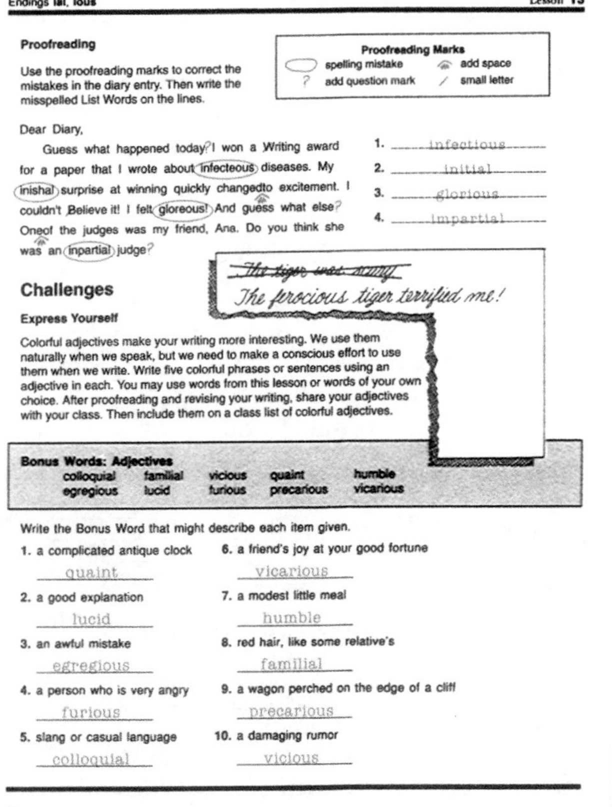

Endings ial, ious — Lesson 13

Proofreading

Use the proofreading marks to correct the mistakes in the diary entry. Then write the misspelled List Words on the lines.

Proofreading Marks: spelling mistake; add question mark; add space; small letter

Dear Diary,

Guess what happened today? I won a Writing award for a paper that I wrote about infecteous diseases. My inishal surprise at winning quickly changedto excitement. I couldn't Believe it! I felt gloreous! And guess what else? Oneof the judges was my friend, Ana. Do you think she was an inpartial judge?

1. infectious
2. initial
3. glorious
4. impartial

Challenges

Express Yourself

Colorful adjectives make your writing more interesting. We use them naturally when we speak, but we need to make a conscious effort to use them when we write. Write five colorful phrases or sentences using an adjective in each. You may use words from this lesson or words of your own choice. After proofreading and revising your writing, share your adjectives with your class. Then include them on a class list of colorful adjectives.

~~The tiger was scary.~~ *The ferocious tiger terrified me!*

Bonus Words: Adjectives colloquial, egregious, familial, lucid, vicious, furious, quaint, precarious, humble, vicarious

Write the Bonus Word that might describe each item given.

1. a complicated antique clock — quaint
2. a good explanation — lucid
3. an awful mistake — egregious
4. a person who is very angry — furious
5. slang or casual language — colloquial
6. a friend's joy at your good fortune — vicarious
7. a modest little meal — humble
8. red hair, like some relative's — familial
9. a wagon perched on the edge of a cliff — precarious
10. a damaging rumor — vicious

56

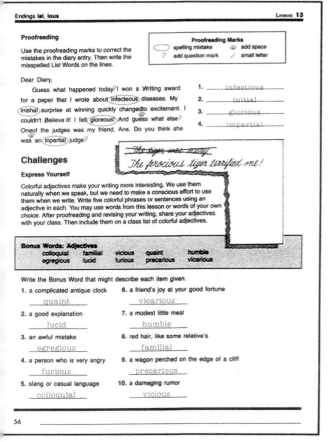

Puzzle (Page 55) Have students discuss strategies for solving crossword puzzles without clues. Then let them complete the puzzle without further help.

Proofreading (Page 56) Use the question *Wasn't that an exeting Book* to demonstrate the proofreading marks that students will be using to correct the diary entry.

Challenges

Express Yourself (Page 56) Have students suggest categories of adjectives, such as color, size, shape, number, and feeling. It may help if they first think of nouns and then try to name adjectives that might describe these. Encourage students to think of vivid or exaggerated scenes or objects. Then have them do the writing independently.

Bonus Words: Adjectives (Page 56) Explain that all the Bonus Words name adjectives. Discuss each word's meaning, using dictionaries if necessary. Have volunteers identify a noun that each adjective could describe. Then have students take turns using the words in oral sentences.

Bonus Word Test

1. The family lived in a humble little cottage.
2. Allan's dog is not vicious and would never hurt you.
3. I was embarrassed to make such an egregious error!
4. We got vicarious joy from their wedding pictures.
5. We heard the colloquial chat, not a formal report.
6. We understood Dr. Chan's lucid explanation.
7. Move the lamp away from such a precarious spot.
8. My uncle and I have a strong familial resemblance.
9. Tourists flocked to visit the quaint little village.
10. The furious battle raged for weeks.

Final Test

1. Is Wanda a conscientious student?
2. Read the financial pages for information on stocks.
3. My initial reaction changed after I met her.
4. The raccoon was tenacious and would not let go.
5. Special rules apply at ceremonial events.
6. Lee's project was the most ambitious in the class.
7. The animal looked ferocious, so I stayed far away.
8. The influential person supported the candidate.
9. Traveling will broaden your provincial attitude.
10. Max's gracious acceptance speech was charming.
11. We are moving to a more spacious apartment.
12. The ruler was surrounded by material comforts.
13. A yawn is infectious and makes others yawn.
14. Will you allow me to read the confidential report?
15. The news reported the burial of a time capsule.
16. Let an impartial jury determine who is right.
17. Do you find the colors harmonious?
18. Art was unconscious of the time until the bell rang.
19. The new leader declared martial law.
20. This is the most glorious sunset in weeks!

Lesson 14

Objective

To spell words with the endings *al, ally, ic, ically, ly*

Pretest

1. Academically, June is a leader in her class.
2. The club's annual meeting will be held in February.
3. Toads are basically very similar to frogs.
4. The sunset cast a dramatic glow on the ocean.
5. Incidentally, Jack will be late for the meeting.
6. The president met with her economic advisors.
7. Tony's response was an emphatic "No, thank you!"
8. Is the Model T a classic American automobile?
9. There has been a gradual decline in temperature.
10. A brick wall is more substantial than a wooden one.
11. The amoeba is microscopic organism.
12. Frantically, I searched for my lost dog.
13. Comically, the clowns scurried into the small car.
14. You acted heroically when you rescued the cat.
15. Father packed the car in a systematic way.
16. Was the decision to go to the movies mutual?
17. Jane Austen was a prolific writer.
18. The drought drastically reduced the water supply.
19. Ideally, the new highway will be finished by May.
20. Did the tragic story touch your heart?

Game Plan

Page 57

Discuss the Game Plan and examples. Then have students analyze each List Word to tell the root or root word, its meaning and part of speech, the ending that was added, and the meaning and part of speech of the new word.

Warm Up

Vocabulary Development (Page 57) Before the exercise, have volunteers identify the List Words that match these definitions: *very sad (tragic); bravely (heroically).*

Dictionary Skills (Page 57) Have students refer to dictionaries to find the sound spellings of *dramatic, emphatic,* and *drastically* and write them on the board.

Practice

Word Analysis (Page 58) Before students complete this two-part exercise, have volunteers add endings to these adjectives to make adverbs: *beautiful (beautifully); final (finally); typical (typically)*; and add endings to these nouns to make adjectives: *democrat (democratic); rent (rental); history (historic).*

Word Application (Page 58) Write these words on the chalkboard: *thorough, practical, congenial.* Have students tell which word belongs in each of these phrases. The answer will be a synonym for the word in parentheses. *a ________ solution (workable); a ________ investigation (complete); a ________ friend (pleasant). (practical; thorough; congenial)*

Analogies (Page 58) Review analogies by writing on the chalkboard: *bird, horse, monkey.* Then read this incomplete analogy aloud and have students select a word to complete it: *Leash is to dog as bridle is to ________. (horse)*

Endings **al, ally, ic, ically, ly** — LESSON **14**

Game Plan

The endings **al**, **ally**, **ic**, **ically**, and **ly** are often added to roots or root words to form new words and new parts of speech.

Root or Root Word	Meaning	Plus Ending	New Meaning
annus (Latin root)	year (noun)	**annual**	yearly (adj)
comic	humorous (adj)	**comically**	humorously (adv.)
ideal	perfect (adj.)	**ideally**	perfectly (adv.)

1. academically
2. annual
3. basically
4. dramatic
5. incidentally
6. economic
7. emphatic
8. classic
9. gradual
10. substantial
11. microscopic
12. frantically
13. comically
14. heroically
15. systematic
16. mutual
17. prolific
18. drastically
19. ideally
20. tragic

Warm Up

Vocabulary Development

Write the List Word that matches each definition.

1. harshly — drastically
2. having to do with education — academically
3. having great substance; solid or firm — substantial
4. invisible to the naked eye; tiny — microscopic
5. very productive; fruitful — prolific
6. shared in common by two or more people — mutual
7. acting in a worried or hurried way — frantically
8. filled with action, emotion, or excitement — dramatic
9. developing little by little, over time — gradual
10. expressed or done with emphasis; forceful — emphatic

Dictionary Skills

Write the List Word that matches each sound-spelling.

1. (klas′ ik) classic
2. (kăm′ i k′l ē) comically
3. (bā′ sik′l ē) basically
4. (ī dē′ əl ē) ideally
5. (traj′ ik) tragic
6. (hi rō′ i k′l ē) heroically
7. (sis tə mat′ ik) systematic
8. (an′ yoo wəl) annual
9. (in si dent′ lē) incidentally
10. (ē kə näm′ ik) economic

57

Endings **al, ally, ic, ically, ly** — Lesson **14**

Practice

Did you know?

The adjective **microscopic** comes to our language from the Greek words *mikros*, meaning "small," and *skopein*, meaning "to watch or view." In our language, a microscope is an instrument which helps us to view tiny objects. *Microscopic* is used to describe objects which cannot be seen with the naked eye.

Word Analysis

Form List Words by adding endings to these adjectives to make adverbs.

1. drastic drastically
2. academic academically
3. incidental incidentally
4. ideal ideally
5. frantic frantically
6. basic basically
7. comic comically
8. heroic heroically

Form List Words by adding endings to these nouns to make adjectives. Some nouns change form before endings are added.

9. system systematic
10. economy economic
11. class classic
12. microscope microscopic
13. drama dramatic
14. substance substantial

Word Application

Write the List Word that is a synonym for the word in parentheses.

1. the annual meeting (yearly)
2. economic security (financial)
3. by mutual consent (shared)
4. a prolific plant (fruitful)
5. a tragic story (extremely sad)
6. a systematic procedure (orderly; planned)
7. the gradual changes (little by little)
8. his emphatic reply (forceful)

Analogies

Write a List Word to complete each analogy.

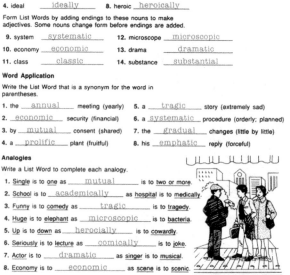

1. Single is to one as mutual is to two or more.
2. School is to academically as hospital is to medically.
3. Funny is to comedy as tragic is to tragedy.
4. Huge is to elephant as microscopic is to bacteria.
5. Up is to down as heroically is to cowardly.
6. Seriously is to lecture as comically is to joke.
7. Actor is to dramatic as singer is to musical.
8. Economy is to economic as scene is to scenic.
9. Slow is to calmly as fast is to frantically.
10. Soft-spoken is to period as emphatic is to exclamation point.

58

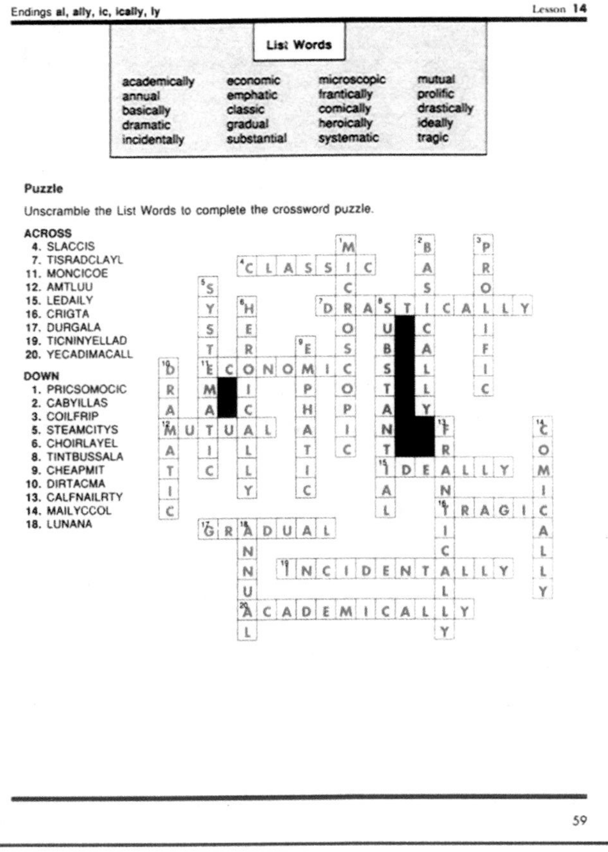
Endings **al, ally, ic, ically, ly** Lesson **14**

List Words

academically	economic	microscopic	mutual
annual	emphatic	frantically	prolific
basically	classic	comically	drastically
dramatic	gradual	heroically	ideally
incidentally	substantial	systematic	tragic

Puzzle

Unscramble the List Words to complete the crossword puzzle.

ACROSS
4. SLACCIS
7. TISRADCLAYL
11. MONCICOE
12. AMTLUU
15. LEDAILY
16. CRIGTA
17. DURGALA
19. TICNINYELLAD
20. YECADIMACALL

DOWN
1. PRICSOMOCIC
2. CABYILLAS
3. COILFRIP
5. STEAMCITYS
6. CHOIRLAYEL
8. TINTBUSSALA
9. CHEAPMIT
10. DIRTACMA
13. CALFNAILRTY
14. MAILYCCOL
18. LUNANA

59

Puzzle (Page 59) Urge students to find clues not only in the scrambled letters, but in the number of spaces in each answer and the letter clues found once some of the words have been entered in the grid.

Proofreading (Page 60) Review the proofreading marks in this lesson emphasizing the use of the delete mark.

Challenges

Express Yourself (Page 60) To review students' knowledge of topic sentences, have them find examples in such content-area texts as social studies and science. When students have finished writing, provide time for discussion of their topic sentences, pointing out the clarity that each adds to the paragraph.

Bonus Words: Automobile Parts (Page 60) With dictionaries and diagrams or illustrations from an encyclopedia, define and discuss the Bonus Words. Urge students to share their knowledge of automobile engines.

Bonus Word Test

1. The mechanic replaced the damaged crankshaft.
2. The distributor sends electricity to the spark plugs.
3. The generator creates a steady flow of electricity.
4. In the carburetor, gasoline is mixed with air.
5. Then the throttle sends fuel vapors onward.
6. Road salt and sand may cause the chassis to rust.
7. Check your speed on the speedometer.
8. Check the odometer to see how far you've driven.
9. Antifreeze will prevent your radiator from freezing.
10. Inside each cylinder is a moving piston.

Final Test

1. Did you notice a gradual decrease in temperature?
2. Are puffins ideally suited to cold environments?
3. Heroically, the man entered the burning store.
4. The principal made a dramatic announcement.
5. Solve math problems in a systematic way.
6. Incidentally, my sister met your cousin last night.
7. Shakespeare wrote a tragic play about Caesar.
8. An atlas is a substantial source of information.
9. Jamal was emphatic in his refusal to wear a hat.
10. We had a terrific harvest from our prolific garden.
11. Frantically, I searched for my lost dog!
12. The company's annual report outlined its profits.
13. Several microscopic organisms exist in water.
14. Tina and I have a mutual friend named Linda.
15. The nation's economic state improved last year.
16. Our school is academically superior to theirs.
17. Is the Kentucky Derby a classic sporting event?
18. Critics gave the movie a basically positive review.
19. The actors behaved comically in that movie.
20. The oil embargo caused prices to rise drastically.

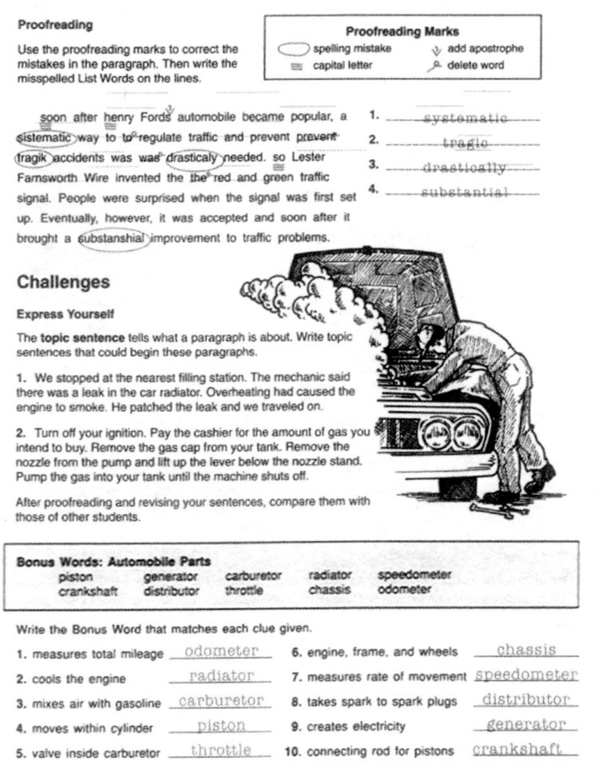
Endings **al, ally, ic, ically, ly** Lesson **14**

Proofreading

Use the proofreading marks to correct the mistakes in the paragraph. Then write the misspelled List Words on the lines.

Proofreading Marks
spelling mistake — add apostrophe
capital letter — delete word

soon after henry Fords automobile became popular, a sistematic way to to regulate traffic and prevent prevent fragik accidents was was drasticaly needed. so Lester Farnsworth Wire invented the the red and green traffic signal. People were surprised when the signal was first set up. Eventually, however, it was accepted and soon after it brought a substanshial improvement to traffic problems.

1. systematic
2. tragic
3. drastically
4. substantial

Challenges

Express Yourself

The **topic sentence** tells what a paragraph is about. Write topic sentences that could begin these paragraphs.

1. We stopped at the nearest filling station. The mechanic said there was a leak in the car radiator. Overheating had caused the engine to smoke. He patched the leak and we traveled on.

2. Turn off your ignition. Pay the cashier for the amount of gas you intend to buy. Remove the gas cap from your tank. Remove the nozzle from the pump and lift up the lever below the nozzle stand. Pump the gas into your tank until the machine shuts off.

After proofreading and revising your sentences, compare them with those of other students.

Bonus Words: Automobile Parts

piston	generator	carburetor	radiator	speedometer
crankshaft	distributor	throttle	chassis	odometer

Write the Bonus Word that matches each clue given.

1. measures total mileage — odometer
2. cools the engine — radiator
3. mixes air with gasoline — carburetor
4. moves within cylinder — piston
5. valve inside carburetor — throttle
6. engine, frame, and wheels — chassis
7. measures rate of movement — speedometer
8. takes spark to spark plugs — distributor
9. creates electricity — generator
10. connecting rod for pistons — crankshaft

60

Lesson 15

Objective

To spell words with Latin roots

Pretest

1. Did animosity between the countries lead to war?
2. The emission of sparks from the wire caused a fire.
3. An inanimate object has no life.
4. His father worked long, hard days at manual labor.
5. His submission for the contest won first prize.
6. Tina received a commission on the stereo she sold.
7. Water is a clear fluid.
8. Use your influence to change Carly's mind.
9. The pilot will manipulate the helicopter controls.
10. The radio transmission was not clear.
11. Animation brings cartoon characters to life.
12. The water supply in our town contains fluoride.
13. Influenza is a horrible illness!
14. I got lost because of the omission of street signs.
15. The decision of the judges was unanimous.
16. Will the new laws emancipate the citizens?
17. The interest payments on the loan will fluctuate.
18. Refreshments were served during intermission.
19. The queen issued a harsh mandate.
20. Is Chan fluent in Chinese, Japanese, and English?

Game Plan

Page 61
Work with students to find the Latin roots of these words inthe dictionary: *magnanimous, admission, affluent, manufacture.* Discuss how the meaning of each word is related to the meaning of the Latin root. Then help students identify the Latin root in each List Word and define each word.

Warm Up

Vocabulary Development (Page 61) Encourage students to refer to the Game Plan to recall the meaning of each root and to determine which List Words contain that root.

Dictionary Skills (Page 61) Remind students that knowing how to pronounce a word may help them remember how to spell the word.

Practice

Word Analysis (Page 62) Point out to students that some words may be used as more than one part of speech. As an example, have students look up *manual* in the dictionary and tell its different parts of speech. When students complete the activity, have them use the words in sentences.

Synonyms and Antonyms (Page 62) If necessary, review the definitions of *synonym* and *antonym* and have students give examples of each.

Word Application (Page 62) Before the exercise, have students use a List Word to replace the underlined word in: *Peace talks were scheduled to relieve the hatred between the two countries. (animosity)*

Latin Roots — LESSON 15

Game Plan

Recognizing Latin roots in words can help you determine the meaning of unfamiliar words and remember how to spell them.

Latin Root and Meaning	English Word and Meaning
miss (to send)	**emission** (the act of sending out)
anim (breath or soul)	**inanimate** (not alive)
flu (flow)	**fluid** (able to flow)
man (hand)	**manipulate** (to operate by hand)

Study these List Words that are based on Latin roots.

1. animosity
2. emission
3. inanimate
4. manual
5. submission
6. commission
7. fluid
8. influence
9. manipulate
10. transmission
11. animation
12. fluoride
13. influenza
14. omission
15. unanimous
16. emancipate
17. fluctuate
18. intermission
19. mandate
20. fluent

Warm Up

Vocabulary Development

Write the List Words that have a Latin root that means to send.

1. emission 4. transmission
2. submission 5. omission
3. commission 6. intermission

Write the List Words that have a Latin root that means breath or soul.

7. animosity 9. animation
8. inanimate 10. unanimous

Write the List Words that have a Latin root that means to flow.

11. fluid 14. influenza
12. influence 15. fluctuate
13. fluoride 16. fluent

Write the List Words that have a Latin root that means hand.

17. manual 19. emancipate
18. manipulate 20. mandate

Dictionary Skills

Write the List Word that matches each sound-spelling.

1. (man´ yoo wəl) manual 4. (floor´ id) fluoride
2. (mə nip´ yə lāt) manipulate 5. (ō mish´ ən) omission
3. (man´ dāt) mandate 6. (floo´ id) fluid

61

Latin Roots — Lesson 15

Practice

Word Analysis

Write the List Words that can be used as verbs.

1. influence 3. emancipate
2. manipulate 4. fluctuate

Write the List Words that can be used as adjectives.

5. inanimate 8. unanimous
6. manual 9. fluent
7. fluid

Write the List Words that can be used as a noun and a verb.

10. influence 11. mandate

Synonyms and Antonyms

Write a List Word that matches each synonym.

1. neglect omission 5. eloquent fluent
2. lifeless inanimate 6. proposal submission
3. hatred animosity 7. cartoon animation
4. operate manipulate 8. change fluctuate

Write a List Word that matches each antonym.

9. solid fluid 11. divided unanimous
10. enslave emancipate 12. automatic manual

Did you know?
Unanimous comes from two Latin words meaning "one" and "the mind." When a vote or decision is *unanimous,* it means that everyone is of "one mind," or everyone thinks the same and agrees completely.

Word Application

Replace the underlined word or words in each sentence with a List Word. Write the List Word on the line.

1. Mr. Roper earned a large amount of money when he sold five cars in one week. commission
2. Insects are responsible for the passing along of many diseases. transmission
3. The sending out of harmful elements into the air has led to the enactment of pollution control laws. emission
4. The dentist recommended that we use a chemical element mouthwash to prevent tooth decay. fluoride
5. There will be a fifteen minute pause in the program. intermission

62

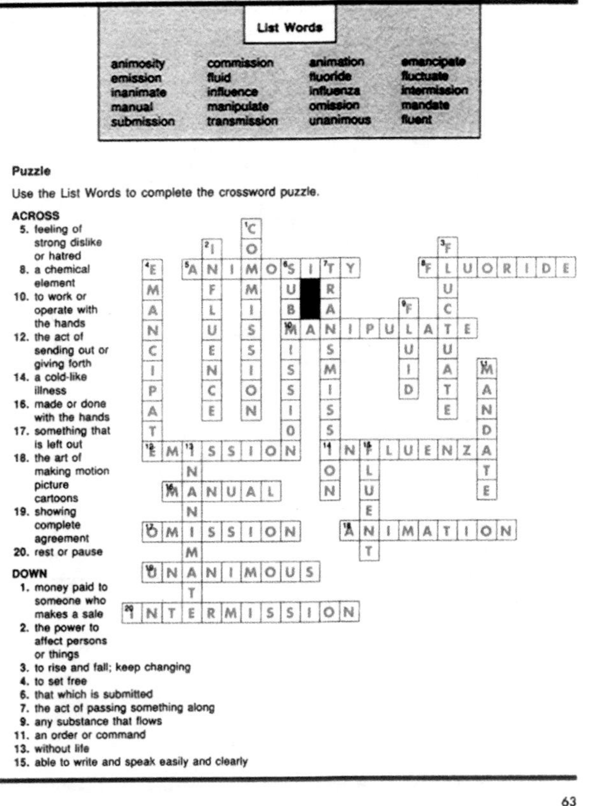

Latin Roots Lesson 15

List Words

animosity	commission	animation	emancipate
emission	fluid	fluoride	fluctuate
inanimate	influence	influenza	intermission
manual	manipulate	omission	mandate
submission	transmission	unanimous	fluent

Puzzle

Use the List Words to complete the crossword puzzle.

ACROSS

5. feeling of strong dislike or hatred
8. a chemical element
10. to work or operate with the hands
12. the act of sending out or giving forth
14. a cold-like illness
16. made or done with the hands
17. something that is left out
18. the art of making motion picture cartoons
19. showing complete agreement
20. rest or pause

DOWN

1. money paid to someone who makes a sale
2. the power to affect persons or things
3. to rise and fall; keep changing
4. to set free
6. that which is submitted
7. the act of passing something along
9. any substance that flows
11. an order or command
13. without life
15. able to write and speak easily and clearly

63

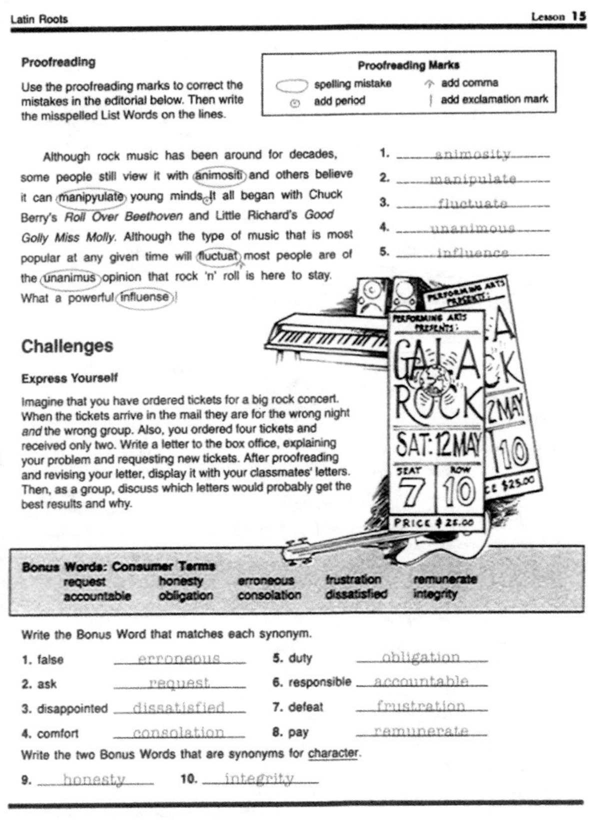

Latin Roots Lesson 15

Proofreading

Use the proofreading marks to correct the mistakes in the editorial below. Then write the misspelled List Words on the lines.

Proofreading Marks
spelling mistake · add comma · add period · add exclamation mark

Although rock music has been around for decades, some people still view it with animositi and others believe it can manipyulate young minds It all began with Chuck Berry's *Roll Over Beethoven* and Little Richard's *Good Golly Miss Molly*. Although the type of music that is most popular at any given time will fluctuat most people are of the unanimus opinion that rock 'n' roll is here to stay. What a powerful influense

1. animosity
2. manipulate
3. fluctuate
4. unanimous
5. influence

Challenges

Express Yourself

Imagine that you have ordered tickets for a big rock concert. When the tickets arrive in the mail they are for the wrong night *and* the wrong group. Also, you ordered four tickets and received only two. Write a letter to the box office, explaining your problem and requesting new tickets. After proofreading and revising your letter, display it with your classmates' letters. Then, as a group, discuss which letters would probably get the best results and why.

Bonus Words: Consumer Terms

request	honesty	erroneous	frustration	remunerate
accountable	obligation	consolation	dissatisfied	integrity

Write the Bonus Word that matches each synonym.

1. false	erroneous	5. duty	obligation
2. ask	request	6. responsible	accountable
3. disappointed	dissatisfied	7. defeat	frustration
4. comfort	consolation	8. pay	remunerate

Write the two Bonus Words that are synonyms for character.

9. honesty 10. integrity

64

Puzzle (Page 63) Encourage students to think carefully about the meaning of each List Word as they complete the crossword puzzle.

Proofreading (Page 64) Write a sentence on the board to demonstrate the proofreading marks students will be using in this lesson.

Challenges

Express Yourself (Page 64) Ask students what they should do if they ordered tickets to a special event and received the wrong tickets in the mail. Lead students to realize that writing a letter complaining of the mix-up and requesting new tickets is one solution. If necessary, review business letter form with students, emphasizing that they should use polite language in their letters.

Bonus Words: Consumer Terms (Page 64) Have students look up the meanings of each Bonus Word in the dictionary. Discuss how these words apply to businesses and customers. Ask volunteers to use the words in oral sentences.

Bonus Word Test

1. The school must remunerate all its guest speakers.
2. As a consolation, the store refunded my money.
3. His honesty led him to return the extra change.
4. The store has an obligation to its valued customers.
5. In frustration, Jason demanded his money back.
6. Linda made a request to see the hat in the window.
7. The store is accountable for inferior merchandise.
8. The store owner was respected for his integrity.
9. A dissatisfied customer returned the shirt.
10. Al was overcharged due to an erroneous sales tag.

Final Test

1. The realtor earns a commission on every sale.
2. Research shows fluoride helps prevent cavities.
3. What terrible animosity between the two teams!
4. Everyone's story submission must be typewritten.
5. Is Patricia a fluent speaker on political issues?
6. The farmer hired manual laborers to pick apples.
7. Is that statue an inanimate object?
8. They detected the emission of radiation.
9. The committee's mandate angered many people.
10. Lincoln worked to emancipate the slaves.
11. An omission from the contract made it invalid.
12. Some new movies mix animation and real life.
13. The teacher has a great influence on his pupils.
14. Are fever and chills symptoms of influenza?
15. Computers quicken the transmission of ideas.
16. A greenish fluid leaked from the car's radiator.
17. The dancers changed costumes at intermission.
18. My report card shows how my grades fluctuate.
19. Ramon can manipulate very complicated machines.
20. Julie was elected by a unanimous class vote.

Lesson 16

Objective

To spell words with the endings *able* and *ible*

Pretest

1. At home I am responsible for feeding the pets.
2. Our class donated money to a charitable group.
3. Today, diseases such as cancer are often curable.
4. What a nice, livable back yard this building has!
5. Sara carries a portable radio in her backpack.
6. The Delgados are amiable people to travel with.
7. Is my VCR compatible with your television?
8. The house needed work to make it habitable.
9. Many notable people were born in Texas.
10. A disposable flashlight is handy when you travel.
11. You can be successful if you set attainable goals.
12. Are colds very communicable?
13. Because of static, the words aren't intelligible.
14. Swimming is permissible in the roped-off area.
15. Many lines from that speech are quotable.
16. Is Paul available for work on Friday?
17. Pack the consumable items in a separate bag.
18. Is your name and address clearly legible?
19. The storm left the village in a pitiable state.
20. Anna is a reliable worker and seldom late.

Game Plan

Page 65
After students have read the Game Plan, have them tell which words contain *s* or soft *g* followed by *ible*. Discuss ways students can remember the spelling of words, and then discuss the words' meanings. Encourage students to use dictionaries for this purpose and to use each word in an oral sentence.

Warm Up

Vocabulary Development (Page 65) By now, students should be familiar with this type of exercise. Have them consult dictionaries if they encounter any difficulties.

Dictionary Skills (Page 65) Review the letters and symbols used in respellings. Encourage students to use a dictionary to check any answers they question.

Practice

Word Analysis (Page 66) Write *I live here.* on the board and ask which word is a verb. (*live*) Point out that the List Word *livable* is the adjective form of the word. Then have students read the directions. You may wish to work through the first item or two with them.

Proofreading (Page 66) Write this sentence on the board and use it to demonstrate the use of the proofreading marks in this lesson: *We will read a a story called Onthe Stairs.* Point out that each sentence has at least two mistakes in it.

Endings **able, ible** — LESSON **16**

Game Plan

The endings **able** and **ible** make adjectives from base words. For instance, pity becomes pitiable. The more common ending is **able**. The ending **ible** is often used after **s** or soft **g**, as in responsible and legible. There are some words, such as compatible, which have to be remembered as exceptions.

1. responsible
2. charitable
3. curable
4. livable
5. portable
6. amiable
7. compatible
8. habitable
9. notable
10. disposable
11. attainable
12. communicable
13. intelligible
14. permissible
15. quotable
16. available
17. consumable
18. legible
19. pitiable
20. reliable

Warm Up

Vocabulary Development

Write the List Word that matches each definition.

1. able to be remedied or cured curable
2. able to be carried around portable
3. able to be thrown away disposable
4. able to get along well together compatible
5. worth noticing notable
6. deserving scorn or contempt pitiable
7. that which can be eaten or used up consumable
8. that which can be understood easily intelligible
9. able to be achieved by hard work attainable
10. worth quoting quotable

Dictionary Skills

Write the List Word that matches each sound-spelling.

1. (liv´ ə b'l) livable
2. (ə vā´ lə b'l) available
3. (lej´ ə b'l) legible
4. (pər mis´ ə b'l) permissible
5. (ri lī´ ə b'l) reliable
6. (kə myōō´ ni kə b'l) communicable
7. (char´ ə tə b'l) charitable
8. (ā´ mē ə b'l) amiable
9. (ri spän´ sə b'l) responsible
10. (hab´ it ə b'l) habitable

65

Endings **able, ible** — Lesson **16**

Practice

Word Analysis

Form List Words by adding endings to these verbs to make adjectives. You will change the form of some verbs before adding the endings.

1. attain attainable
2. pity pitiable
3. dispose disposable
4. communicate communicable
5. avail available
6. quote quotable
7. rely reliable
8. consume consumable
9. cure curable
10. habitat habitable
11. permit permissible
12. respond responsible

Did you know?

The word **portable** is derived from the Latin word *portus* which originally meant "a mountain pass," and later "a gate, or a door." *Portus* eventually came to be *port*, or what we today call a harbor. The word *port* came to refer to transportation, and carrying goods. So *port*, meaning "carry," together with the suffix *able*, came to mean "able to be carried around easily."

Proofreading

Use the proofreading marks to correct the mistakes in the sentences. Then write the misspelled words correctly on the lines.

Proofreading Marks
spelling mistake — delete word
add space — add quotation marks
add period, question mark, or exclamation mark

1. Several notable businessprofessionals made charitible donations. charitable
2. As a result, the homeless now have a habitible place to live habitable
3. The mayor said, This house is really quite liveable." livable
4. An amiable staff helps each family find a a compatable apartment. compatible
5. Are portible televisions available for families that want them portable
6. Pets are permissable only only for elderly residents. permissible
7. Each family is responsable for cleaning its ownunit. responsible
8. The tenants have been quite relyable, said the superintendent. reliable
9. "What a notible achievement this is" declared one public leader. notable
10. Could it be that homelessness is curible in the this city? curable
11. Citizens havemade several donations of consumible goods. consumable
12. Many use disposible products until theyfind permanent homes. disposable
13. One resident said, "Last year I was in a piteable state. pitiable
14. Thatresident was highly quoteable and often appeared on the news. quotable
15. For that person, self-sufficiency is now a an attainnable goal. attainable

66

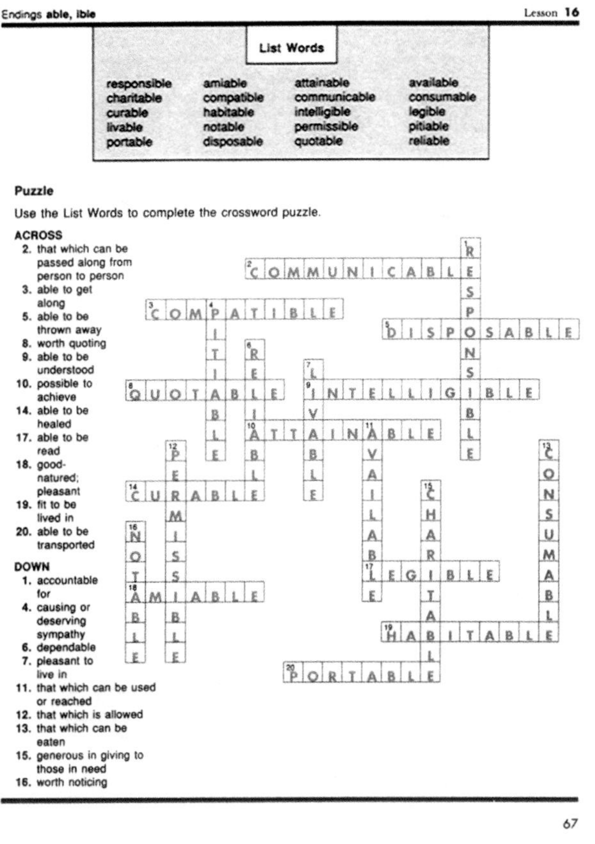
Endings **able, ible** Lesson **16**

List Words

responsible	amiable	attainable	available
charitable	compatible	communicable	consumable
curable	habitable	intelligible	legible
livable	notable	permissible	pitiable
portable	disposable	quotable	reliable

Puzzle

Use the List Words to complete the crossword puzzle.

ACROSS
2. that which can be passed along from person to person
3. able to get along
5. able to be thrown away
8. worth quoting
9. able to be understood
10. possible to achieve
14. able to be healed
17. able to be read
18. good-natured; pleasant
19. fit to be lived in
20. able to be transported

DOWN
1. accountable for
4. causing or deserving sympathy
6. dependable
7. pleasant to live in
11. that which can be used or reached
12. that which is allowed
13. that which can be eaten
15. generous in giving to those in need
16. worth noticing

67

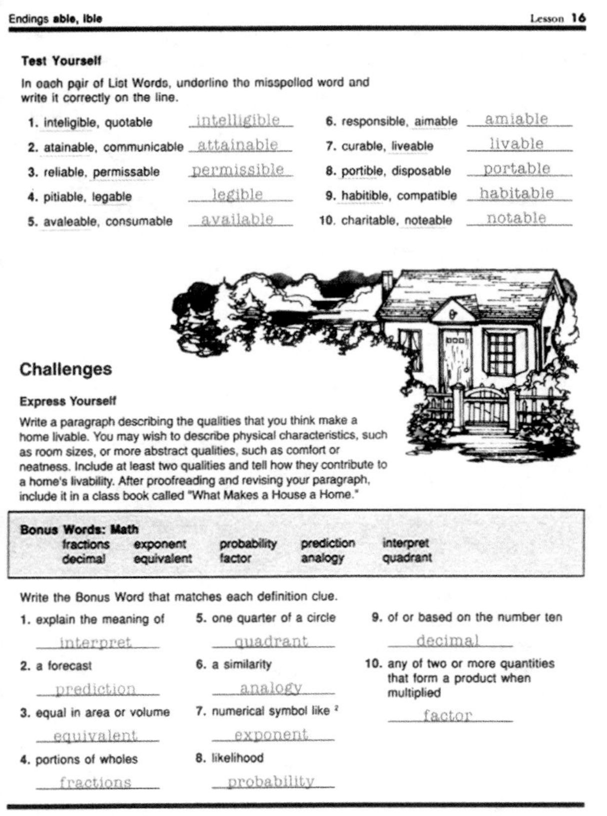
Endings **able, ible** Lesson **16**

Test Yourself

In each pair of List Words, underline the misspelled word and write it correctly on the line.

1. inteligible, quotable — intelligible
2. atainable, communicable — attainable
3. reliable, permissable — permissible
4. pitiable, legable — legible
5. avaleable, consumable — available
6. responsible, aimable — amiable
7. curable, liveable — livable
8. portible, disposable — portable
9. habitible, compatible — habitable
10. charitable, noteable — notable

Challenges

Express Yourself

Write a paragraph describing the qualities that you think make a home livable. You may wish to describe physical characteristics, such as room sizes, or more abstract qualities, such as comfort or neatness. Include at least two qualities and tell how they contribute to a home's livability. After proofreading and revising your paragraph, include it in a class book called "What Makes a House a Home."

Bonus Words: Math

fractions, decimal, exponent, equivalent, probability, factor, prediction, analogy, interpret, quadrant

Write the Bonus Word that matches each definition clue.

1. explain the meaning of — interpret
2. a forecast — prediction
3. equal in area or volume — equivalent
4. portions of wholes — fractions
5. one quarter of a circle — quadrant
6. a similarity — analogy
7. numerical symbol like ² — exponent
8. likelihood — probability
9. of or based on the number ten — decimal
10. any of two or more quantities that form a product when multiplied — factor

68

Puzzle (Page 67) Have students briefly review strategies for solving crossword puzzles. Remind them to use neatly printed upper-case letters.

Test Yourself (Page 68) Have volunteers tell how this test is to be taken. Students should check their own answers against the List Words on page 67.

Challenges

Express Yourself (Page 68) Discuss the difference between *habitable,* or fit to be lived in, and *livable,* which implies comfort. Have students brainstorm qualities that contribute to livability. Encourage them to think of both physical characteristics and more abstract qualities. Then have them do the writing independently.

Bonus Words: Math (Page 68) Explain that all the Bonus Words are related to mathematics. Through discussion and dictionary use, help students understand each word's meaning. Math books may provide examples of some terms.

Bonus Word Test

1. An analogy is a kind of comparison.
2. While not identical, the areas are equivalent.
3. Jan is very quick at multiplying fractions.
4. The number two is a factor in all even numbers.
5. One quarter of a circle is called a quadrant.
6. The decimal point separates dollars from cents.
7. If the exponent is two, the number is squared.
8. A prediction may or may not prove to be true.
9. A bar graph is easier to interpret than many lists.
10. The laws of probability explain what is likely.

Final Test

1. That candidate gave a highly quotable speech.
2. Is borrowing reference books permissible?
3. I heard sounds, but no intelligible speech.
4. Communicable diseases are easily spread.
5. Your goals seem realistic and attainable.
6. We have a fire extinguisher available at all times.
7. I shop frequently for consumable groceries.
8. That handwriting is barely legible!
9. The animal shelter had taken in a pitiable puppy.
10. My car has always provided reliable transportation.
11. Darla is certainly an amiable companion on a trip.
12. That color is not compatible with the red rug.
13. The hut wasn't fancy, but it was habitable.
14. Nothing notable happened all weekend.
15. Bring disposable utensils to the picnic.
16. Two people are responsible for today's victory.
17. Does Gregario donate time to charitable groups?
18. Luckily, you have an easily curable condition.
19. Your apartment has a nice livable feeling to it.
20. Did you bring along your portable radio?

Lesson 17

Objective

To spell difficult words with unusual spelling patterns

Pretest

1. Icebergs are common in Arctic climates.
2. The actor will endeavor to learn his lines.
3. Your cat may feel jealousy if you get a new kitten.
4. When the meteorite landed, it created a crater.
5. The police sergeant spoke about highway safety.
6. The newspaper prints a calendar of local events.
7. Is vitamin C an essential daily nutrient?
8. Barb is the best player in the soccer league.
9. I'd hate to be an elephant with a nasal infection!
10. *Angry* is a synonym for *furious*.
11. He watched the wobbly tower of blocks collapse.
12. Tell the postal worker that this package is fragile.
13. Let's maneuver our way to the front of the crowd.
14. Instead of taking sides, I think I'll remain neutral.
15. May I help you carry your valise onto the train?
16. The debtor was given one year to repay the loan.
17. The temperature gauge reads 82 degrees.
18. Tomorrow's matinee will begin at two o'clock.
19. Halley's Comet is a rarely seen phenomenon.
20. Please put mayonnaise on my sandwich.

Game Plan

Page 69

Discuss the Game Plan. Point out that students should memorize the spellings of "hurdle words" in order to prevent mistakes. Then have students analyze each List Word, identifying the "trick" in each one. Work with them to define the words. Have volunteers use them in oral sentences.

Warm Up

Vocabulary Development (Page 69) Before the exercise, have volunteers identify the List Words that match the synonym *measure (gauge)* and the definition *move according to a plan (maneuver).*

Dictionary Skills (Page 69) Before students begin work, use a dictionary to review guide words, pointing out examples and explaining their function.

Practice

Word Analysis (Page 70) Point out that this exercise will help students analyze the "tricks" in some of the hurdle words. Urge them to check the List Words on page 71 carefully to find the various letter components.

Classification (Page 70) To review classification skills, have students select a List Word to complete this series: *consumer, lender, ________. (debtor)*

Word Application (Page 70) Urge students to use context clues to find the List Word that best completes each sentence. They may enjoy creating similar sentences for other List Words to present as challenges to classmates.

Hurdle Words — LESSON 17

Game Plan

Some words are hard to spell because they have silent letters or unusual vowel spellings or double consonants. Other "hurdle words" contain the schwa sound /ə/ in unstressed syllables. Although it sounds like short **e**, it may be spelled with any of the five vowels.

Hurdle Word	"Trick"	Hurdle Word	"Trick"
debtor	silent **b**	**jealousy**	**ea** = /e/; **ou** = /ə/
matinee	**ee** = /ä/	**mayonnaise**	**o** = /ə/; double **n**
calendar	**ar** = /ər/	**synonym**	**y** = /i/; **o** = /ə/

1. arctic
2. endeavor
3. jealousy
4. meteorite
5. sergeant
6. calendar
7. essential
8. league
9. nasal
10. synonym
11. collapse
12. fragile
13. maneuver
14. neutral
15. valise
16. debtor
17. gauge
18. matinee
19. phenomenon
20. mayonnaise

Warm Up

Vocabulary Development

Write the List Word that matches each synonym or definition.

1. borrower debtor
2. envy jealousy
3. necessary essential
4. breakable fragile
5. suitcase valise
6. attempt endeavor
7. breakdown collapse
8. afternoon event matinee
9. not taking sides neutral
10. rare occurrence phenomenon
11. a spread mayonnaise
12. group of teams league
13. schedule calendar
14. of the nose nasal

Dictionary Skills

Write the List Word that comes between each pair of dictionary guide words.

1. senior/settle sergeant
2. matrimony/maze mayonnaise
3. game/get gauge
4. empathy/escrow endeavor
5. main/market maneuver
6. endive/estate essential
7. swim/system synonym
8. merge/metric meteorite
9. arbor/argue arctic

Hurdle Words — Lesson 17

Practice

Word Analysis

Write List Words to answer the following questions.

Which words contain the vowel combination **ea**?

1. endeavor
2. jealousy
3. sergeant
4. league

Which words contain the vowel combination **eu**?

5. maneuver
6. neutral

Which words contain these vowel combinations?

7. **ou** jealousy
8. **eo** meteorite
9. **au** gauge
10. **ee** matinee
11. **ai** mayonnaise
12. **ia** essential

Which words contain these double consonants?

13. **nn** mayonnaise
14. **ll** collapse
15. **ss** essential

Classification

Write a List Word to complete each series.

1. dainty, breakable, fragile
2. handbag, luggage, valise
3. polar, icy, arctic
4. visual, oral, nasal
5. clock, datebook, calendar
6. star, comet, meteorite
7. necessary, critical, essential
8. lieutenant, colonel, sergeant
9. oddity, surprise, phenomenon
10. antonym, homonym, synonym
11. player, team, league
12. mustard, catsup, mayonnaise

Word Application

Write a List Word to complete each sentence.

1. Check the calendar to find the day on which your birthday will occur this year.
2. We went to a matinee performance of the play last Saturday afternoon.
3. By remaining a neutral country, Switzerland does not take sides in a conflict.
4. The tent may collapse if the stakes are not hammered into the ground firmly.
5. A person who owes money is called a debtor.
6. A person with a cold might have a sore throat and nasal congestion.
7. A total eclipse of the sun is a strange and dramatic phenomenon to experience.

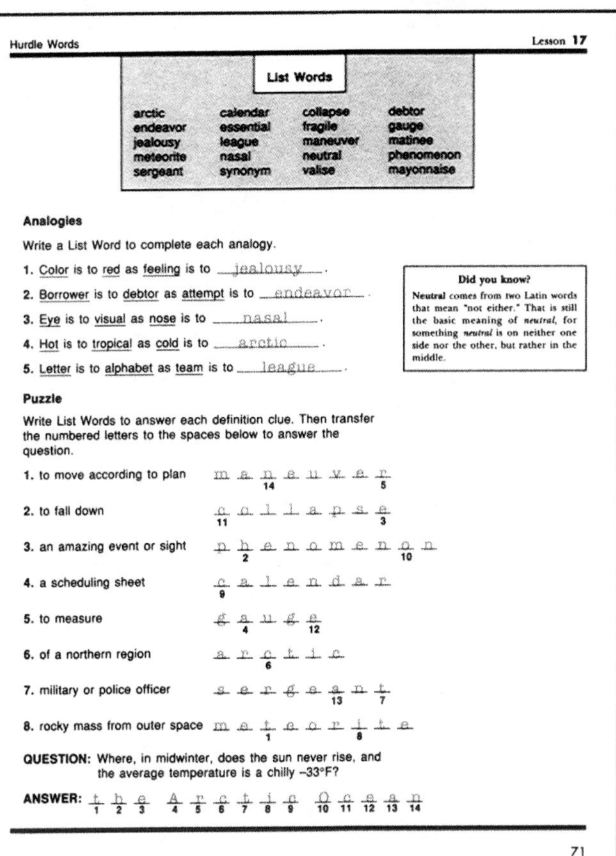

Hurdle Words — Lesson 17

List Words

arctic	calendar	collapse	debtor
endeavor	essential	fragile	gauge
jealousy	league	maneuver	matinee
meteorite	nasal	neutral	phenomenon
sergeant	synonym	valise	mayonnaise

Analogies

Write a List Word to complete each analogy.

1. Color is to red as feeling is to jealousy.
2. Borrower is to debtor as attempt is to endeavor.
3. Eye is to visual as nose is to nasal.
4. Hot is to tropical as cold is to arctic.
5. Letter is to alphabet as team is to league.

Did you know?

Neutral comes from two Latin words that mean "not either." That is still the basic meaning of *neutral*, for something *neutral* is on neither one side nor the other, but rather in the middle.

Puzzle

Write List Words to answer each definition clue. Then transfer the numbered letters to the spaces below to answer the question.

1. to move according to plan — m a n(14) e u v e r(5)
2. to fall down — c(11) o l l a p s e(3)
3. an amazing event or sight — p h(2) e n o m e n o(10) n
4. a scheduling sheet — c(9) a l e n d a r
5. to measure — g a(4) u g e(12)
6. of a northern region — a r c(6) t i c
7. military or police officer — s e r g e a(13) n t(7)
8. rocky mass from outer space — m e t(1) e o r i(8) t e

QUESTION: Where, in midwinter, does the sun never rise, and the average temperature is a chilly −33°F?

ANSWER: t h e A r c t i c O c e a n

71

Analogies (Page 71) Review analogies by writing on the board: *adjective, homonym, synonym.* Then read this incomplete analogy aloud and have students complete it: *Lender is to debtor as antonym is to________. (synonym)*

Puzzle (Page 71) Remind students to write their answers carefully, one letter to each space. They may enjoy reading and discussing additional facts concerning the bleakness of winter in the Arctic Circle.

Proofreading (Page 72) Write the question *Are your freinds comingon tuesday* and demonstrate the proofreading marks students will use to correct the letter.

Challenges

Express Yourself (Page 72) Discuss jobs that students might enjoy, including job descriptions and qualifications. Review the form of a business letter, and urge each student to write in a way that puts his or her "best foot forward." Remind students that they each have talents and personality factors that would be of interest to potential employers. Once they have finished writing, provide time for discussion.

Bonus Words: Job Applications (Page 72) Relate the Bonus Words to the writing project and to students' knowledge and experience. Discuss the features of a job application form and, if possible, display an example. Students may enjoy creating resumés to accompany their letters of inquiry.

Bonus Word Test

1. My career aspiration is to be a doctor.
2. We accept your letter of resignation with sorrow.
3. Carlos is extremely proficient in math.
4. List all your job experiences on your resumé.
5. You've got the qualifications to be an able cook.
6. Peg listed two of her teachers as references.
7. Relax and stay calm during your job interview.
8. I am determined to become a chemical engineer.
9. Hal's job gives him an opportunity to travel.
10. The sales manager read Jane's application form.

Hurdle Words — Lesson 17

Proofreading

Use the proofreading marks to correct the mistakes in the letter below. Then write the misspelled List Words on the lines.

Proofreading Marks
spelling mistake — add space — capital letter — ? add question mark

Dear Mom and Dad,

guess what I'm working as a camp counselor for the summer. It is definitely a challenging endeevor. I have been assigned ashead of one cabin and also as captain ofthe baseball leegue. The longer I'm here, the more I realize that it's essenchal I stay organized. When are you coming fora visit When youget here, you can watch me herd these campers around like a sargeant and wipe mayonaize stains offcamp shirts like a champ. Hope to see you soon.

Love,

1. endeavor
2. league
3. essential
4. sergeant
5. mayonnaise

Challenges

Express Yourself

If you could have any summer job this year, what would you choose? A camp counselor, a soccer coach, a pet sitter, a computer operator—the sky's the limit! Write a letter to a prospective employer. Tell about your job aspirations. Explain what skills and personality traits would make you a good candidate for the job. Be sure to proofread and revise your letter. Then, as a group, discuss what an employer's reaction might be to your letter.

Bonus Words: Job Applications

resumé	application	references	resignation	determined
opportunity	qualifications	interview	aspiration	proficient

Write the Bonus Word that matches each definition clue.

1. decided; resolved — determined
2. recommendations — references
3. summary of job experiences — resumé
4. form for requesting a job — application
5. face-to-face meeting — interview
6. act of quitting a job — resignation
7. chance; good fortune — opportunity
8. skilled; competent; adept — proficient
9. specific skills required — qualifications
10. hope; ambition; desire — aspiration

72

Final Test

1. Each month, the debtor pays back part of the loan.
2. The calendar featured beautiful photographs.
3. Push this button to collapse the umbrella.
4. Arctic temperatures are rarely above freezing.
5. Joy will maneuver the boat through the channel.
6. Our basketball league competes in tournaments.
7. Jealousy can be a harmful emotion.
8. A meteorite usually looks like metallic rock.
9. The peace talks were held at a neutral site.
10. A falling star is a phenomenon many enjoy seeing.
11. Sinusitis can cause a nasal infection.
12. Is there a matinee on Wednesday at two o'clock?
13. The sergeant carried the flag during the parade.
14. Is *enormous* a synonym for *large*?
15. You can check your valise at the ticket counter.
16. Mario stirred mayonnaise into the chicken salad.
17. The pilot used radar to help gauge her position.
18. For a writer, a good dictionary is an essential tool.
19. How did the police endeavor to solve the crime?
20. Careful! Those dishes are fragile.

Lesson 18

Objective
To review spelling patterns of words from Lessons 13–17

Game Plan
Page 73
This lesson will help students review the spelling patterns of words they studied in Lessons 13–17. Read and discuss the Game Plan with students, having them identify root words and endings, where appropriate. Then have students give other examples of hurdle words, telling what makes each hard to spell.

Practice
Lesson 13 (Page 73) Use the words *luscious, glorious, special, impartial* as examples of words in which *ial* and *ious* are suffixes or endings. Then have students identify the List Words that have suffixes. Point out the additional write-on lines and encourage students to add two words from Lesson 13 that they found especially difficult, or select and assign certain words that seem difficult for everyone. (Repeat this procedure for each lesson review in the Replay.)

Lesson 14 (Page 74) Use these words to review the endings *al, ally, ic, ically,* and *ly: emphatic, emphatically, mutual, mutually, simply.* Then have students identify the ending each List Word has. Before students begin the exercise, remind them to use the number of letters in each word as a clue.

Lesson 15 (Page 74) Write *manuscript, animated, fluency, missile* on the board. Use the words to review the Latin roots *miss, anim, flu,* and *man.* Before assigning the exercise, have students tell the meaning of each word. Then have them identify which root helps form each List Word.

Lesson 16 (Page 75) Review the endings *able* and *ible,* using these words as examples: *washable, admissible, edible, eligible.* Discuss the meaning of each word and ask which ending is more common. (*able*) Then ask which two letters often come before the ending *ible.* (s *or soft* g) Before students complete the activity, have them note which letter precedes each ending in the List Words.

Lesson 17 (Page 75) Write the words *endeavor, jealousy, nasal, collapse,* and *debtor* on the board. Use them to discuss ways in which hurdle words may be hard to spell. Have students suggest other words that are not spelled the way they sound, and then discuss different ways to remember the spelling of such words.

Mixed Practice (Page 76) Remind students that the words given may have had new prefixes and suffixes added. If necessary, work the first item with students. To extend, elicit from students additional words containing the same roots as the words given.

Test Yourself (Page 76) Remind students that this test will help them know if they have mastered the words in Lessons 13-17. Have a volunteer restate the directions and tell which word in the first item should be marked. (*nutral*)

INSTANT REPLAY — LESSON **18**

Game Plan

Learning how to spell word endings can help you spell many words correctly. Some endings are suffixes, such as the **ial** and **ious** at the end of burial and gracious. Other words have endings that look like suffixes, but aren't, such as material and ferocious.

Many endings change words to form other parts of speech. Notice the endings on these words and how each changes the root or root word:

substantial – substantially
classic – classical, classically

The endings **able** and **ible** both turn root words into adjectives. They sound alike, but remember that **able** is the more common ending, as in notable. When the ending is **ible**, it often follows **s** or soft **g**, as in intelligible and permissible.

A knowledge of Latin roots can help you spell and understand many words. Read each word below and notice the meaning of its Latin root, which has been underlined.

Word with Latin Root	Meaning of Root
annual	year
emission	to send
animation	breath or soul
fluidity	flow
manage	hand

A few words are tricky to spell because they have some unusual features, such as a silent letter, an odd vowel spelling, a double consonant, or the schwa sound spelled with an **a, i, o,** or **u**. Read each word below and notice what makes it hard to spell.

mayonnaise arctic matinee debtor

Study carefully the spelling of such words.

Practice
Replace the underlined word in each sentence with a List Word. Write the List Word on the line.

1. Carla consulted a money expert to help her make investment decisions. financial
2. What a pleasing sound those voices make! harmonious
3. This house has very roomy closets. spacious
4. Duane is a reliable student. conscientious
5. My cold is no longer catching. infectious
6. The family was unaware of the noise. unconscious
7. Please capitalize the first letter. initial
8. The doctor assured me that the information would be kept private. confidential
9. The most powerful advisors had the candidate's full attention. influential
10. Most of the countrified regions had narrow roads. provincial

Lesson **13**

conscientious	spacious
confidential	infectious
harmonious	initial
influential	financial
unconscious	provincial

73

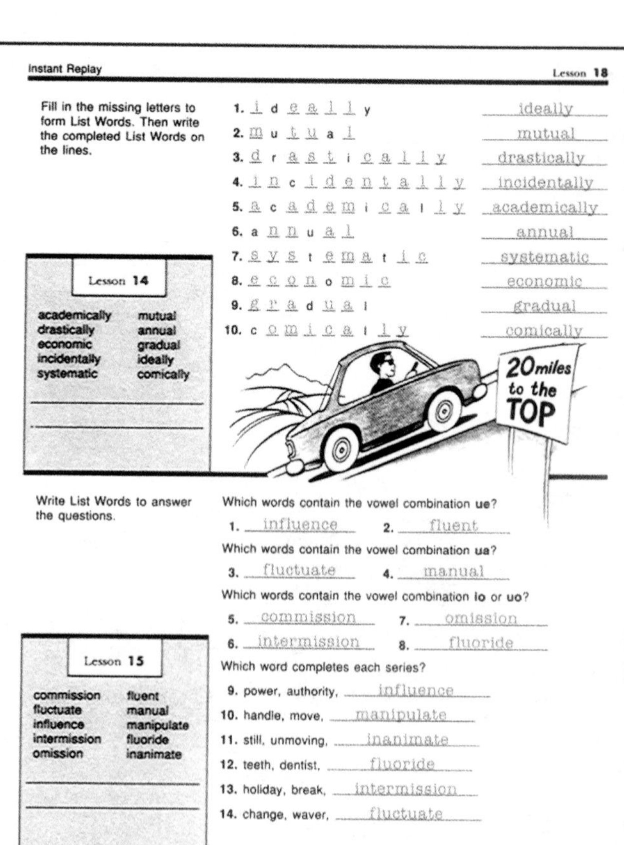
Instant Replay — Lesson **18**

Fill in the missing letters to form List Words. Then write the completed List Words on the lines.

1. i d e a l l y — ideally
2. m u t u a l — mutual
3. d r a s t i c a l l y — drastically
4. i n c i d e n t a l l y — incidentally
5. a c a d e m i c a l l y — academically
6. a n n u a l — annual
7. s y s t e m a t i c — systematic
8. e c o n o m i c — economic
9. g r a d u a l — gradual
10. c o m i c a l l y — comically

Lesson **14**

academically	mutual
drastically	annual
economic	gradual
incidentally	ideally
systematic	comically

Write List Words to answer the questions.

Which words contain the vowel combination **ue**?
1. influence 2. fluent

Which words contain the vowel combination **ua**?
3. fluctuate 4. manual

Which words contain the vowel combination **io** or **uo**?
5. commission 7. omission
6. intermission 8. fluoride

Which word completes each series?
9. power, authority, influence
10. handle, move, manipulate
11. still, unmoving, inanimate
12. teeth, dentist, fluoride
13. holiday, break, intermission
14. change, waver, fluctuate

Lesson **15**

commission	fluent
fluctuate	manual
influence	manipulate
intermission	fluoride
omission	inanimate

74

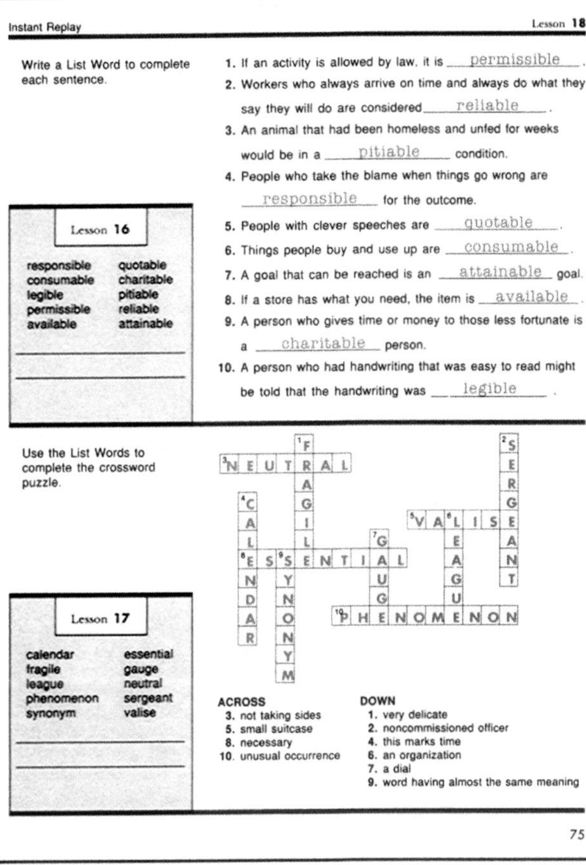

Instant Replay — Lesson 18

Write a List Word to complete each sentence.

1. If an activity is allowed by law, it is permissible.
2. Workers who always arrive on time and always do what they say they will do are considered reliable.
3. An animal that had been homeless and unfed for weeks would be in a pitiable condition.
4. People who take the blame when things go wrong are responsible for the outcome.
5. People with clever speeches are quotable.
6. Things people buy and use up are consumable.
7. A goal that can be reached is an attainable goal.
8. If a store has what you need, the item is available.
9. A person who gives time or money to those less fortunate is a charitable person.
10. A person who had handwriting that was easy to read might be told that the handwriting was legible.

Lesson 16

responsible, consumable, legible, permissible, available, quotable, charitable, pitiable, reliable, attainable

Use the List Words to complete the crossword puzzle.

1 FRAGILE, 2 SERGEANT, 3 NEUTRAL, 4 CALENDAR, 5 VALISE, 6 LEAGUE, 7 GAUGE, 8 ESSENTIAL, 9 SYNONYM, 10 PHENOMENON

Lesson 17

calendar, fragile, league, phenomenon, synonym, essential, gauge, neutral, sergeant, valise

ACROSS
3. not taking sides
5. small suitcase
8. necessary
10. unusual occurrence

DOWN
1. very delicate
2. noncommissioned officer
4. this marks time
6. an organization
7. a dial
9. word having almost the same meaning

75

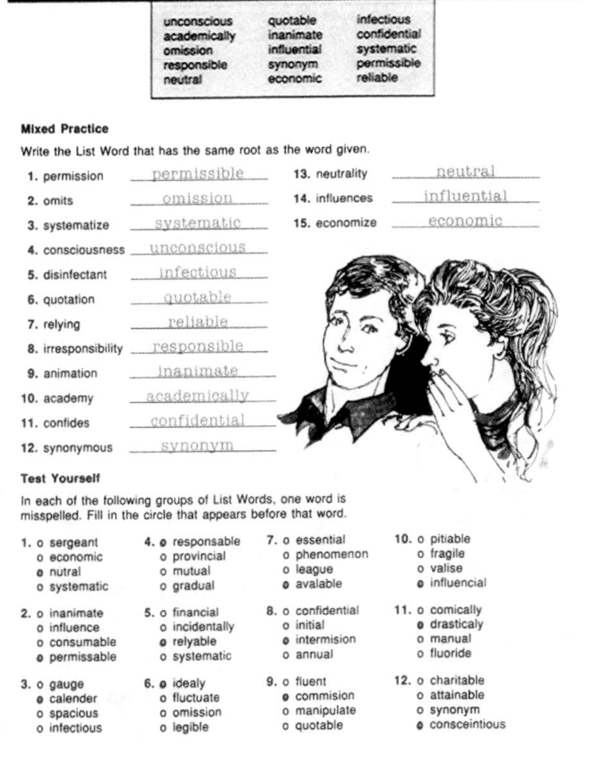

Instant Replay — Lesson 18

unconscious, academically, omission, responsible, neutral, quotable, inanimate, influential, synonym, economic, infectious, confidential, systematic, permissible, reliable

Mixed Practice

Write the List Word that has the same root as the word given.

1. permission — permissible
2. omits — omission
3. systematize — systematic
4. consciousness — unconscious
5. disinfectant — infectious
6. quotation — quotable
7. relying — reliable
8. irresponsibility — responsible
9. animation — inanimate
10. academy — academically
11. confides — confidential
12. synonymous — synonym
13. neutrality — neutral
14. influences — influential
15. economize — economic

Test Yourself

In each of the following groups of List Words, one word is misspelled. Fill in the circle that appears before that word.

1. o sergeant / o economic / ● nutral / o systematic
2. o inanimate / o influence / o consumable / ● permissable
3. o gauge / ● calender / o spacious / o infectious
4. ● responsable / o provincial / o mutual / o gradual
5. o financial / o incidentally / ● relyable / o systematic
6. ● idealy / o fluctuate / o omission / o legible
7. o essential / o phenomenon / o league / ● avalable
8. o confidential / o initial / ● intermision / o annual
9. o fluent / ● commision / o manipulate / o quotable
10. o pitiable / o fragile / o valise / ● influencial
11. o comically / ● drasticaly / o manual / o fluoride
12. o charitable / o attainable / o synonym / ● consceintious

76

Final Replay Test

1. Incidentally, we both attended the same lecture.
2. Tien's family came from a provincial village.
3. At our initial meeting, we exchanged information.
4. That information is highly confidential!
5. The signature on this contract is barely legible.
6. After my fluoride treatment, I can't eat for an hour.
7. Our state budget has been cut drastically this year.
8. Is your rash very infectious?
9. What a beautiful spacious apartment!
10. Make a systematic list of every drawer's contents.
11. My sister is fluent in three languages.
12. I have a manual typewriter, not an electric one.
13. You may have to manipulate the pieces into place.
14. We tried to solve our economic problems.
15. This artist paints inanimate objects, like rocks.
16. Will Kate be responsible for setting up the chairs?
17. Fruit is a consumable product.
18. Is this class for academically talented students?
19. I paid the agent a commission to sell my house.
20. A consultant will be available to help you decide.
21. Be careful with that fragile statue!
22. A mediator tries to stay neutral during arguments.
23. My brother has now achieved the rank of sergeant.
24. I think *habit* is a synonym for *custom*.
25. The moon has a direct influence on high tide.
26. Eric has always been a conscientious worker.
27. The bank questioned my financial history.
28. Those three colors make a harmonious pattern.
29. The president's secretary is very influential.
30. The boy was knocked unconscious by the ball.
31. A treaty is a mutual agreement between countries.
32. Mark the date of the party on your calendar.
33. Learning is a gradual process that never ends.
34. Is camping permissible in this park?
35. In one skit, the character was comically dressed.
36. Let me carry your valise to the train.
37. The prices of stocks and bonds fluctuate daily.
38. Lee told one particularly quotable story.
39. During intermission, we all bought popcorn.
40. The omission of your name can be corrected easily.
41. Mom's company has an annual picnic each July.
42. Several charitable groups asked for donations.
43. Many homeless people live in a pitiable state.
44. This clock is not reliable, so don't depend on it.
45. If I have help, this goal will be attainable.
46. Ideally, everyone will arrive at the same time.
47. The surtcase is full, so bring only essential clothes.
48. Keep the needle out of the red area on the gauge.
49. Scientists studied the phenomenon thoroughly.
50. Our baseball league is comprised of seven teams.

Lesson 19

Objective

To spell words from geography

Pretest

1. Danielle owns one acre of land near Lake Boone.
2. Southerners speak with a regional dialect.
3. A healthy plant should have thick, green foliage.
4. A narrow isthmus links the two larger islands.
5. We had a dry June, with no precipitation.
6. I took aerial photographs from a helicopter.
7. That massive oil spill was an ecological disaster!
8. The teacher drew horizontal lines across the map.
9. Are meridian lines used to measure longitude?
10. We must protect our nation's natural resources.
11. The earth rotates on an imaginary axis.
12. Columbus led an expedition to new lands.
13. The hurricane brought high winds and heavy rains.
14. We tasted a variety of ethnic foods at the festival.
15. Is the reservoir low because of the drought?
16. She paddled through the marshy bayou waters.
17. Mr. Lee planted vegetables in the rich, fertile soil.
18. The farmer learned new ways to irrigate crops.
19. The hikers set up camp on a wide plateau.
20. Here is a map of New York City and the vicinity.

Game Plan

Page 77

Discuss the Game Plan. Encourage students to name other words that they know come from geography. Then have volunteers say the List Words and define them. For unfamiliar words, have students consult a dictionary or geography book to learn the definitions. Point out that words from geography and other content areas are often more difficult to spell because they are not used regularly. Emphasize that they must study and practice these words.

Warm Up

Vocabulary Development (Page 77) Stress that students should think carefully about the meaning of each word as they complete the exercise. Then encourage students to use the words in oral sentences.

Dictionary Skills (Page 77) In this activity, students will focus on each syllable of the List Words as they appear in the pronunciation guide in the dictionary. You may wish to discuss the diacritical marks and the sounds they stand for in words such as *horizontal* and *hurricane.*

Practice

Word Analysis (Page 78) Remind students that many words are based on a common root. As an example, write on the board: *observe, reserve, preserve.* When students have completed the written work, you may wish to have them look up the definitions of the given words to learn how they differ in meaning from the List Words.

Words from Geography

LESSON 19

Game Plan

Every subject you study in school has its own specific vocabulary. Words such as isthmus, meridian, and axis are words you often encounter when you study geography.

All the List Words are from geography. Memorize and practice spelling these words.

1. *acre*
2. *dialect*
3. *foliage*
4. *isthmus*
5. *precipitation*
6. *aerial*
7. *ecological*
8. *horizontal*
9. *meridian*
10. *resources*
11. *axis*
12. *expedition*
13. *hurricane*
14. *ethnic*
15. *reservoir*
16. *bayou*
17. *fertile*
18. *irrigate*
19. *plateau*
20. *vicinity*

Warm Up

Vocabulary Development

Write the List Word that matches each definition.

1. relating to a group with a common cultural heritage ethnic
2. a narrow strip of land with water on either side isthmus
3. a place where water is stored reservoir
4. a broad stretch of high level land plateau
5. a form of a language used by a certain group dialect
6. producing much fruit or crops fertile
7. a measure of land acre
8. a long journey or voyage expedition
9. a marshy body of water bayou
10. to water by means of canals or ditches irrigate
11. opposite of vertical horizontal
12. snow, hail, sleet, rain precipitation

Dictionary Skills

Write the List Word that matches each sound spelling.

1. (və sin′ ə tē) vicinity
2. (fō′ lē ij) foliage
3. (ak′ sis) axis
4. (mə rid′ ē ən) meridian
5. (ek′ ə läj′ i k'l) ecological
6. (hur′ ə kān′) hurricane
7. (er′ ē əl) aerial
8. (rē′ sôrs ez) resources

77

Words from Geography

Lesson 19

Practice

Did you know?

Acre meant "field" in Old English. It is related to *ager,* the Latin word for field, and to the word *agriculture.*

Word Analysis

Write the List Word that contains the same root word as the word given.

1. precipitate precipitation
2. reservation reservoir
3. defoliate foliage
4. irrigation irrigate
5. horizon horizontal
6. aerialist aerial
7. resourceful resources
8. expedite expedition
9. ecology ecological
10. dialogue dialect

Analogies

Write a List Word to complete each analogy.

1. Desert is to sand as forest is to foliage.
2. Canal is to water as isthmus is to land.
3. Grain is to silo as rainfall is to reservoir.
4. Wet is to dry as precipitation is to drought.
5. Gallon is to liquid as acre is to land.
6. Terrestrial is to land as aerial is to sky.
7. Breeze is to hurricane as snow flurry is to blizzard.
8. Swamp is to bayou as tornado is to twister.
9. Fertilize is to plant food as irrigate is to water.
10. Explorer is to expedition as sailor is to voyage.

Classification

Write a List Word to complete each series.

1. neighborhood, environment, vicinity
2. vertical, diagonal, horizontal
3. language, accent, dialect
4. tornado, cyclone, hurricane
5. rainfall, snowfall, precipitation
6. productive, fruitful, fertile
7. rotation, earth, axis
8. longitude, latitude, meridian

78

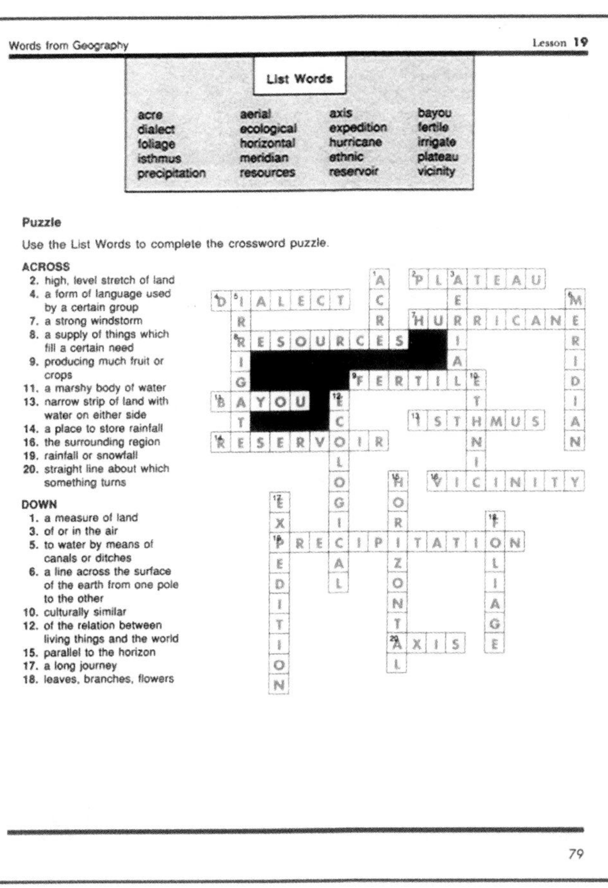
Words from Geography — Lesson 19

List Words

acre	aerial	axis	bayou
dialect	ecological	expedition	fertile
foliage	horizontal	hurricane	irrigate
isthmus	meridian	ethnic	plateau
precipitation	resources	reservoir	vicinity

Puzzle

Use the List Words to complete the crossword puzzle.

ACROSS
2. high, level stretch of land
4. a form of language used by a certain group
7. a strong windstorm
8. a supply of things which fill a certain need
9. producing much fruit or crops
11. a marshy body of water
13. narrow strip of land with water on either side
14. a place to store rainfall
16. the surrounding region
19. rainfall or snowfall
20. straight line about which something turns

DOWN
1. a measure of land
3. of or in the air
5. to water by means of canals or ditches
6. a line across the surface of the earth from one pole to the other
10. culturally similar
12. of the relation between living things and the world
15. parallel to the horizon
17. a long journey
18. leaves, branches, flowers

79

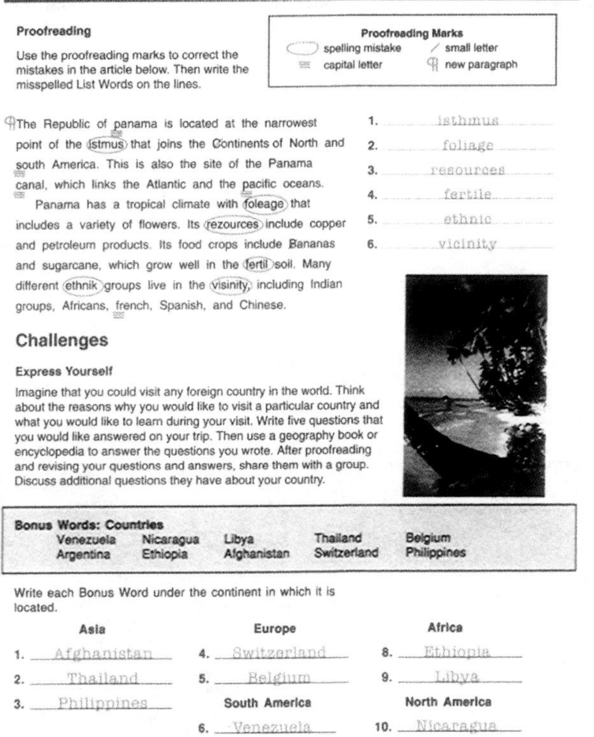
Words from Geography — Lesson 19

Proofreading

Use the proofreading marks to correct the mistakes in the article below. Then write the misspelled List Words on the lines.

Proofreading Marks: spelling mistake; capital letter; / small letter; ¶ new paragraph

¶The Republic of panama is located at the narrowest point of the istmus that joins the Continents of North and south America. This is also the site of the Panama canal, which links the Atlantic and the pacific oceans. Panama has a tropical climate with foleage that includes a variety of flowers. Its rezources include copper and petroleum products. Its food crops include Bananas and sugarcane, which grow well in the fertil soil. Many different ethnik groups live in the visinity, including Indian groups, Africans, french, Spanish, and Chinese.

1. isthmus
2. foliage
3. resources
4. fertile
5. ethnic
6. vicinity

Challenges

Express Yourself

Imagine that you could visit any foreign country in the world. Think about the reasons why you would like to visit a particular country and what you would like to learn during your visit. Write five questions that you would like answered on your trip. Then use a geography book or encyclopedia to answer the questions you wrote. After proofreading and revising your questions and answers, share them with a group. Discuss additional questions they have about your country.

Bonus Words: Countries
Venezuela, Nicaragua, Libya, Thailand, Belgium, Argentina, Ethiopia, Afghanistan, Switzerland, Philippines

Write each Bonus Word under the continent in which it is located.

Asia: 1. Afghanistan 2. Thailand 3. Philippines
Europe: 4. Switzerland 5. Belgium
South America: 6. Venezuela 7. Argentina
Africa: 8. Ethiopia 9. Libya
North America: 10. Nicaragua

80

Analogies (Page 78) Elicit from students that an analogy compares two pairs of things to show the relationship between two things. Help students complete the first item.

Classification (Page 78) To review classification, ask students to name another word that belongs with the following items and explain why the word belongs: mountains, valleys, __________. *(Answers may include rivers, hills, streams, and other landscape words.)*

Puzzle (Page 79) Tell students to use capital letters and to print neatly as they complete the puzzle.

Proofreading (Page 80) Review with students the proofreading marks in this lesson. Point out that students will use these marks to correct the article.

Challenges

Express Yourself (Page 80) Have students name a country they would like to visit and tell one thing they know about that country. Provide time for students to read their work aloud.

Bonus Words: Countries (Page 80) Help students locate each country on a map. Be sure students notice on which continent each country is located. You may wish to have pairs of students consult an encyclopedia to find some significant facts about each country to report back to the class.

Bonus Word Test

1. Agriculture is the main industry of Nicaragua.
2. The capital of Venezuela is Caracas.
3. Many people of Ethiopia speak English or Arabic.
4. Patagonia is a dry plateau in southern Argentina.
5. Thailand was once known as Siam.
6. There are over twenty ethnic tribes in Afghanistan.
7. Switzerland was neutral during World War II.
8. Libya was once a part of the Roman Empire.
9. Belgium is a densely populated country in Europe.
10. More than 7,000 islands comprise the Philippines.

Final Test

1. The sheep grazed on the low mountain plateau.
2. The hurricane ripped trees out of the ground.
3. Some people in Quebec have a French dialect.
4. Is there an airport in the vicinity of the city?
5. The farmer planted corn on one acre of land.
6. Swimming is forbidden in the reservoir!
7. The gyroscope spun around on a steel axis.
8. Coal is one of our natural resources.
9. Scientists did ecological research on the island.
10. This maps gives an aerial view of Cape Cod.
11. Are snow and rain forms of precipitation?
12. A path was cut through the thick jungle foliage.
13. The prime meridian passes through England.
14. Horizontal and vertical lines mark the chart.
15. The Isthmus of Panama connects two continents.
16. Dad installed a pipeline to irrigate his crops.
17. Mae Jemison was a member of a space expedition.
18. Is the water in a bayou stagnant?
19. Fertile soil contains nutrients that help plants grow.
20. The festival musicians performed ethnic songs.

Lesson 20

Objective

To spell words from science

Pretest

1. The chemist will analyze the compound.
2. I used a compass to find my way back to camp.
3. The diagram shows how to assemble the bicycle.
4. The frequency of rainfall is often unpredictable.
5. Every living creature has its own specific features.
6. We learn about past cultures through archaeology.
7. The shadow softened the contour of her face.
8. Health officials predict a flu epidemic this winter.
9. At what temperature will wax liquefy?
10. Dr. Won listened to my heart with a stethoscope.
11. Medical instruments are sterilized to kill bacteria.
12. It is crucial that they reach the hospital soon.
13. Will this class study the evolution of a frog?
14. My sociology report was on the homeless situation.
15. Toxic gases are harmful to people and animals.
16. Do botanists study the characteristics of plants?
17. The four seasons of the year complete a cycle.
18. The doctor showed us a facsimile of a heart.
19. The landscape artist used good spatial proportions.
20. That explosion caused a huge earth tremor!

Game Plan

Page 81

Discuss the Game Plan. Encourage students to name and define other words that they know that come specifically from science. Then have volunteers define the List Words. Have students consult a dictionary or science book for any words that are unfamiliar. Point out to students that because scientific words are often difficult to pronounce and spell, it is important to study and practice these words.

Warm Up

Vocabulary Development (Page 81) Have a volunteer explain the directions. To be sure students understand what they are to do, do the first item with them.

Dictionary Skills (Page 81) Remind students that knowing how to divide a multisyllabic word into individual syllables will help them learn how to spell that word.

Practice

Proofreading (Page 82) Review the proofreading marks in the box, focusing on the paragraph indent mark. Remind students that this mark is used to show where a new paragraph begins and should be indented. Have volunteers practice making the mark on the board. Point out to students that not all the List Words that appear in the article are misspelled.

Words from Science — LESSON 20

Game Plan

When studying science, you may encounter some unfamiliar words. Words such as archaeology, stethoscope, and characteristics may seem complicated and difficult to spell. With practice, you can master these challenging words.

All the List Words are from science. Memorize and practice spelling these words.

1. analyze
2. compass
3. diagram
4. frequency
5. specific
6. archaeology
7. contour
8. epidemic
9. liquefy
10. stethoscope
11. bacteria
12. crucial
13. evolution
14. sociology
15. toxic
16. characteristics
17. cycle
18. facsimile
19. spatial
20. tremor

Warm Up

Vocabulary Development

Write the List Word from column B that matches the synonym in column A.

A		B
1. copy	facsimile	toxic
2. traits	characteristics	tremor
3. exact	specific	liquefy
4. examine	analyze	diagram
5. chart	diagram	facsimile
6. outline	contour	specific
7. melt	liquefy	crucial
8. earthquake	tremor	analyze
9. poisonous	toxic	characteristics
10. critical	crucial	contour

Dictionary Skills

Write the List Word that matches each sound-spelling.

1. (steth´ ə skōp)	stethoscope	6. (spā´ shəl)	spatial
2. (sō sē äl´ ə jē)	sociology	7. (kum´ pəs)	compass
3. (sī´ k l)	cycle	8. (bak tir´ ē ə)	bacteria
4. (är kē äl´ ə jē)	archaeology	9. (ep ə dem´ ik)	epidemic
5. (ev ə lōō´ shən)	evolution	10. (frē´ kwən sē)	frequency

81

Words from Science — Lesson 20

Practice

Word Analysis

Write List Words to answer the following questions.

Which words contain the **ia** vowel combination?

1. diagram 3. crucial
2. bacteria 4. spatial

Which word contains the **ae** vowel combination?

5. archaeology

Which words contain the letter combination **que**?

6. frequency 7. liquefy

Did you know?

Toxic comes from a Greek word for a poison in which arrows were dipped before they were used. In turn, the word for this poison comes from the Greek word *toxon*, for the bow from which an arrow is shot.

Proofreading

Use the proofreading marks to correct the mistakes in the paragraphs. Then write the misspelled List Words correctly on the lines.

The study of archaelogy explores and examines the characterestics of ancient times and peoples. By unearthing ruinsand gravesites, scientists gather artifacts that can reveal crushal information about the evalution of mankind, and the ever-changing cycle of life.
Advances in technology have enabled scientists to analize human remains from centuries past, and and identify specific bactiria or toxic waste that once could have polluted the environment They can also study the frequincy of natural disasters such as as earthquakes and tremors Through their findings, we may well determine how to predict an earthquake, or to prevent the spread of of an epademic.

1. archaeology 5. analyze
2. characteristics 6. bacteria
3. crucial 7. frequency
4. evolution 8. epidemic

Proofreading Marks

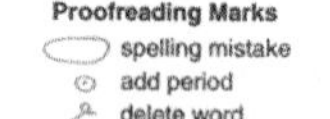

spelling mistake
add period
delete word
add space
new paragraph

82

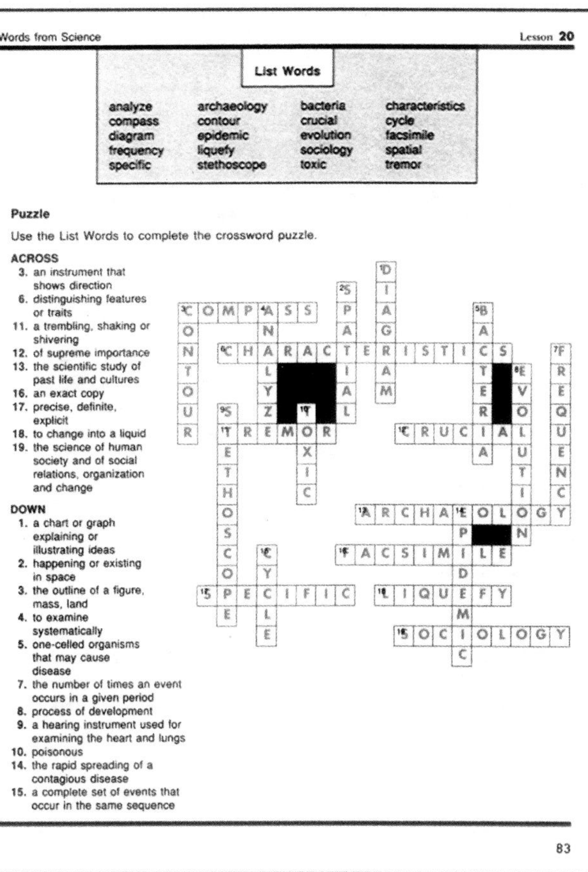
Words from Science — Lesson 20

List Words

analyze	archaeology	bacteria	characteristics
compass	contour	crucial	cycle
diagram	epidemic	evolution	facsimile
frequency	liquefy	sociology	spatial
specific	stethoscope	toxic	tremor

Puzzle

Use the List Words to complete the crossword puzzle.

ACROSS
3. an instrument that shows direction
6. distinguishing features or traits
11. a trembling, shaking or shivering
12. of supreme importance
13. the scientific study of past life and cultures
16. an exact copy
17. precise, definite, explicit
18. to change into a liquid
19. the science of human society and of social relations, organization and change

DOWN
1. a chart or graph explaining or illustrating ideas
2. happening or existing in space
3. the outline of a figure, mass, land
4. to examine systematically
5. one-celled organisms that may cause disease
7. the number of times an event occurs in a given period
8. process of development
9. a hearing instrument used for examining the heart and lungs
10. poisonous
14. the rapid spreading of a contagious disease
15. a complete set of events that occur in the same sequence

83

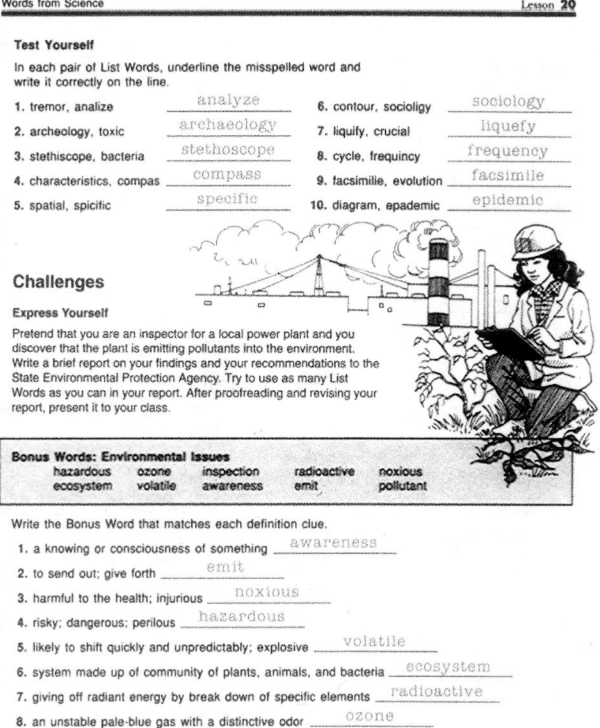
Words from Science — Lesson 20

Test Yourself

In each pair of List Words, underline the misspelled word and write it correctly on the line.

1. tremor, analize — analyze
2. archeology, toxic — archaeology
3. stethiscope, bacteria — stethoscope
4. characteristics, compas — compass
5. spatial, spicific — specific
6. contour, socioligy — sociology
7. liquify, crucial — liquefy
8. cycle, frequincy — frequency
9. facsimilie, evolution — facsimile
10. diagram, epademic — epidemic

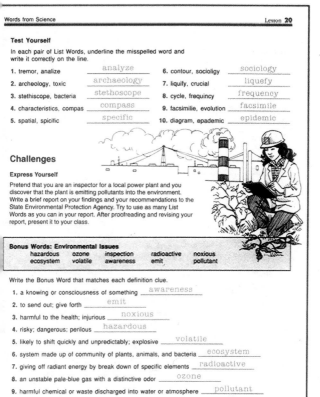

Challenges

Express Yourself

Pretend that you are an inspector for a local power plant and you discover that the plant is emitting pollutants into the environment. Write a brief report on your findings and your recommendations to the State Environmental Protection Agency. Try to use as many List Words as you can in your report. After proofreading and revising your report, present it to your class.

Bonus Words: Environmental Issues

hazardous	ozone	inspection	radioactive	noxious
ecosystem	volatile	awareness	emit	pollutant

Write the Bonus Word that matches each definition clue.

1. a knowing or consciousness of something — awareness
2. to send out; give forth — emit
3. harmful to the health; injurious — noxious
4. risky; dangerous; perilous — hazardous
5. likely to shift quickly and unpredictably; explosive — volatile
6. system made up of community of plants, animals, and bacteria — ecosystem
7. giving off radiant energy by break down of specific elements — radioactive
8. an unstable pale-blue gas with a distinctive odor — ozone
9. harmful chemical or waste discharged into water or atmosphere — pollutant
10. an official examination — inspection

84

Puzzle (Page 83) Students will be familiar with the process for completing a crossword puzzle. Encourage them to print neatly and clearly as they write the letters in the boxes.

Test Yourself (Page 84) Have students work independently to complete the activity. When they have finished, encourage them to check their spelling with the List Words on page 84.

Challenges

Express Yourself (Page 84) To prepare students to write, encourage them to tell what they know about current environmental issues. Lead students to focus on the kinds of environmental problems caused by factories and chemical and industrial plants. Encourage students to think of possible ways of correcting these pollution problems.

Bonus Words: Environmental Issues (Page 84) Have students look up the meanings of each Bonus Word in the dictionary. Discuss how these words apply to the environment and pollution. For example, although *hazardous* means *risky or dangerous,* it is often used in the phrase *hazardous waste.* You may also wish to invite an environmental specialist to visit the class and discuss local ecological issues.

Bonus Word Test

1. Radon is a radioactive gas found in the earth.
2. Careless dumping of hazardous waste causes pollution.
3. There is a delicate balance of life in the ecosystem.
4. A pollutant is a harmful waste.
5. Noxious gases can cause health problems.
6. After the rain, we could smell the ozone.
7. The chemical plant will emit pollutants into the air.
8. Nitroglycerine is volatile and will explode easily.
9. There is a great awareness of ecological issues.
10. After the inspection, the factory was shut down.

Final Test

1. Did you feel that earth tremor shake the house?
2. She had to make a crucial decision under stress.
3. The block of ice will liquefy into a puddle of water.
4. The chemical explosion produced toxic fumes.
5. Spring begins a new cycle of life in the garden.
6. A compass shows which direction you're traveling.
7. This diagram shows the human skeletal system.
8. What is the frequency of earthquakes in California?
9. The map showed the contour of the coastline.
10. Each experiment will produce specific results.
11. The archaeology professor visited the ancient ruins.
12. Every person has different physical characteristics.
13. The lawyer sent us a facsimile of the document.
14. Some bacteria are used to make medicines.
15. He has poor spatial vision.
16. A psychiatrist will analyze a person's behavior.
17. We discussed family life in sociology class.
18. Does evolution explain the development of life?
19. The doctor used a stethoscope to hear my heart.
20. That flu epidemic spread rapidly at school!

Lesson 21

Objective

To spell words from math

Pretest

1. Tell me the absolute truth!
2. Use this equation for calculating the area of a circle.
3. Don't waste! Use a minimum amount of paint.
4. A mistake will skew all the results.
5. I will show you how to prove this theorem.
6. Do these two triangles have congruent sides?
7. Draw an equilateral triangle and label the sides.
8. The angle will either be obtuse or acute.
9. Is a ball one kind of sphere?
10. A trapezoid always has four sides.
11. The denominator is the bottom number of a fraction.
12. The diagram shows the inequality of the two sides.
13. Use your protractor to draw an arc.
14. A symmetrical design is balanced and proportioned.
15. The answers will be variable.
16. Draw a diagonal line from one corner to the other.
17. Does an isosceles triangle have two equal sides?
18. All angles, except right angles, are oblique.
19. Draw the circle and the tangent described.
20. This vertical line is perpendicular to the base.

Game Plan

Page 85
After students have read the Game Plan, have them discuss the meanings of the List Words that they know. For unfamiliar words, have students consult a dictionary or math book. Show them how to find the mathematical meaning of words with multiple meanings by looking for the field labels *math*, *algebra*, or *geometry*. Then discuss how they can best learn to spell the words.

Warm Up

Vocabulary Development (Page 85) Have students write the List Words which can easily be matched to the given definitions first. For items with which they encounter difficulties urge students to consult dictionaries.

Dictionary Skills (Page 85) Review the letters and symbols used in respellings. Point out the importance of appropriately placing the accent.

Practice

Word Analysis (Page 86) Remind students that analyzing words makes it easier to remember how to spell them. Remind students that the number of syllables in a word can be determined by the number of vowel sounds heard.

Proofreading (Page 86) Ask a volunteer to paraphrase the directions. Remind students that every phrase may not contain an error.

Words from Math — LESSON 21

Game Plan

The world of mathematics has its own language. Some of its words, such as isosceles, are not used except in mathematics. Other words, such as obtuse, have meanings within mathematics and outside of it. All the List Words are used in math. Many follow spelling rules you have already learned. Others will have to be memorized.

1. absolute
2. equation
3. minimum
4. skew
5. theorem
6. congruent
7. equilateral
8. obtuse
9. sphere
10. trapezoid
11. denominator
12. inequality
13. protractor
14. symmetrical
15. variable
16. diagonal
17. isosceles
18. oblique
19. tangent
20. vertical

Warm Up

Vocabulary Development

Write the List Word that matches each definition.

1. anything that changes or varies ____variable____
2. slanting from one corner to the other ____diagonal____
3. corresponding; in agreement or harmony ____congruent____
4. having an angle greater than 90° ____obtuse____
5. a law or principle ____theorem____
6. having symmetry or balance ____symmetrical____
7. a line touching a curved plane ____tangent____
8. a round object ____sphere____
9. four-sided figure with two parallel sides ____trapezoid____
10. triangle with two equal sides ____isosceles____
11. triangle with all sides equal ____equilateral____
12. instrument for measuring angles ____protractor____

Dictionary Skills

Write the List Word that matches each sound-spelling.

1. (skyo͞o) ____skew____
2. (vur´ ti k'l) ____vertical____
3. (ī säs´ ə lēz) ____isosceles____
4. (ə blēk´) ____oblique____
5. (ab´ sə lo͞ot) ____absolute____
6. (prō trak´ tər) ____protractor____
7. (min´ ə məm) ____minimum____
8. (di näm´ ə nāt´ ər) ____denominator____
9. (i kwā´ zhən) ____equation____
10. (in´ i kwäl´ ə tē) ____inequality____

85

Words from Math — Lesson 21

Practice

Word Analysis

Write List Words to answer the following questions.

Which List Words contain **equa** or **equi**?

1. ____equation____
2. ____equilateral____
3. ____inequality____

Which List Words end with the adjectival ending **al**?

4. ____equilateral____
5. ____symmetrical____
6. ____diagonal____
7. ____vertical____

Which List Words contain five syllables?

8. ____equilateral____
9. ____denominator____
10. ____inequality____

Did you know?

When you have been absolved, you have been set free from something. If you have been set free from all ties, you are acting wholly on your own and are absolutely free. You have **absolute** power over yourself. The word *absolutely* comes from the Latin prefix *ab*, meaning "from," and *solvere*, meaning "to set free."

Proofreading

Proofread the following phrases. Circle any misspelled List Words and write the words correctly on the lines. If there are no errors, place a check mark on the line.

1. verticle angles ____vertical____
2. symmetrical triangles ____✓____
3. a similar theorim ____theorem____
4. regular trapizoid ____trapezoid____
5. diagonel lines ____diagonal____
6. equalateral triangles ____equilateral____
7. complex equasion ____equation____
8. perfect sphere ____✓____
9. compass and protracter ____protractor____
10. congruant numbers ____congruent____
11. lowest common denominater ____denominator____

86

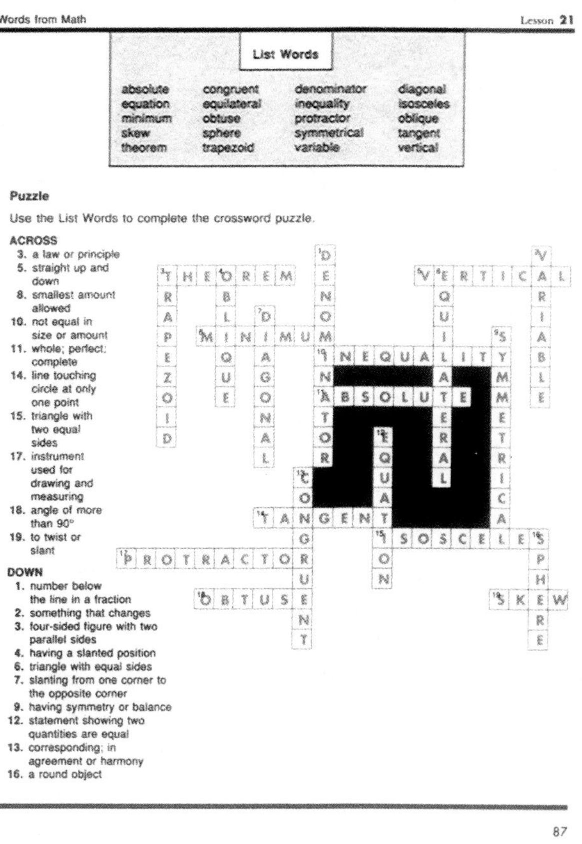

Words from Math — Lesson 21

List Words

absolute	congruent	denominator	diagonal
equation	equilateral	inequality	isosceles
minimum	obtuse	protractor	oblique
skew	sphere	symmetrical	tangent
theorem	trapezoid	variable	vertical

Puzzle

Use the List Words to complete the crossword puzzle.

ACROSS
3. a law or principle
5. straight up and down
8. smallest amount allowed
10. not equal in size or amount
11. whole; perfect; complete
14. line touching circle at only one point
15. triangle with two equal sides
17. instrument used for drawing and measuring
18. angle of more than 90°
19. to twist or slant

DOWN
1. number below the line in a fraction
2. something that changes
3. four-sided figure with two parallel sides
4. having a slanted position
6. triangle with equal sides
7. slanting from one corner to the opposite corner
9. having symmetry or balance
12. statement showing two quantities are equal
13. corresponding; in agreement or harmony
16. a round object

87

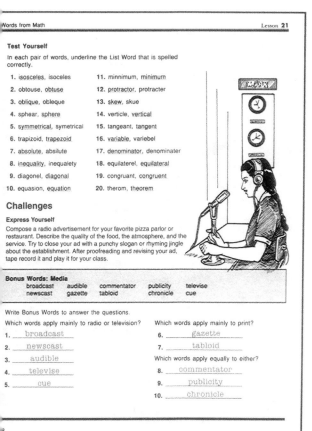

Puzzle (Page 87) By now, students should be able to complete the puzzle independently. Remind them to print neatly.

Test Yourself (Page 88) Have volunteers explain how this test is to be taken. Students should check their own answers against the List Words on page 87.

Challenges

Express Yourself (Page 88) Have the students form small groups to brainstorm lists of restaurants and their features. You may wish to point out that a ten-second radio advertisement is approximately 26 words long; a thirty-second spot approximately 78 words; and a one-minute spot approximately 156 words long. Students may enjoy reading their ads as if on radio.

Bonus Words: Media (Page 88) Explain that all the Bonus Words are related to media, the forms of communication. Discuss familiar words and have students use dictionaries to find the meanings of unfamiliar terms. Point out, if necessary, that a commentator can use any media form, as can a chronicle.

Bonus Word Test

1. This story will be a chronicle of our trip.
2. The studio has a new commentator.
3. Our latest broadcast begins at midnight.
4. At the cue, Richard says his lines.
5. We bought an ad in a local weekly tabloid.
6. That story came in too late for the noon newscast.
7. The announcer spoke in a barely audible voice.
8. Channel 3 will televise the debates.
9. Look for our ad on page two of the local gazette.
10. Without publicity, the show would have failed.

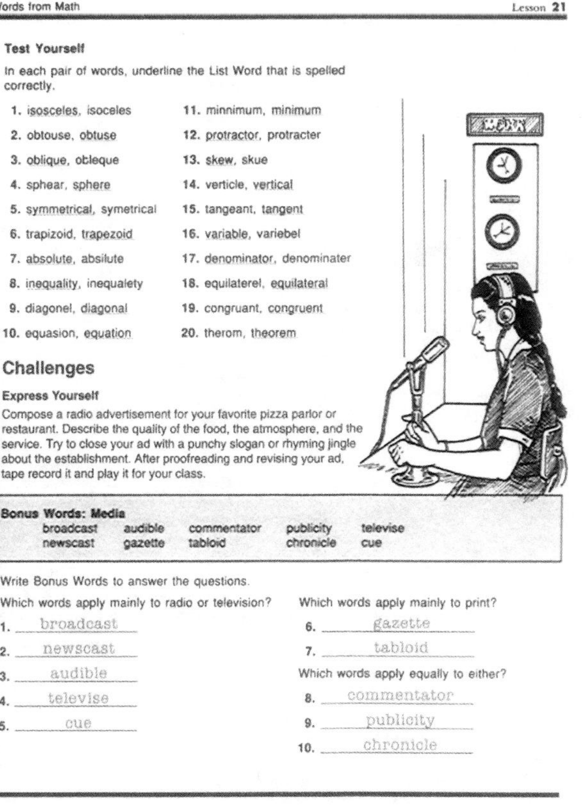

Words from Math — Lesson 21

Test Yourself

In each pair of words, underline the List Word that is spelled correctly.

1. isosceles, isoceles
2. obtouse, obtuse
3. oblique, obleque
4. sphear, sphere
5. symmetrical, symetrical
6. trapizoid, trapezoid
7. absolute, absilute
8. inequality, inequalety
9. diagonel, diagonal
10. equasion, equation
11. minnimum, minimum
12. protractor, protracter
13. skew, skue
14. verticle, vertical
15. tangeant, tangent
16. variable, variebel
17. denominator, denominater
18. equilaterel, equilateral
19. congruant, congruent
20. therom, theorem

Challenges

Express Yourself

Compose a radio advertisement for your favorite pizza parlor or restaurant. Describe the quality of the food, the atmosphere, and the service. Try to close your ad with a punchy slogan or rhyming jingle about the establishment. After proofreading and revising your ad, tape record it and play it for your class.

Bonus Words: Media

broadcast, audible, commentator, publicity, televise, newscast, gazette, tabloid, chronicle, cue

Write Bonus Words to answer the questions.

Which words apply mainly to radio or television?
1. broadcast
2. newscast
3. audible
4. televise
5. cue

Which words apply mainly to print?
6. gazette
7. tabloid

Which words apply equally to either?
8. commentator
9. publicity
10. chronicle

88

Final Test

1. Is the denominator equal to the numerator?
2. Notice the inequality between the numbers.
3. A protractor will help you measure an angle.
4. The two halves of this figure are symmetrical.
5. The weight is variable, depending on the size.
6. Draw a vertical line down the left side of the page.
7. The tangent touches the circle in one place only.
8. An oblique figure has a tilted axis.
9. Is this figure called an isosceles triangle?
10. The two diagonal lines cross in the center.
11. You can see that the two figures are congruent.
12. An equilateral figure has equal sides.
13. This angle is obtuse and that one is acute.
14. Our planet is not really a perfect sphere.
15. This trapezoid looks like a slanted box.
16. The absolute value of negative three is three.
17. Here is a very simple equation you will recognize.
18. Use a minimum amount of sugar in your food.
19. Be careful or you will skew those figures!
20. Can the theorem be proven to be true or false?

Lesson 22

Objective

To spell words related to history

Pretest

1. The aggressor fought to conquer new territory.
2. The leaders held a caucus to select a candidate.
3. My aunt served in the state legislature of Ohio.
4. The propaganda about the candidate was untrue.
5. Socialist theory seeks to aid disadvantaged people.
6. The United States and Canada enjoy an alliance.
7. The government of China promotes communism.
8. Are atoms split to form nuclear energy?
9. The rebellion forces fought against the government.
10. We developed a strategic plan to build our profits.
11. Support your opinions with an arsenal of facts.
12. Was grandmother born in a European ghetto?
13. The peasant lives in a hut near the stream.
14. Did the recession cause interest rates to fall?
15. The admiral proved that he was not a traitor.
16. A capitalist believes in free enterprise.
17. They will inaugurate the president in January.
18. The Puritans believed in the prohibition of dancing.
19. Vote "No" on the referendum to lower taxes!
20. Representatives of the nations signed the armistice.

Game Plan

Page 89

Relate the Game Plan to a current social studies unit, having students name words that have crucial significance to the events and issues being studied. Then discuss the List Words, relying on dictionaries and history texts for definitions, examples, and contextual references.

Warm Up

Vocabulary Development (Page 89) Before the exercise, have volunteers suggest short definitions for these words related to history: *democracy, migration, monarchy.*

Dictionary Skills (Page 89) Before students begin, have a volunteer summarize the function of guide words and point out examples in a dictionary.

Practice

Word Analysis (Page 90) To extend this activity, you may wish to have students separate the words into syllables, using dictionaries to check their work.

Classification (Page 90) To review classification skills, have students select a List Word to complete this series: *Meeting, discussion, ________. (caucus)*

Word Application (Page 90) Urge students to use context clues to find the List Word that best completes each sentence. They may enjoy creating similar sentences for other List Words to present as challenges to classmates.

Game Plan

The List Words are related to government, politics, and social issues. Knowledge and use of such words as referendum, recession, and rebellion will help you in your study and discussion of historical events, and your analysis of the causes and effects of those events.

1. aggressor
2. caucus
3. legislature
4. propaganda
5. socialist
6. alliance
7. communism
8. nuclear
9. rebellion
10. strategic
11. arsenal
12. ghetto
13. peasant
14. recession
15. traitor
16. capitalist
17. inaugurate
18. prohibition
19. referendum
20. armistice

Warm Up

Vocabulary Development

Write the List Word that matches each definition.

1. an agreement to stop a conflict armistice
2. a collection, usually of weapons arsenal
3. a meeting to choose a leader or set policy caucus
4. the person or group who starts a conflict aggressor
5. one who betrays his or her country traitor
6. a revolt or revolution rebellion
7. to install an official or establish a policy inaugurate
8. showing sound planning strategic
9. a period of declining business activity recession
10. persuasive language used to promote ideas propaganda

Dictionary Skills

Write the List Word that comes between each pair of dictionary guide words.

1. soap/soft socialist
2. can/carry capitalist
3. reef/regular referendum
4. color/cope communism
5. gem/give ghetto
6. nuance/nugget nuclear
7. patter/pepper peasant
8. problem/project prohibition
9. left/legitimate legislature
10. ago/apartment alliance

Practice

Word Analysis

Write each List Word under the correct category.

Words of Two Syllables	Words of Three Syllables	Words of Four Syllables
1. caucus	5. aggressor	14. legislative
2. ghetto	6. socialist	15. propaganda
3. peasant	7. alliance	16. communism
4. traitor	8. nuclear	17. capitalist
	9. rebellion	18. inaugurate
	10. strategic	19. prohibition
	11. arsenal	20. referendum
	12. recession	
	13. armistice	

Classification

Write a List Word to complete each series.

1. careful, logical, strategic
2. prevention, ban, prohibition
3. attacker, conqueror, aggressor
4. assembly, senate, legislature
5. electric, solar, nuclear
6. peace, victory, armistice
7. fort, garrison, arsenal
8. partnership, association, alliance
9. capitalism, socialism, communism
10. strike, uprising, rebellion

Word Application

Write a List Word to complete each sentence.

1. Benedict Arnold is considered a traitor who betrayed the American patriots' cause.
2. The voters were given a referendum on whether or not a new library should be built.
3. Advertisements often contain propaganda designed to persuade consumers to buy a product.
4. Under communism, all property is owned by the community as a whole.
5. A capitalist believes in free enterprise, competitive business, and private ownership.
6. A socialist believes that all members of society should share work and profits equally.
7. Political leaders hold a caucus to select candidates and establish platforms.
8. A ghetto is an urban neighborhood in which many members of an ethnic group live.

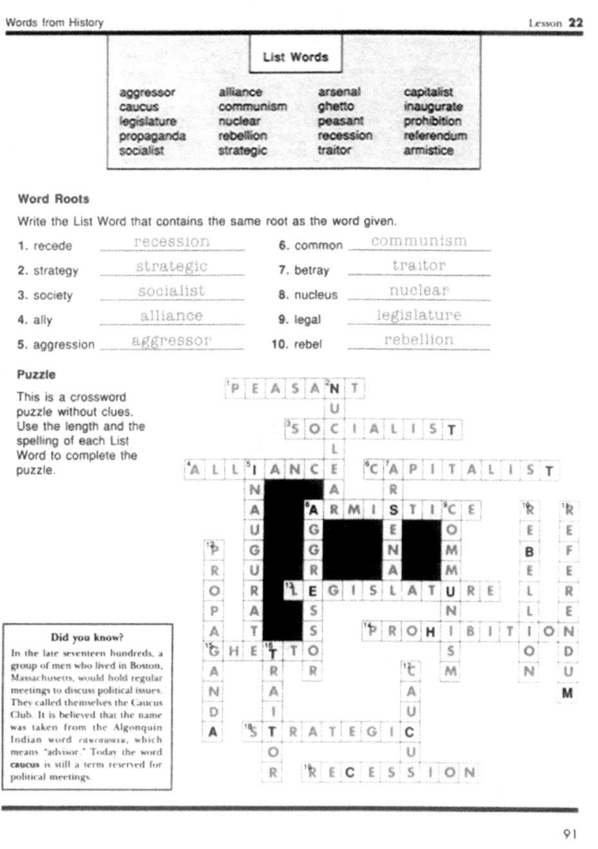

Words from History — Lesson 22

List Words

aggressor	alliance	arsenal	capitalist
caucus	communism	ghetto	inaugurate
legislature	nuclear	peasant	prohibition
propaganda	rebellion	recession	referendum
socialist	strategic	traitor	armistice

Word Roots

Write the List Word that contains the same root as the word given.

1. recede	recession	6. common	communism
2. strategy	strategic	7. betray	traitor
3. society	socialist	8. nucleus	nuclear
4. ally	alliance	9. legal	legislature
5. aggression	aggressor	10. rebel	rebellion

Puzzle

This is a crossword puzzle without clues. Use the length and the spelling of each List Word to complete the puzzle.

Did you know?

In the late seventeen hundreds, a group of men who lived in Boston, Massachusetts, would hold regular meetings to discuss political issues. They called themselves the Caucus Club. It is believed that the name was taken from the Algonquin Indian word *caucauasu*, which means "advisor." Today the word **caucus** is still a term reserved for political meetings.

91

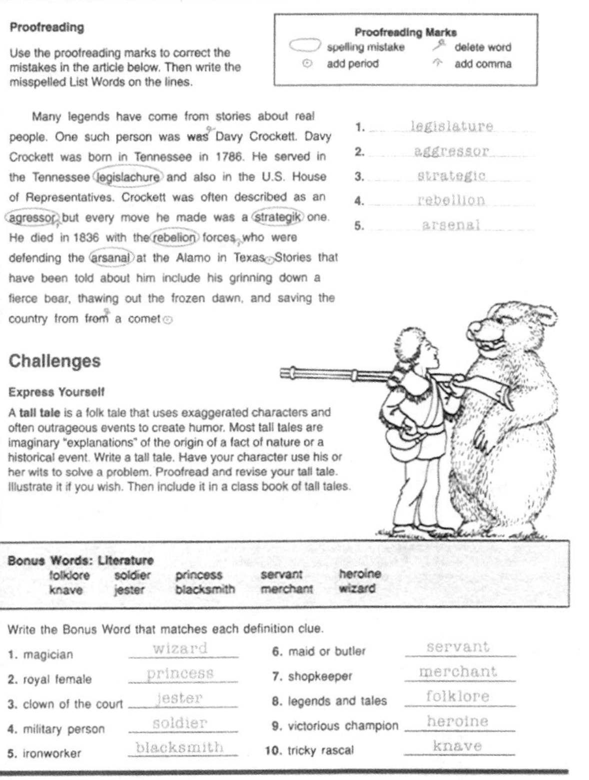

Words from History — Lesson 22

Proofreading

Use the proofreading marks to correct the mistakes in the article below. Then write the misspelled List Words on the lines.

Proofreading Marks
spelling mistake — delete word
add period — add comma

Many legends have come from stories about real people. One such person was was Davy Crockett. Davy Crockett was born in Tennessee in 1786. He served in the Tennessee legislachure and also in the U.S. House of Representatives. Crockett was often described as an agressor but every move he made was a strategik one. He died in 1836 with the rebelion forces who were defending the arsanal at the Alamo in Texas Stories that have been told about him include his grinning down a fierce bear, thawing out the frozen dawn, and saving the country from from a comet

1. legislature
2. aggressor
3. strategic
4. rebellion
5. arsenal

Challenges

Express Yourself

A **tall tale** is a folk tale that uses exaggerated characters and often outrageous events to create humor. Most tall tales are imaginary "explanations" of the origin of a fact of nature or a historical event. Write a tall tale. Have your character use his or her wits to solve a problem. Proofread and revise your tall tale. Illustrate it if you wish. Then include it in a class book of tall tales.

Bonus Words: Literature

folklore, soldier, princess, servant, heroine, knave, jester, blacksmith, merchant, wizard

Write the Bonus Word that matches each definition clue.

1. magician	wizard	6. maid or butler	servant
2. royal female	princess	7. shopkeeper	merchant
3. clown of the court	jester	8. legends and tales	folklore
4. military person	soldier	9. victorious champion	heroine
5. ironworker	blacksmith	10. tricky rascal	knave

92

Word Roots (Page 91) Point out that understanding the meanings of roots will help students to understand the technical words that they encounter in history, science, and geography texts.

Puzzle (Page 91) Urge students to count the number of spaces in each answer blank to help them to solve the puzzle. Point out that each List Word appears once.

Proofreading (Page 92) Write this sentence on the board to demonstrate the proofreading marks for this lesson: *Please go to the libray the store, and the bank*

Challenges

Express Yourself (Page 92) Read and discuss the features of a popular tall tale, such as one featuring Pecos Bill or Paul Bunyan. Have students cite examples of exaggeration and outrageous events. Then brainstorm story ideas with them. Encourage them to jot down notes to help them organize their tales. Invite them to share their finished work orally, and create a bulletin board or a classroom anthology.

Bonus Words: Literature (Page 92) Discuss the Bonus Words, relating them to the writing project, to familiar folk tales, and to students' own knowledge and experiences. Have students use the words in oral sentences.

Bonus Word Test

1. The blacksmith worked over an open forge.
2. In many folk tales, a servant becomes a great hero.
3. A wizard appears in the King Arthur legends.
4. In a famous tale, a princess falls in love with a frog.
5. The court jester was the castle's resident comedian.
6. The tin soldier is the hero of a well-known tale.
7. Germany is a country that is rich in folklore.
8. In one tale, a knave pretends that he's a king.
9. In another tale, a merchant is granted three wishes.
10. A young shepherdess is the heroine of this tale.

Final Test

1. The coach explained her strategic game plan.
2. All were jubilant when the armistice was signed.
4. Was the traitor exiled from the country?
5. Karl Marx was a German philosopher and socialist.
6. Our company was hit hard by the recession.
7. There are two referendum questions on the ballot.
8. The queen lowered taxes to prevent a rebellion.
9. Don't be swayed by propaganda!
10. At the caucus, Roberto presented his views.
11. The people of the ghetto formed a citizen's group.
12. Russia turned to communism in 1922.
13. We will inaugurate our new class officers today.
14. The bordering nations formed a trade alliance.
15. Andrew Carnegie was a major American capitalist.
16. A knight's arsenal of weapons included lances.
17. I ran away from the aggressor to avoid a fight.
18. Is there a nuclear power plant south of the city?
19. The peasant works in the field every day.
20. Many people support the prohibition of fireworks.

Lesson 23

Objective
To spell words from business

Pretest
1. The administration of the business requires skill.
2. Mr. Inez added up the receipts on a calculator.
3. Ana receives a monthly dividend on her investment.
4. He had to justify his monthly expenses to his boss.
5. If you miss loan payments, they'll repossess the car.
6. Did the office supervisor authorize your raise?
7. Teachers must have proper certification to teach.
8. The company's executive offices are upstairs.
9. Trucks deliver merchandise to stores every day.
10. Leah's promotion meant an increase in salary.
11. That business tycoon is worth a billion dollars!
12. The bank requires collateral on the personal loan.
13. Italics are used to set off or emphasize an idea.
14. The invoice shows that part of the order is missing.
15. Is a signature required to cash a check?
16. The credit bureau ran a check on Al's credit rating.
17. We exchanged U.S. dollars for German currency.
18. Will my statement show the interest that I earned?
19. Lin enclosed a copy of the bill with her remittance.
20. Statistics show that the business is booming.

Game Plan
Page 93
Discuss the Game Plan. You may wish to focus on the process of obtaining a bank loan, discussing the reasons people seek loans, what they use for collateral, how payments are made, etc. Have volunteers define the List Words. Encourage them to consult a dictionary for any unfamiliar words.

Warm Up
Vocabulary Development (Page 93) When students have finished the exercise they may wish to find synonyms for other List Words, such as *calculator (adding machine), dividend (profit), certification (verification).*

Dictionary Skills (Page 93) Emphasize that students should be careful not to drop letters from any of the syllables as they write the words.

Practice
Word Analysis (Page 94) Students should refer to the List Words on page 93 to find each letter combination. You may wish to have students identify the words that contain *st* letter combinations. *(administration, justify, interest, statistics)*

Proofreading (Page 94) As you review the use of the proofreading marks, focus on the mark for showing lower case. Write this sentence on the board as an example: The Company sent its employees home early. You may also wish to review the use of commas in a letter. Point out to students that not every List Word in the letter is misspelled.

Puzzle (Page 95) Encourage students to think about the meanings of the List Words as they complete the puzzle.

Words from Business — LESSON 23

Game Plan
The world of business and finance has its own particular vocabulary. Collateral, interest, and repossess are words associated with bank loans. The words administration and executive suggest big business.

All the List Words are related to business. Some words you will recognize. Some may be unfamiliar. Study all the words. Memorize and practice spelling them.

1. administration
2. calculator
3. dividend
4. justify
5. repossess
6. authorize
7. certification
8. executive
9. merchandise
10. salary
11. billion
12. collateral
13. italics
14. invoice
15. signature
16. bureau
17. currency
18. interest
19. remittance
20. statistics

Warm Up
Vocabulary Development

Write the List Word from column B that matches the synonym in column A.

A		B
1. autograph	signature	currency
2. money	currency	administration
3. bill	invoice	merchandise
4. manager	executive	salary
5. recover	repossess	statistics
6. empower	authorize	executive
7. figures	statistics	authorize
8. pay	salary	signature
9. goods	merchandise	repossess
10. management	administration	invoice

Dictionary Skills

Rewrite each of the following List Words to show how they are divided into syllables.

1. remittance	re mit tance	6. italics	i tal ics
2. calculator	cal cu la tor	7. bureau	bu reau
3. dividend	div i dend	8. interest	in ter est
4. collateral	col lat er al	9. billion	bil lion
5. certification	cer ti fi ca tion	10. justify	jus ti fy

93

Words from Business — Lesson 23

Practice
Word Analysis

Write List Words to answer the following questions.

Which words contain these double consonants?

1. ss repossess 2. rr currency 3. tt remittance

Which words contain the **er** letter combination?

4. certification 5. merchandise 6. collateral 7. interest

Did you know?
Salary comes from a Latin word that means "money for salt," as part of a Roman soldier's pay. To be worth one's salt is to be worth one's salary or wages.

Proofreading

Use the proofreading marks to correct the mistakes in the letter. Then write the misspelled List Words correctly on the lines.

Proofreading Marks
- spelling mistake
- capital letter
- small letter
- add comma
- new paragraph

Sunshine Computers

Mr. Mark Casey
1701 Broadway
Readville NC 28409

Dear Mr. Casey:

Thank you for your patronage in our company. Sunshine computers welcomes you to become a shareholder in one of the world's fastest growing Corporations with over a bilion clients. Our superior merchandize is sold in over fifty countries. Perhaps you are familiar with our famous pocket calculater and our portable word processor. These products alone are enough to justefy an investment with us. Our shareholders profit from substantial yearly divedend payments which reflect sales from World markets, regardless of international currancy levels.
We hope that you will join us for an investment in your future. If needed, I will forward further statistcs to you. Please do not forget to enclose your signiture with your remitence as certification of your intent.

Sincerely

M. Hernandez
Exicutive Vice president

1. billion
2. merchandise
3. calculator
4. justify
5. dividend
6. currency
7. statistics
8. signature
9. remittance
10. Executive

94

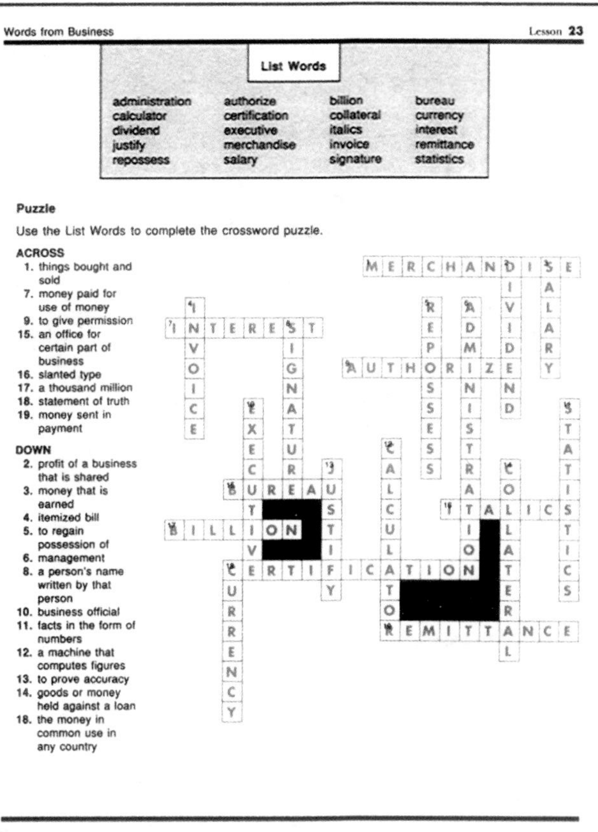
Words from Business Lesson **23**

List Words

administration	authorize	billion	bureau
calculator	certification	collateral	currency
dividend	executive	italics	interest
justify	merchandise	invoice	remittance
repossess	salary	signature	statistics

Puzzle

Use the List Words to complete the crossword puzzle.

ACROSS
1. things bought and sold
7. money paid for use of money
9. to give permission
15. an office for certain part of business
16. slanted type
17. a thousand million
18. statement of truth
19. money sent in payment

DOWN
2. profit of a business that is shared
3. money that is earned
4. itemized bill
5. to regain possession of
6. management
8. a person's name written by that person
10. business official
11. facts in the form of numbers
12. a machine that computes figures
13. to prove accuracy
14. goods or money held against a loan
18. the money in common use in any country

95

Words from Business Lesson **23**

Test Yourself

In each pair of List Words, underline the misspelled word and write it correctly on the line.

1. repossess, statistecs	statistics	6. signiture, salary	signature
2. executive, merchandize	merchandise	7. curency, dividend	currency
3. autherize, interest	authorize	8. justify, italecs	italics
4. administration, billion	administration	9. invoice, remitance	remittance
5. colaterel, certification	collateral	10. bureau, calculater	calculator

Challenges

Express Yourself

Imagine that you have invented a brand new product. It may be a breakfast cereal that provides enough nutrients for three meals or a fantastic all-purpose cleaning agent. Write a letter to a manufacturing firm, persuading them to produce your product. Describe your product or invention in detail. Tell them why you think it will be a big seller. You may wish to create a slogan for your new product. Proofread and revise your letter. Then present it to a group who is acting on behalf of the manufacturing firm. See if you are able to convince them to produce your product.

Bonus Words: Inventions

laboratory	experiment	development	originate	devise
formula	inventive	generate	insight	analysis

Write the Bonus Word that matches each definition clue.

1. ability to see the inner nature of things insight
2. a bringing of something into reality development
3. a room where research is conducted laboratory
4. an examination of the parts of something analysis
5. a test or trial of something experiment
6. skilled in thinking up new and creative things inventive
7. directions for preparing something formula

Write the words that are synonyms or near-synonyms for invent.

8. generate 9. originate 10. devise

96

Test Yourself (Page 96) When students complete the activity, encourage them to check their spelling with the List Words on page 95.

Challenges

Express Yourself (Page 96) To stimulate students to write, discuss their ideas for inventions or new products. Ask students to describe their product, what made them think of inventing it, how it works or what it does, and why they think that it is important. Students may also enjoy creating ads for their products and sharing them with the class.

Bonus Words: Inventions (Page 96) Work with students to define the Bonus Words. Discuss with them how these words apply to inventions. Encourage students to use each word in an oral sentence. Lead them to notice that three of the words mean nearly the same thing. (*generate, originate, devise*)

Bonus Word Test

1. After careful analysis I solved the problem.
2. As an experiment, she mixed the liquids together.
3. The formula for the new fuel was kept secret.
4. Jane is an inventive person with a creative mind.
5. Becky tried to devise a new way to package cereal.
6. Many new inventions originate out of necessity.
7. Paul worked in his laboratory on his new invention.
8. She assisted in the development of a new computer.
9. Inventors have insight into the needs of the future.
10. One invention may generate ideas for others.

Final Test

1. Mr. Hall must justify his annual tax deductions.
2. Did you receive a dividend on your stock?
3. Mrs. Vance is a top executive at the company.
4. The bank will repossess a car if you miss payments.
5. The restaurant has served over a billion meals.
6. The first paragraph of the contract was set in italics.
7. The workers agreed to a temporary cut in salary.
8. Did you use a calculator to compute your taxes?
9. The bank will exchange foreign currency for a fee.
10. Businesses rely on statistics to chart their growth.
11. The company grew under the new administration.
12. Ms. Wang's signature appears on our paychecks.
13. John used his car as collateral for a bank loan.
14. Did Leona check the figures listed on the invoice?
15. Full remittance on the bill is due in 30 days.
16. The state requires certification of all its plumbers.
17. The floor supervisor will authorize your refund.
18. The interest rate on our mortgage is 8.5 percent.
19. What a great sale on that merchandise!
20. Our Seattle bureau handles all our product sales.

Lesson 24

Objective

To review spelling patterns of words from Lessons 19–23

Game Plan

Page 97
Tell students that in this lesson they will review the skills and spelling words they studied in Lessons 19–23. You may wish to have students refer to previous Game Plans to review the information on cross-curriculum words from geography, science, math, history, and business.

Practice

Lesson 19 (Page 97) Have students identify what the following words have in common: meridian, bayou, axis, ecological, precipitation. (They are all words related to the study of geography.) Then discuss the geographical references of the List Words. Point out the additional write-on lines to students and encourage them to add two words from Lesson 19 that they found especially difficult, or select and assign certain words that seemed to be difficult for everyone. (Repeat this procedure for each lesson review that follows in the Replay.) Emphasize that students should think of the meaning of each word as they complete the activity.

Lesson 20 (Page 98) Have students tell what subject they would be studying if they encountered these words: tremor, cycle, characteristics, stethoscope. (science) Elicit that the List Words are also from science and discuss their meanings. Point out to students that the first part of each sentence contains a clue to the answer.

Lesson 21 (Page 98) Write on the board: theorem, equilateral, oblique, tangent. Elicit from students that these words are math terms and have volunteers define the words. Point out that the List Words are math terms and have students define each word. Students should look closely at the spelling patterns of each word as they answer the questions.

Lesson 22 (Page 99) Ask students which of these words is not related to the study of history: communism, socialist, therapy, armistice. (therapy) Elicit from students that the List Words are from history and discuss the meanings of the words.

Lesson 23 (Page 99) Have volunteers tell how each of the following words relates to business and finance: dividend, invoice, interest, merchandise. Then write these words on the board: itch, and laugh. Have students tell which of the following words would come between these words in the dictionary: italics, itemize, interest, justify, merchandise.

Mixed Practice (Page 100) Before students begin the activity, elicit synonyms for the following words: rapid (fast), maximum (most), pacifist (peacemaker).

Test Yourself (page 100) You may wish to write additional test items on the board for specific words with which students encountered difficulty.

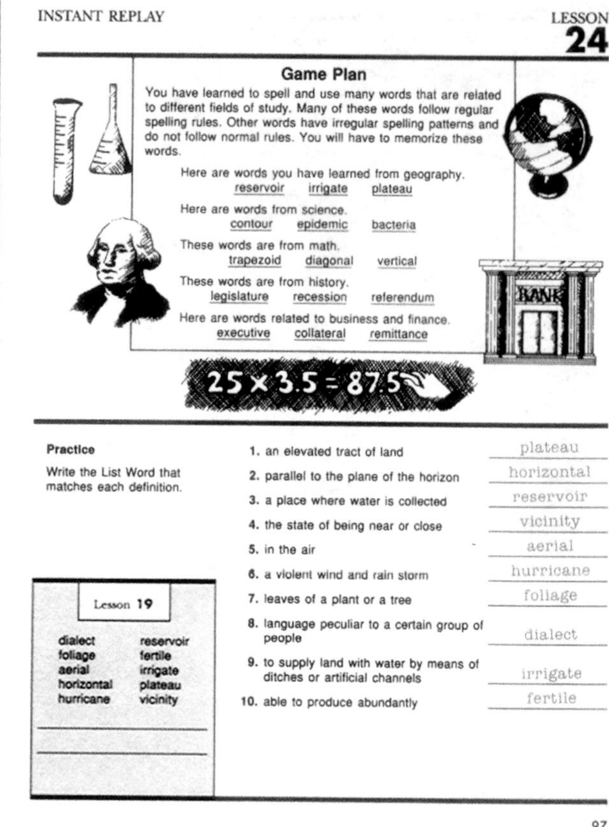

INSTANT REPLAY — LESSON 24

Game Plan

You have learned to spell and use many words that are related to different fields of study. Many of these words follow regular spelling rules. Other words have irregular spelling patterns and do not follow normal rules. You will have to memorize these words.

Here are words you have learned from geography.
reservoir irrigate plateau

Here are words from science.
contour epidemic bacteria

These words are from math.
trapezoid diagonal vertical

These words are from history.
legislature recession referendum

Here are words related to business and finance.
executive collateral remittance

Practice
Write the List Word that matches each definition.

1. an elevated tract of land — plateau
2. parallel to the plane of the horizon — horizontal
3. a place where water is collected — reservoir
4. the state of being near or close — vicinity
5. in the air — aerial
6. a violent wind and rain storm — hurricane
7. leaves of a plant or a tree — foliage
8. language peculiar to a certain group of people — dialect
9. to supply land with water by means of ditches or artificial channels — irrigate
10. able to produce abundantly — fertile

Lesson 19

dialect	reservoir
foliage	fertile
aerial	irrigate
horizontal	plateau
hurricane	vicinity

97

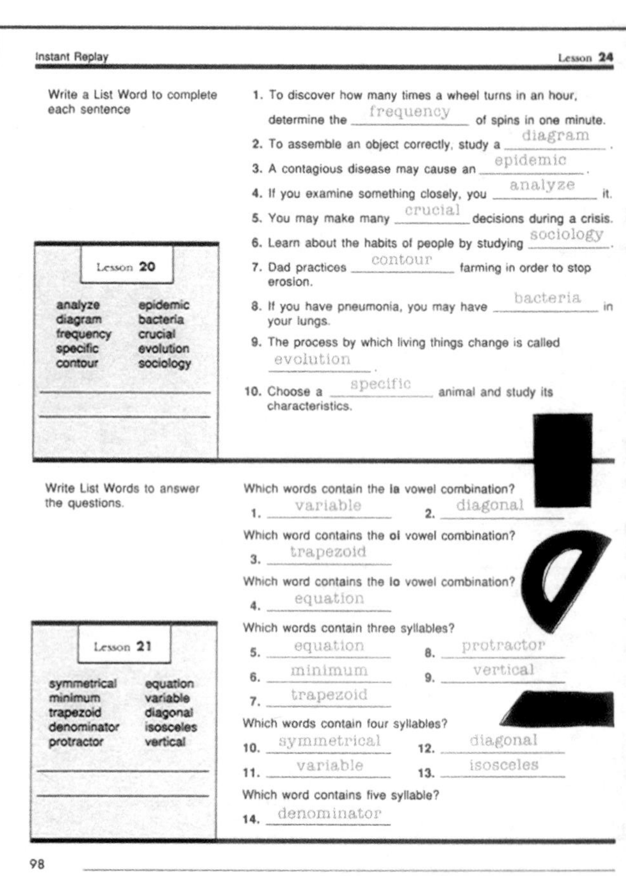

Instant Replay — Lesson 24

Write a List Word to complete each sentence.

1. To discover how many times a wheel turns in an hour, determine the frequency of spins in one minute.
2. To assemble an object correctly, study a diagram.
3. A contagious disease may cause an epidemic.
4. If you examine something closely, you analyze it.
5. You may make many crucial decisions during a crisis.
6. Learn about the habits of people by studying sociology.
7. Dad practices contour farming in order to stop erosion.
8. If you have pneumonia, you may have bacteria in your lungs.
9. The process by which living things change is called evolution.
10. Choose a specific animal and study its characteristics.

Lesson 20

analyze	epidemic
diagram	bacteria
frequency	crucial
specific	evolution
contour	sociology

Write List Words to answer the questions.

Which words contain the **ia** vowel combination?
1. variable 2. diagonal

Which word contains the **oi** vowel combination?
3. trapezoid

Which word contains the **io** vowel combination?
4. equation

Which words contain three syllables?
5. equation 8. protractor
6. minimum 9. vertical
7. trapezoid

Which words contain four syllables?
10. symmetrical 12. diagonal
11. variable 13. isosceles

Which word contains five syllable?
14. denominator

Lesson 21

symmetrical	equation
minimum	variable
trapezoid	diagonal
denominator	isosceles
protractor	vertical

98

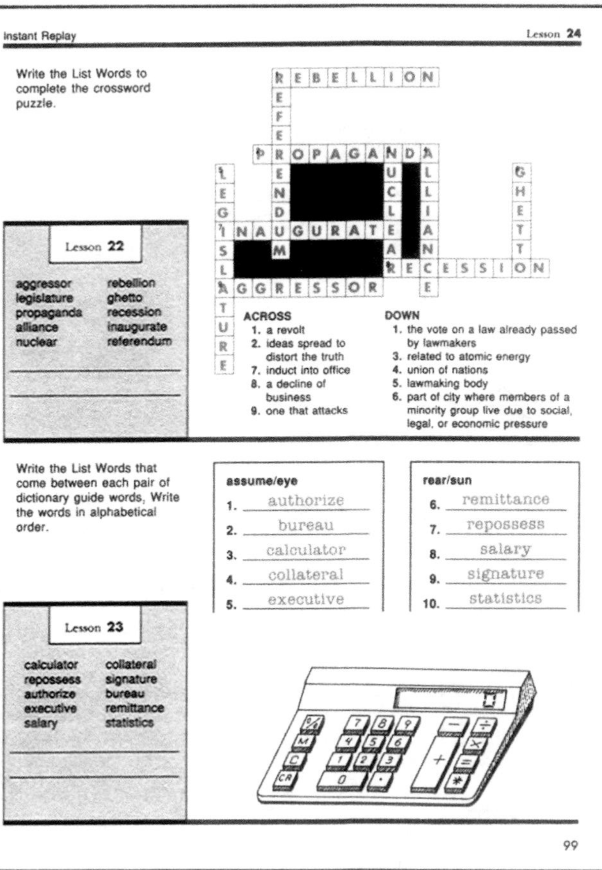

Instant Replay — Lesson **24**

Write the List Words to complete the crossword puzzle.

Lesson **22**

aggressor	rebellion
legislature	ghetto
propaganda	recession
alliance	inaugurate
nuclear	referendum

ACROSS
1. a revolt
2. ideas spread to distort the truth
7. induct into office
8. a decline of business
9. one that attacks

DOWN
1. the vote on a law already passed by lawmakers
3. related to atomic energy
4. union of nations
5. lawmaking body
6. part of city where members of a minority group live due to social, legal, or economic pressure

Write the List Words that come between each pair of dictionary guide words. Write the words in alphabetical order.

assume/eye
1. authorize
2. bureau
3. calculator
4. collateral
5. executive

rear/sun

6. remittance
7. repossess
8. salary
9. signature
10. statistics

Lesson **23**

calculator	collateral
repossess	signature
authorize	bureau
executive	remittance
salary	statistics

99

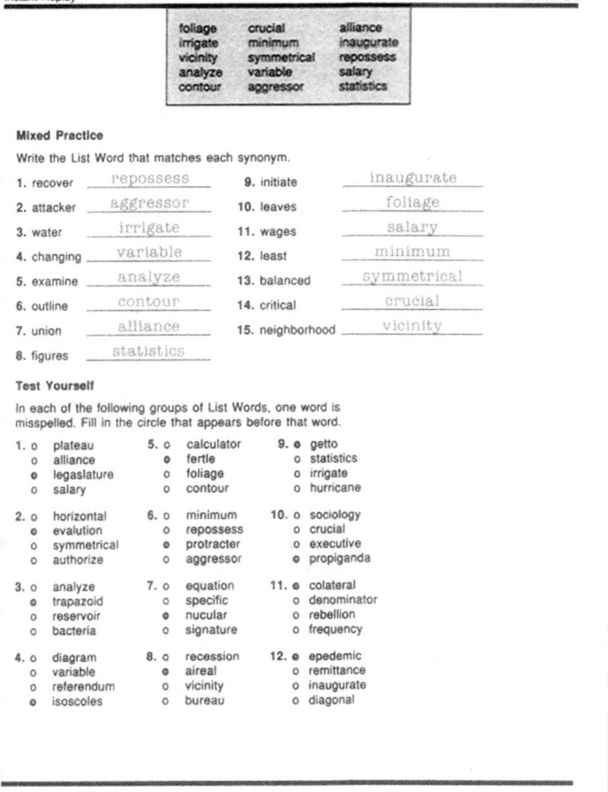

Instant Replay — Lesson **24**

foliage	crucial	alliance
irrigate	minimum	inaugurate
vicinity	symmetrical	repossess
analyze	variable	salary
contour	aggressor	statistics

Mixed Practice

Write the List Word that matches each synonym.

1. recover — repossess
2. attacker — aggressor
3. water — irrigate
4. changing — variable
5. examine — analyze
6. outline — contour
7. union — alliance
8. figures — statistics
9. initiate — inaugurate
10. leaves — foliage
11. wages — salary
12. least — minimum
13. balanced — symmetrical
14. critical — crucial
15. neighborhood — vicinity

Test Yourself

In each of the following groups of List Words, one word is misspelled. Fill in the circle that appears before that word.

1. o plateau, o alliance, ● legaslature, o salary
2. o horizontal, ● evalution, o symmetrical, o authorize
3. o analyze, ● trapazoid, o reservoir, o bacteria
4. o diagram, o variable, o referendum, ● isoscoles
5. o calculator, ● fertle, o foliage, o contour
6. o minimum, o repossess, ● protracter, o aggressor
7. o equation, o specific, ● nucular, o signature
8. o recession, ● aireal, o vicinity, o bureau
9. ● getto, o statistics, o irrigate, o hurricane
10. o sociology, o crucial, o executive, ● propiganda
11. ● colateral, o denominator, o rebellion, o frequency
12. ● epedemic, o remittance, o inaugurate, o diagonal

100

Final Replay Test

1. Rosaria speaks the dialect of her native island.
2. Dr. Fermi will analyze the results of the blood test.
3. He wrote the mathematical equation on the board.
4. The aggressor nation was criticized by Congress.
5. Tim checked his addition with a calculator.
6. The tree's foliage turns bright orange in the fall.
7. The diagram shows all the bones of the hand.
8. The minimum speed limit on a highway is 45 mph.
9. The state legislature enacts the laws of the state.
10. The store agreed not to repossess their furniture.
11. What a great aerial view!
12. They determined the frequency of rain in the area.
13. A trapezoid is a four-sided figure.
14. Is the newspaper spreading propaganda?
15. Mr. Juarez will have to authorize this loan.
16. A horizontal streak of red ran across the sky.
17. She researched the specific traits of mammals.
18. In the fraction 5/6, six is the denominator.
19. The two nations formed a political alliance.
20. The company sent a top executive to the meeting.
21. What a ferocious hurricane!
22. The scenic road follows the contour of the coast.
23. Should I use a protractor to measure the angle?
24. The treaty called for nuclear disarmament.
25. With an increase in salary, I can afford a new car.
26. Heavy rains increased the water in the reservoir.
27. Schools closed during the measles epidemic.
28. The symmetrical design is attractive.
29. The government worked to prevent a rebellion.
30. The Changs used their car as collateral for a loan.
31. The fertile land can support many species of plants.
32. Only a few bacteria lead to serious disease.
33. Weather in that region is quite variable.
34. Will the candidate campaign in the ghetto?
35. Ms. Town's signature appeared on the contract.
36. Dad will irrigate the corn fields.
37. That information is crucial for my report!
38. A diagonal line connects two corners of a rectangle.
39. Many economists predict a long recession.
40. Sueann works at the federal bureau in the city.
41. The wind howled across the mountain plateau.
42. Fossils give proof to some theories of evolution.
43. An isosceles triangle has two or more equal sides.
44. When will we inaugurate our new president?
45. She sent her remittance in the form of a check.
46. Is there a restaurant in the vicinity of the hotel?
47. Sociology is the study of people and their behavior.
48. He drew a vertical line down the sidewalk.
49. The people voted on the seat belt referendum.
50. Statistics show that business is declining.

Lesson 25

Objective

To spell words with *ei, ie*

Pretest

1. Is that antique bowl a family heirloom?
2. The corner store has convenient weekend hours.
3. What a fiend that evil wizard is!
4. Macbeth committed the heinous crime of murder.
5. This receipt shows I paid for the sweater.
6. The curtains are made of beige and white fabric.
7. My new secretary is a very efficient person.
8. Speak to a financier about a savings program.
9. Will this chart illustrate the company hierarchy?
10. The storm gave us a brief reprieve from the heat.
11. Don't besiege Mrs. Delgado with questions.
12. Water freezes at thirty-two degrees Fahrenheit.
13. American settlers journeyed across the frontier.
14. The dentist spoke to us about good oral hygiene.
15. Let's walk out onto the pier and watch the boats.
16. Will too much caffeine make you nervous?
17. That sunset turned the sky a fiery red!
18. People do not always cry when they grieve.
19. The train is a little late, so please have patience.
20. The police used a surveillance camera.

Game Plan

Page 101

After students have read the Game Plan, discuss which List Words follow the rule and which do not. Make sure students know the meaning and pronunciation of unfamiliar words, referring them to dictionaries when needed. Point out that *Fahrenheit* is capitalized because it comes from the name of a German scientist, Gabriel Daniel Fahrenheit, who developed the measurement scale.

Warm Up

Vocabulary Development (Page 101) Remind students to pay attention to the spelling of each word, as well as its meaning.

Dictionary Skills (Page 101) Briefly review the symbols used in respellings. When students have completed the exercise, have them check any answers they are unsure about against a dictionary's respellings.

Practice

Word Analysis (Page 102) This exercise will help students remember the spelling of words that are exceptions to this lesson's rule, as well as ones that follow it.

Word Application (Page 102) Point out to students that the answers they choose must make sense in the sentences and be spelled correctly.

Game Plan

Words containing the letter combinations **ie** and **ei** are tricky and must be studied carefully. Many, but not all, follow the rule expressed by this jingle:

> I before E, except after C,
> unless sounded like A, as in neighbor and weigh.

Remember, there are numerous exceptions to this rule, such as efficient and caffeine. These will have to be memorized.

1. heirloom
2. convenient
3. fiend
4. heinous
5. receipt
6. beige
7. efficient
8. financier
9. hierarchy
10. reprieve
11. besiege
12. Fahrenheit
13. frontier
14. hygiene
15. pier
16. caffeine
17. fiery
18. grieve
19. patience
20. surveillance

Warm Up

Vocabulary Development

Write the List Word that matches each definition.

1. close watch kept over someone surveillance
2. to give temporary relief reprieve
3. border between two countries frontier
4. structure built over water pier
5. stimulant found in coffee caffeine
6. type of thermometer Fahrenheit
7. group with positions of power hierarchy
8. handy or easily accessible convenient
9. to mourn grieve
10. very evil or cruel person fiend
11. treasured family possession heirloom
12. outrageously evil heinous

Dictionary Skills

Write the List Word that matches each sound-spelling.

1. (ə fish´ ənt) efficient	6. (bi sēj´) besiege
2. (ri prēv´) reprieve	7. (hā´ nəs) heinous
3. (fī´ ər ē) fiery	8. (fin´ ən sir´) financier
4. (pā´ shəns) patience	9. (hī´ jēn´) hygiene
5. (ri sēt´) receipt	10. (bāzh) beige

Practice

Word Analysis

Write the List Words that are spelled with **ie**.

1. convenient	8. frontier
2. fiend	9. hygiene
3. efficient	10. pier
4. financier	11. fiery
5. hierarchy	12. grieve
6. reprieve	13. patience
7. besiege	

Write the List Words that are spelled with **ei**.

14. heirloom	18. Fahrenheit
15. heinous	19. caffeine
16. receipt	20. surveillance
17. beige	

Did you know?

The word **hierarchy** has its roots in the Greek language. It comes from the Greek words *hieros*, meaning "holy," and *archos*, meaning "ruler." *Hierarchy*, which once meant "a government by officers of the church, or a holy government," now means "a system of graded authority."

ie?

ei?

Word Application

Replace the underlined words with List Words and write them on the lines.

1. Maintaining watch on a suspect requires a great deal of endurance by a police officer.
   surveillance patience
2. The carpet, a family treasure, has a light tan background.
   heirloom beige
3. Professor Moriarty, the famous villain, was guilty of many wicked crimes.
   fiend heinous
4. The club's officials gave a relief to members who have not yet paid their dues.
   hierarchy reprieve
5. The town's fishing wharf is easily accessible to many of the public buses and train.
   pier convenient

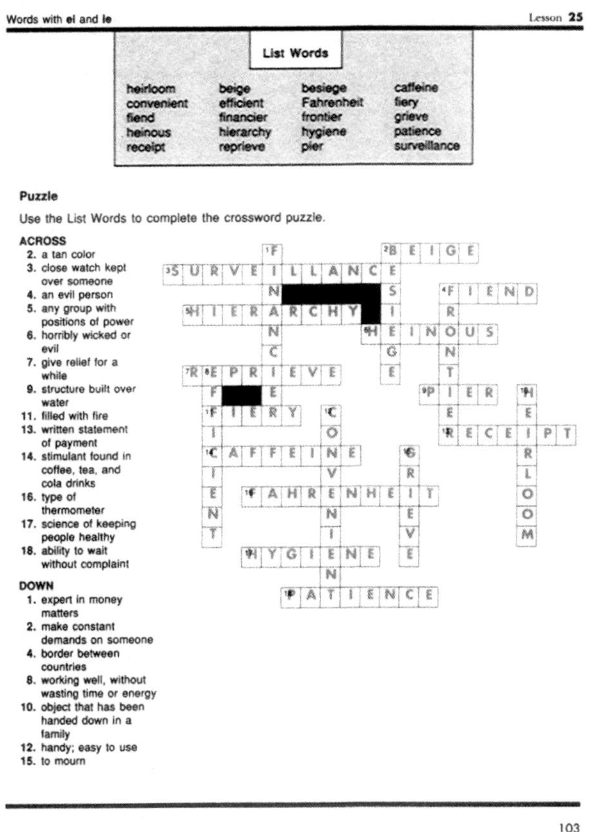

Words with **ei** and **ie** | Lesson **25**

List Words

heirloom	beige	besiege	caffeine
convenient	efficient	Fahrenheit	fiery
fiend	financier	frontier	grieve
heinous	hierarchy	hygiene	patience
receipt	reprieve	pier	surveillance

Puzzle

Use the List Words to complete the crossword puzzle.

ACROSS
2. a tan color
3. close watch kept over someone
4. an evil person
5. any group with positions of power
6. horribly wicked or evil
7. give relief for a while
9. structure built over water
11. filled with fire
13. written statement of payment
14. stimulant found in coffee, tea, and cola drinks
16. type of thermometer
17. science of keeping people healthy
18. ability to wait without complaint

DOWN
1. expert in money matters
2. make constant demands on someone
4. border between countries
8. working well, without wasting time or energy
10. object that has been handed down in a family
12. handy; easy to use
15. to mourn

103

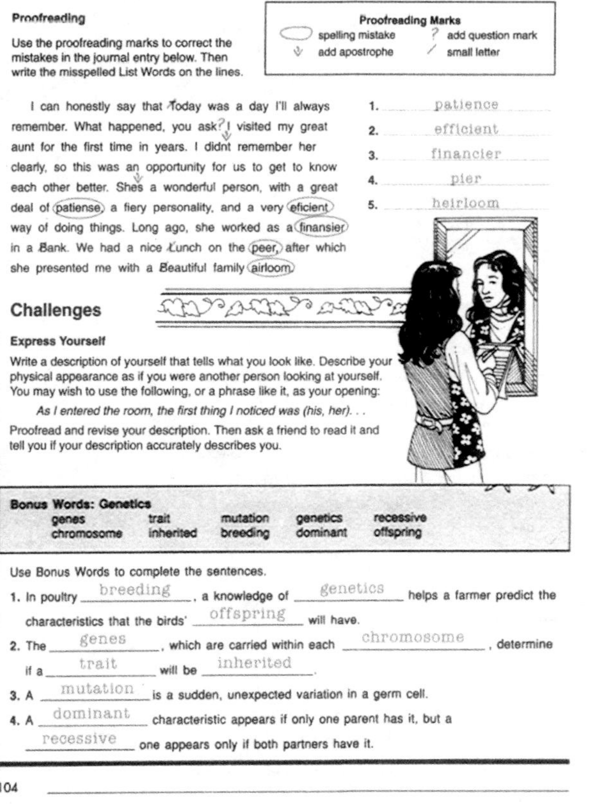

Words with **ei** and **ie** | Lesson **25**

Proofreading

Use the proofreading marks to correct the mistakes in the journal entry below. Then write the misspelled List Words on the lines.

Proofreading Marks
spelling mistake — add question mark — add apostrophe — small letter

I can honestly say that Today was a day I'll always remember. What happened, you ask I visited my great aunt for the first time in years. I didnt remember her clearly, so this was an opportunity for us to get to know each other better. Shes a wonderful person, with a great deal of patiense, a fiery personality, and a very eficient way of doing things. Long ago, she worked as a finansier in a Bank. We had a nice Lunch on the peer, after which she presented me with a Beautiful family airloom.

1. patience
2. efficient
3. financier
4. pier
5. heirloom

Challenges

Express Yourself

Write a description of yourself that tells what you look like. Describe your physical appearance as if you were another person looking at yourself. You may wish to use the following, or a phrase like it, as your opening:

As I entered the room, the first thing I noticed was (his, her). . .

Proofread and revise your description. Then ask a friend to read it and tell you if your description accurately describes you.

Bonus Words: Genetics

genes	trait	mutation	genetics	recessive
chromosome	inherited	breeding	dominant	offspring

Use Bonus Words to complete the sentences.

1. In poultry breeding, a knowledge of genetics helps a farmer predict the characteristics that the birds' offspring will have.
2. The genes, which are carried within each chromosome, determine if a trait will be inherited.
3. A mutation is a sudden, unexpected variation in a germ cell.
4. A dominant characteristic appears if only one parent has it, but a recessive one appears only if both partners have it.

104

Puzzle (Page 103) Tell students to use all capital letters, and remind them to print neatly.

Proofreading (Page 104) Write *Wheres my Blue jackit* on the board and use it to demonstrate the proofreading marks in this lesson. Point out to students that they will use these marks to correct the journal entry.

Challenges

Express Yourself (Page 104) As a group, discuss characteristic students might write about, including ones they might not think of, such as gait, posture, and gesture. Have them imagine that they are looking at videotapes of themselves entering a room. After students have finished, you may wish to have them exchange papers, read them aloud, and try to guess the identity of each subject.

Bonus Words: Genetics (Page 104) Explain that all the Bonus Words are related to genetics, the branch of biology that deals with heredity. By using dictionaries and biology books, help students learn the meanings of the words. Before they complete the written exercise, have them use each word in an oral sentence.

Bonus Word Test

1. Blue eyes is a recessive characteristic.
2. These cattle are being kept as breeding stock.
3. I inherited my left-handedness from my mother.
4. My father says artistic talent is in my genes.
5. Each chromosome carries genetic material.
6. One of the dog's offspring may have spots.
7. In some dogs, herding is a desirable trait.
8. That color is a normal variation, not a mutation.
9. Brown eyes is a dominant characteristic.
10. The average farmer today knows about genetics.

Final Test

1. Please don't besiege me with so much work!
2. Can you convert from Fahrenheit to Celsius?
3. Beyond the town is unexplored frontier.
4. Good hygiene helps prevent disease.
5. Is that your boat at the end of the pier?
6. This herbal tea has no caffeine.
7. The sun is actually a large fiery star.
8. I would prefer to mourn privately.
9. My patience was rewarded with a great photograph.
10. We kept the beehive under constant surveillance.
11. This pocket watch is an old family heirloom.
12. You look very attractive in that shade of beige.
13. Will the six o'clock train be the most convenient?
14. An efficient person can finish that task in an hour.
15. Dr. Jekyll became a fiend named Mr. Hyde.
16. A banker is only one kind of financier.
17. Such heinous crimes deserve long prison terms.
18. Anna worked her way up through the hierarchy.
19. I will need a receipt for that purchase.
20. Weekends are a reprieve from long work weeks.

Lesson 26

Objective

To spell words with the endings *ance, ence, ce*

Pretest

1. At what age does adolescence officially begin?
2. What a coincidence to meet you here!
3. A marathon runner needs to build up endurance.
4. The opening performance of the play is tonight.
5. I admire the brilliance of O'Keeffe's paintings.
6. The ambulance pulled up to the hospital entrance.
7. Will the meeting commence promptly at noon?
8. The forest possessed the essence of tranquility.
9. Dr. Thompson recently moved to a new residence.
10. Is it your preference to stay home?
11. Arrogance is not a positive personal quality.
12. I've kept all my correspondence from Uncle Ken.
13. The district attorney presented the evidence.
14. What is the significance of the stripes on the flag?
15. The ballerina moves with grace and elegance.
16. There is little clearance under that bridge.
17. In defiance of my command, my dog refused to sit.
18. You should take your dog to obedience school.
19. Anger and vengeance can lead to many problems.
20. The sudden occurrence of thunder startled the cat.

Game Plan

Page 105
Discuss the Game Plan. As further examples of verbs that take *ance* or *ence* to form nouns, use *allow, exist, excel.* For adjectives ending in *ant* or *ent* that take *ce* to form nouns, use *silent, ignorant, constant.* Then work with students to discuss and define each List Word.

Warm Up

Vocabulary Development (Page 105) Before the exercise, have volunteers identify the List Words that match the synonym *incident (occurrence)* and the definition *act of obeying; submission (obedience).*

Dictionary Skills (Page 105) Have students begin by writing the List Words in alphabetical order. Next, have them separate the words into syllables. Finally, have them check their syllabication in a dictionary.

Practice

Word Analysis (Page 106) To show verbs that do or do not change when endings are added, use *disturb/disturbance; excel/excellence; insure/insurance.* To show how adjectives change, use *silent/silence; ignorant/ignorance.*

Classification (Page 106) To review classification skills, have students select a List Word to complete this series: *proof, confirmation,* ________. *(evidence)*

Word Application (Page 106) Context clues will help students decide which word best completes each sentence. To extend the activity, have them write sentences for the distractors.

Endings **ance, ence, ce** LESSON **26**

Game Plan

The endings **ance**, **ence**, and **ce** usually mean "the act of." The endings **ance** and **ence** are usually added to verbs to make nouns. The ending **ce** is usually added to adjectives to make nouns.

Root Word	Meaning	Plus Ending	New Meaning
occur (v.)	to happen	**occurrence**	the act of occurring (n.)
endure (v.)	to last	**endurance**	the act of lasting (n.)
arrogant (adj.)	haughty	**arrogance**	the act of being haughty (n.)

1. *adolescence*
2. *coincidence*
3. *endurance*
4. *performance*
5. *brilliance*
6. *ambulance*
7. *commence*
8. *essence*
9. *residence*
10. *preference*
11. *arrogance*
12. *correspondence*
13. *evidence*
14. *significance*
15. *elegance*
16. *clearance*
17. *defiance*
18. *obedience*
19. *vengeance*
20. *occurrence*

Warm Up

Vocabulary Development

Write the List Word that matches each synonym or definition.

1. revenge vengeance
2. begin commence
3. teen years adolescence
4. proof evidence
5. importance significance
6. medical vehicle ambulance
7. richness; grace elegance
8. letter writing correspondence
9. one's first choice preference
10. brightness brilliance

Dictionary Skills

Write the List Words in alphabetical order. Then insert slashes to show how they are divided into syllables.

1. ad/o/les/cence
2. am/bu/lance
3. ar/ro/gance
4. bril/liance
5. clear/ance
6. co/in/ci/dence
7. com/mence
8. cor/re/spond/ence
9. de/fi/ance
10. el/e/gance
11. en/dur/ance
12. es/sence
13. ev/i/dence
14. o/be/di/ence
15. oc/cur/rence
16. per/form/ance
17. pref/er/ence
18. res/i/dence
19. sig/nif/i/cance
20. venge/ance

105

Endings **ance, ence, ce** Lesson **26**

Practice

Word Analysis

Form List Words by adding endings to these verbs to make nouns. You will change the form of some verbs before adding the ending.

1. clear clearance
2. correspond correspondence
3. endure endurance
4. prefer preference
5. defy defiance
6. reside residence
7. perform performance
8. occur occurrence

Form List Words by adding endings to these adjectives to make nouns. You will change the form of each adjective before adding the ending.

9. brilliant brilliance
10. coincident coincidence
11. significant significance
12. adolescent adolescence
13. arrogant arrogance
14. elegant elegance
15. obedient obedience
16. evident evidence

Classification

Write a List Word to complete each series.

1. go, start, commence
2. being, substance, essence
3. fire truck, police car, ambulance
4. punishment, fury, vengeance
5. home, apartment, residence
6. infancy, childhood, adolescence
7. pride, disdain, arrogance
8. beauty, refinement, elegance
9. play, concert, performance
10. choice, selection, preference
11. survival, stamina, endurance
12. cards, letters, correspondence

Word Application

Select a List Word from the choices in parentheses to complete each sentence. Write your answer on the line.

1. Ken's brilliance as a student is evident by his A+ average. (vengeance, brilliance)
2. Because it was going out of business, the store had a clearance sale. (coincidence, clearance)
3. The play will commence at two o'clock this afternoon. (commence, occurrence)
4. I took my dog to obedience school because he was difficult to control. (obedience, vengeance)

106

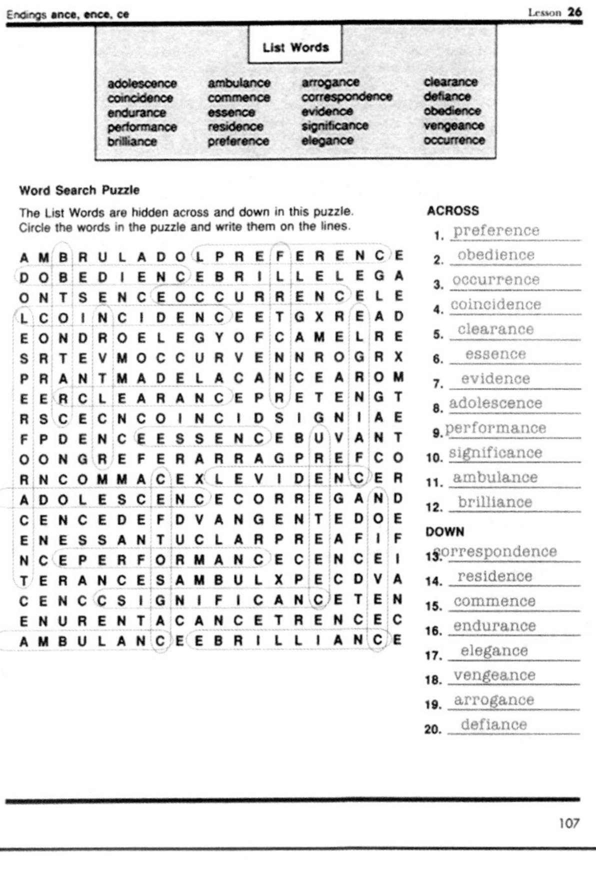

Endings **ance, ence, ce** — Lesson **26**

List Words

adolescence	ambulance	arrogance	clearance
coincidence	commence	correspondence	defiance
endurance	essence	evidence	obedience
performance	residence	significance	vengeance
brilliance	preference	elegance	occurrence

Word Search Puzzle

The List Words are hidden across and down in this puzzle. Circle the words in the puzzle and write them on the lines.

A M B R U L A D O L P R E F E R E N C E
D O B E D I E N C E B R I L L E L E G A
O N T S E N C E O C C U R R E N C E L E
L C O I N C I D E N C E E T G X R E A D
E O N D R O E L E G Y O F C A M E L R E
S R T E V M O C C U R V E N N R O G R X
P R A N T M A D E L A C A N C E A R O M
E E R C L E A R A N C E P R E T E N G T
R S C E C N C O I N C I D S I G N I A E
F P D E N C E E S S E N C E B U V A N T
O O N G R E F E R A R R A G P R E F C O
R N C O M M A C E X L E V I D E N C E R
A D O L E S C E N C E C O R R E G A N D
C E N C E D E F D V A N G E N T E D O E
E N E S S A N T U C L A R P R E A F I F
N C E P E R F O R M A N C E C E N C E I
T E R A N C E S A M B U L X P E C D V A
C E N C C S I G N I F I C A N C E T E N
E N U R E N T A C A N C E T R E N C E C
A M B U L A N C E E B R I L L I A N C E

ACROSS

1. preference
2. obedience
3. occurrence
4. coincidence
5. clearance
6. essence
7. evidence
8. adolescence
9. performance
10. significance
11. ambulance
12. brilliance

DOWN

13. correspondence
14. residence
15. commence
16. endurance
17. elegance
18. vengeance
19. arrogance
20. defiance

107

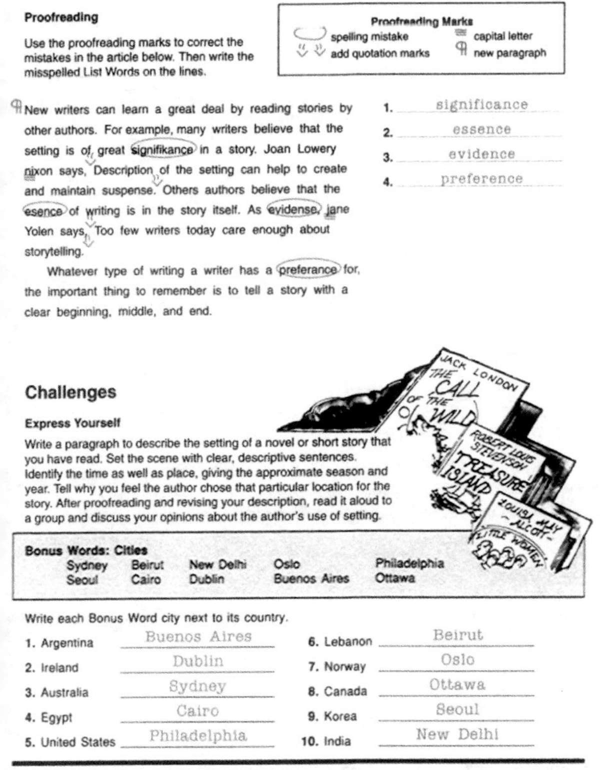

Endings **ance, ence, ce** — Lesson **26**

Proofreading

Use the proofreading marks to correct the mistakes in the article below. Then write the misspelled List Words on the lines.

Proofreading Marks
spelling mistake — capital letter
add quotation marks — new paragraph

¶ New writers can learn a great deal by reading stories by other authors. For example, many writers believe that the setting is of great signifikance in a story. Joan Lowery nixon says, Description of the setting can help to create and maintain suspense. Others authors believe that the esence of writing is in the story itself. As evidense, jane Yolen says, Too few writers today care enough about storytelling.

Whatever type of writing a writer has a preferance for, the important thing to remember is to tell a story with a clear beginning, middle, and end.

1. significance
2. essence
3. evidence
4. preference

Challenges

Express Yourself

Write a paragraph to describe the setting of a novel or short story that you have read. Set the scene with clear, descriptive sentences. Identify the time as well as place, giving the approximate season and year. Tell why you feel the author chose that particular location for the story. After proofreading and revising your description, read it aloud to a group and discuss your opinions about the author's use of setting.

Bonus Words: Cities

Sydney	Beirut	New Delhi	Oslo	Philadelphia
Seoul	Cairo	Dublin	Buenos Aires	Ottawa

Write each Bonus Word city next to its country.

1. Argentina	Buenos Aires	6. Lebanon	Beirut
2. Ireland	Dublin	7. Norway	Oslo
3. Australia	Sydney	8. Canada	Ottawa
4. Egypt	Cairo	9. Korea	Seoul
5. United States	Philadelphia	10. India	New Delhi

108

Word Search Puzzle (Page 107) Make sure students understand that the words appear both horizontally and vertically and that after they find and circle them, they are to write them on the lines accompanying the puzzle.

Proofreading (Page 108) Review with students the proofreading marks they will be using in this lesson, emphasizing the use of quotation marks.

Challenges

Express Yourself (Page 108) Remind students that setting is a combination of time and place. Call on volunteers who have read the pictured books to describe in oral sentences aspects of their settings. Then work with students to draw prewriting cluster maps to brainstorm ideas about the settings of their chosen books. When students have finished writing, provide time for presentation and discussion.

Bonus Words: Cities (Page 108) Help students to locate the cities on a globe or atlas. Point out the continent and country in which each is located. Then have students work in groups to research the cities and create brief paragraphs to describe such aspects of their settings as appearance and climate.

Bonus Word Test

1. Beirut is the capital and chief port of Lebanon.
2. Cairo, the capital of Egypt, is at the Nile delta.
3. A museum of Viking ships exists in Oslo, Norway.
4. Philadelphia was founded in 1682.
5. Ottawa, Canada, is in the province of Ontario.
6. Sydney is Australia's oldest and largest city.
7. The Summer Olympics were held in Seoul, Korea.
8. Buenos Aires, Argentina, was founded in 1536.
9. Dublin, Ireland, is located on the Liffey River.
10. New Delhi is the capital of India.

Final Test

1. My dentist maintains an office at her residence.
2. That grizzly bear fought with vengeance!
3. The Constitution is a document of significance.
4. The actors took a bow after their performance.
5. The essence of Thoreau's message is freedom.
6. Obedience and loyalty are attributes of dogs.
7. Did the witness present the letter as evidence?
8. Exercise will increase your physical endurance.
9. Boys' voices grow deeper during adolescence.
10. Her arrogance made her lose the election.
11. Dad drives an ambulance for the fire department.
12. The road crew is responsible for snow clearance.
13. I enjoy my correspondence with my pen pal.
14. The show will commence after these commercials.
15. By coincidence, Mr. Jones lives on Jones Street.
16. Defiance of the laws may lead to a person's arrest.
17. I admire the brilliance of the poet Maya Angelou.
18. The elegance of the queen's chamber is legendary.
19. Please cast your vote to indicate your preference.
20. Is the sighting of a comet a rare occurrence?

Lesson 27

Objective

To spell words in which *y* is a vowel

Pretest

1. Is *gleeful* an antonym for *sorrowful*?
2. It was unkind of her to make that cynical remark.
3. Pan is a Greek mythical god of forests and fields.
4. The python is a very large, nonpoisonous snake.
5. Write a two-paragraph synopsis of the novel.
6. The crystals in her earrings reflected the sunlight.
7. Use an encyclopedia to verify facts in your report.
8. Is oxygen gas the main component of air?
9. The sauce will solidify if it isn't stirred.
10. Is nylon a synthetic fabric?
11. That cyclone is a violent windstorm!
12. Hydrogen gas explodes when exposed to a flame.
13. A blizzard can paralyze a city.
14. A sympathetic friend cares about your problems.
15. Hot humid summers are typical in the South.
16. This juice can is an example of a cylinder.
17. A pyramid has triangular sides that meet at a point.
18. The physician examined Toby's sore throat.
19. We analyzed the symbolic elements of the painting.
20. Erica played the cymbals in the school orchestra.

Game Plan

Page 109

Discuss the Game Plan with students. Then say the following words: *sinister, lyric, physical, disaster, dynamite, chimes, Wyoming.* Ask students if they can tell whether the long *i* or short *i* sounds in the words are spelled with a *y*. Then write the words on the board. Emphasize that the only way to know whether a word is spelled with a *y* is to study and practice the word. Have students identify the sound for *y* in the List Words. Then help students define the words and have them use the words in oral sentences.

Warm Up

Vocabulary Development (Page 109) When students have finished the exercise, you may wish to have them find antonyms for the following List Words: *mythical (real), sympathetic (uncaring), solidify (melt),* and *synthetic (natural).*

Dictionary Skills (Page 109) If there is sufficient time when students complete the activity, have them look in the dictionary to find the sound spellings for additional List Words.

Practice

Word Analysis (Page 110) Encourage students to refer to the dictionary if they are not sure of the pronunciation of the *y* in any of the List Words.

Classification (Page 110) When students have completed the written work, have them suggest other words that belong in each series.

Analogies (Page 110) To review analogies, write on the board *Hawk is to bird as ________ is to snake.* Elicit from students the List Word that completes the analogy (*python*), and have students explain the answer.

---

y as a Vowel — LESSON 27

Game Plan

When the letter **y** comes in the middle or at the end of a word, it is usually a vowel. The vowel **y** can spell the long **e** sound, the long **i** sound, or the short **i** sound.

everything dry python mythical

In the List Words, **y** spells either the /ī/ sound or the /i/ sound. There is no consistent rule to help you know when a word is spelled with an **i** or with a **y**. You will have to memorize and practice spelling the words.

1. antonym
2. cynical
3. mythical
4. python
5. synopsis
6. crystals
7. encyclopedia
8. oxygen
9. solidify
10. synthetic
11. cyclone
12. hydrogen
13. paralyze
14. sympathetic
15. typical
16. cylinder
17. pyramid
18. physician
19. symbolic
20. cymbals

Warm Up

Vocabulary Development

Write the List Word from column B that matches the definition or synonym in column A.

A		B
1. harden	solidify	paralyze
2. tornado	cyclone	mythical
3. doctor	physician	synthetic
4. outline	synopsis	cyclone
5. usual	typical	encyclopedia
6. mocking	cynical	cymbals
7. legendary	mythical	physician
8. artificial	synthetic	synopsis
9. caring	sympathetic	cynical
10. reference book	encyclopedia	sympathetic
11. instruments	cymbals	typical
12. immobilize	paralyze	solidify

Dictionary Skills

Write the List Word that matches each sound spelling.

1. (äk′ si jən) oxygen
2. (an′ tə nim) antonym
3. (kris′ t'lz) crystals
4. (sim bäl′ ik) symbolic
5. (hī′ drə jən) hydrogen
6. (sil′ ən dər) cylinder
7. (pir′ ə mid) pyramid
8. (pī′ thän) python

109

---

y as a Vowel — Lesson 27

Practice

Word Analysis

Write the List Words in which **y** spells the short **i** sound.

1. antonym
2. cynical
3. mythical
4. synopsis
5. crystals
6. oxygen
7. synthetic
8. sympathetic
9. typical
10. cylinder
11. pyramid
12. physician
13. symbolize
14. cymbals

Write the List Words in which **y** spells the long **i** sound.

15. python
16. encyclopedia
17. solidify
18. cyclone
19. hydrogen
20. paralyze

Did you know?

The Greek word from which we get **encyclopedia** is made up of three words, *en* meaning "in," *kyklos* meaning "a circle," and *paidea* meaning "education." An *encyclopedia* is, therefore, a work that deals with all subjects that lie within the circle of education.

Classification

Write a List Word to complete each series.

1. fake, artificial, synthetic
2. diamonds, minerals, crystals
3. Egypt, sphinx, pyramid
4. thesaurus, dictionary, encyclopedia
5. hurricane, tornado, cyclone
6. surgeon, doctor, physician
7. boa constrictor, rattler, python
8. homonym, synonym, antonym
9. drums, bells, cymbals
10. stun, stupefy, paralyze
11. summary, condensation, synopsis
12. disdainful, scornful, cynical

Analogies

Write a List Word to complete each analogy.

1. Real is to factual as imaginary is to mythical.
2. Oxygen is to breathe as food is to eat.
3. Melt is to solidify as hot is to cold.
4. Sympathetic is to friend as uncaring is to enemy.
5. Square is to box as cylinder is to tin can.

110

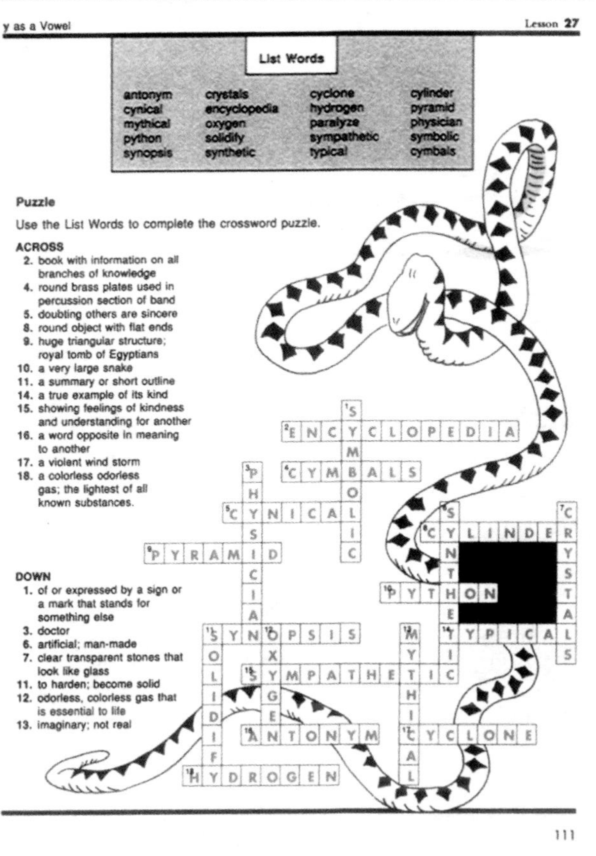

y as a Vowel — Lesson 27

List Words

antonym, cynical, mythical, python, synopsis, crystals, encyclopedia, oxygen, solidify, synthetic, cyclone, hydrogen, paralyze, sympathetic, typical, cylinder, pyramid, physician, symbolic, cymbals

Puzzle

Use the List Words to complete the crossword puzzle.

ACROSS
2. book with information on all branches of knowledge
4. round brass plates used in percussion section of band
5. doubting others are sincere
8. round object with flat ends
9. huge triangular structure; royal tomb of Egyptians
10. a very large snake
11. a summary or short outline
14. a true example of its kind
15. showing feelings of kindness and understanding for another
16. a word opposite in meaning to another
17. a violent wind storm
18. a colorless odorless gas; the lightest of all known substances.

DOWN
1. of or expressed by a sign or a mark that stands for something else
3. doctor
6. artificial; man-made
7. clear transparent stones that look like glass
11. to harden; become solid
12. odorless, colorless gas that is essential to life
13. imaginary; not real

111

y as a Vowel — Lesson 27

Proofreading

Use the proofreading marks to correct the mistakes in the want ad. Then write the misspelled List Words on the lines.

Proofreading Marks	
spelling mistake	delete word
add apostrophe	add space

Americas first computer, called ENIAC, was invented in in the late 1800s. The ENIAC had more than 100,000 parts and was as as large as a two-car garage. But don't let its size fool you. This machine couldnt store the information inone ensyclopedia and burned out tubes wouldquickly parralyze it. Todays tipical computers can outperform ENIAC.

1. encyclopedia
2. paralyze
3. typical

Challenges

Express Yourself

Computers have become indispensable in modern society. People crave faster computers with greater capabilities. Think about what you would like a computer to do. Create an ad that describes this ultra machine and tell why people need it. Give it a name. Then proofread and revise your ad and display it in your class.

Bonus Words: Computers

data processing, graphic, printout, modem, storage, conversion, cursor, documentation, management, structured

Write the Bonus Word that matches each definition clue.

1. computer memory, especially on a disk storage
2. put together systematically structured
3. visual representation graphic
4. written material describing how to run a program or operate a computer documentation
5. the act of controlling or handling management
6. rapid recording and handling of large amounts of information by a computer data processing
7. a device for transmitting computer information by telephone modem
8. the printed output of a computer by a printer onto paper printout
9. a movable indicator light on a computer screen cursor
10. changing a disk from one computer to make it readable by another computer conversion

112

Puzzle (Page 111) Remind students to use each puzzle clue and the number of letter boxes provided to determine each answer.

Proofreading (Page 112) Write *Mias newcomputer isnt to working.* on the board to demonstrate the proofreading marks that students will use to correct the paragraph.

Challenges

Express Yourself (Page 112) Discuss with students what they already know about computers. Then invite students to suggest functions that they would like computers to perform. Encourage students to be creative, and write their best ideas on the board. Students may use these ideas as they complete the writing activity. You may wish to have students assemble their ads in a computer magazine.

Bonus Words: Computers (Page 112) Work with students to define the Bonus Words. Discuss with them how these words apply to computers. If possible, illustrate some or all of the words with a computer demonstration.

Bonus Word Test

1. I converse with computer pals by using a modem.
2. A computer allows management of our records.
3. His computer came with much documentation.
4. This screen provides greater graphic capabilities.
5. Disk conversion makes computers compatible.
6. This program is structured for beginners.
7. This hard disk provides 40 megabytes of storage.
8. The store sent me a printout of my charges.
9. Our data processing department is upstairs.
10. Julio moved the cursor to the third line of the text.

Final Test

1. A heart is a symbolic expression of love.
2. Som built a pyramid of cards on the kitchen table.
3. We'll briefly paralyze the lion so that we can tag it.
4. Is a tornado an example of a cyclone?
5. Karen gave us a synopsis of the play she saw.
6. The Land of the Little People is a mythical place.
7. An antonym for *exciting* is *dull.*
8. What a loud crashing sound those cymbals make!
9. She was sympathetic to everyone's complaints.
10. Hydrogen is the lightest of all known substances.
11. Crystals were once used to build radios.
12. A cynical person mocks other people's ideas.
13. A python can coil around its victim and crush it.
14. Mercury does not solidify at room temperature.
15. I found information about Asia in the encyclopedia.
16. Are red blood cells rich in oxygen?
17. Synthetic fibers are man-made substances.
18. A typical picnic includes chicken and watermelon.
19. The young physician will open a walk-in clinic.
20. Is a cylinder round with two flat ends?

Lesson 28

Objective

To spell words from music

Pretest

1. The singer sang an aria from my favorite opera.
2. Do the number of decibels represent the volume?
3. After playing, the maestro bowed to the audience.
4. The conductor stood at the podium.
5. Six trumpets played the sharp staccato notes.
6. Our school auditorium has a large stage.
7. For an encore, the band played its theme song.
8. Listen to this medley of songs about summer.
9. I play violin for two groups, a trio and a quartet.
10. Our new car radio has stereophonic sound.
11. Is the ballerina in pink the lead dancer?
12. Last week a local jazz ensemble gave a concert.
13. This is easy to sing, because it is so melodic.
14. My next selection will be a Russian rhapsody.
15. A synthesizer can sound like many instruments.
16. My brother wanted me to hear this concerto.
17. The fugue is a form of music best for many voices.
18. Does the pianist think that the piano needs tuning?
19. That music has great rhythm!
20. On a xylophone, each bar makes a different sound.

Game Plan

Page 113
After students have read the Game Plan, discuss which List Words are familiar and which are not. Through discussion and dictionary use, help them understand the meanings of the words. Discuss the spelling of each word and how students can best remember it.

Warm Up

Vocabulary Development (Page 113) Encourage students to check their answers against the spelling and definitions in their dictionaries.

Dictionary Skills (Page 113) To check mastery of respelling symbols and letters, encourage students to try to complete this exercise without any review. When written work is done, discuss any problems they had.

Practice

Word Analysis (Page 114) As an extension activity, you may wish to have students find other words beginning with *deci, quar, syn, pod,* and *stereo.*

Word Application (Page 114) Point out to students that although more than one answer might possibly be correct, one word will make the most sense in each sentence. When written work is complete, discuss the answers and the reasons for them.

Words from Music — LESSON 28

Game Plan

The world of music has a language of its own. Many musical words, such as medley, are also used in other contexts. These List Words are all related to music. Many of the words follow spelling rules that you know. Some will have to be learned by memory.

1. aria
2. decibels
3. maestro
4. podium
5. staccato
6. auditorium
7. encore
8. medley
9. quartet
10. stereophonic
11. ballerina
12. ensemble
13. melodic
14. rhapsody
15. synthesizer
16. concerto
17. fugue
18. pianist
19. rhythm
20. xylophone

Warm Up

Vocabulary Development

Write the List Word that matches each definition.

1. electronic sound reproducer synthesizer
2. reproduction of sound with two speakers stereophonic
3. form or pattern of music rhythm
4. one who plays the piano pianist
5. selection of songs played as one piece medley
6. room where an audience gathers auditorium
7. female ballet dancer ballerina
8. selection for solo instrument plus orchestra concerto
9. master composer or conductor maestro
10. group of singers or musicians ensemble

Dictionary Skills

Write the List Word that matches each sound-spelling.

1. (stə kät′ ō) staccato	6. (mə läd′ ik) melodic
2. (kwôr tet′) quartet	7. (är′ ē ə) aria
3. (des′ ə bəlz) decibels	8. (fyo͞og) fugue
4. (rap′ sə dē) rhapsody	9. (äng′ kôr) encore
5. (zī′ lə fōn) xylophone	10. (pō′ dē əm) podium

113

Words from Music — Lesson 28

Practice

Word Analysis

Write the List Word that contains the same prefix or root as the word given.

1. telephone xylophone	5. decimal decibels
2. quarter quartet	6. piano pianist
3. stereogram stereophonic	7. podiatry podium
4. synthetic synthesizer	8. audition auditorium

Write the List Words containing the elements given below.

ia	ue or ae
9. aria	11. maestro
10. pianist	12. fugue

Write the List Words containing one or two syllables.

13. maestro	16. quartet
14. encore	17. fugue
15. medley	18. rhythm

Did you know?

A **rhapsody** in ancient Greece was a long epic poem that was recited without interruption. It came from a word meaning "one who strings songs together," from a Greek word meaning "to stitch." Probably each *rhapsody* was so long as to seem like many songs "stitched together."

Word Application

Write a List Word to complete each sentence.

1. The ballerina strode to the center stage and began to dance.
2. The diva will sing an aria from the opera "La Boheme."
3. A synthesizer can sound like any of a number of instruments.
4. Tina taught Matt how to play a scale on his toy xylophone.
5. Often the decibels at a rock concert can be harmful to hearing.
6. The chorale's last selection was a medley of three popular songs.
7. As the pianist sat down at the keyboard, the audience cheered.
8. Use the headset and you can listen in stereophonic sound.
9. At the end of the concert, the audience asked for an encore.
10. Nick stood at the podium, ready to conduct his first symphony.
11. The lively rhythm soon had audience members tapping their feet.
12. For the final concert, every seat in the auditorium was filled.

114

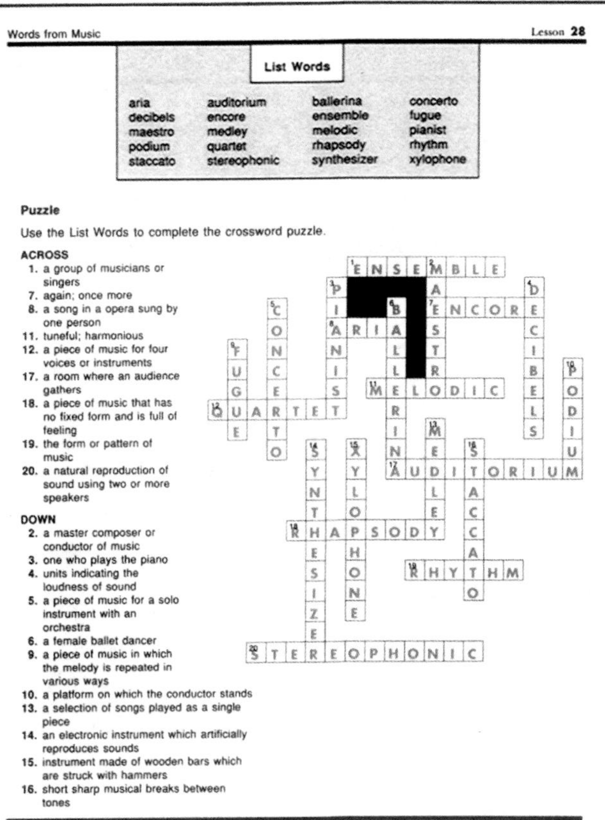
Words from Music — Lesson 28

List Words

aria, decibels, maestro, podium, staccato, auditorium, encore, medley, quartet, stereophonic, ballerina, ensemble, melodic, rhapsody, synthesizer, concerto, fugue, pianist, rhythm, xylophone

Puzzle

Use the List Words to complete the crossword puzzle.

ACROSS

1. a group of musicians or singers
7. again; once more
8. a song in a opera sung by one person
11. tuneful; harmonious
12. a piece of music for four voices or instruments
17. a room where an audience gathers
18. a piece of music that has no fixed form and is full of feeling
19. the form or pattern of music
20. a natural reproduction of sound using two or more speakers

DOWN

2. a master composer or conductor of music
3. one who plays the piano
4. units indicating the loudness of sound
5. a piece of music for a solo instrument with an orchestra
6. a female ballet dancer
9. a piece of music in which the melody is repeated in various ways
10. a platform on which the conductor stands
13. a selection of songs played as a single piece
14. an electronic instrument which artificially reproduces sounds
15. instrument made of wooden bars which are struck with hammers
16. short sharp musical breaks between tones

115

Words from Music — Lesson 28

Proofreading

Use the proofreading marks to correct the mistakes in the article below. Then write the misspelled List Words on the lines.

Proofreading Marks: spelling mistake; add period; add comma; small letter

One of the most complex forms of Western Music is the fuege Developed as an independent form of music in the 1600s it is performed by an ensembel of voices that sing different parts at different times The rythem is often quite fast making the notes sound somewhat stakato This form of music reached new heights when maistro J.S. Bach used it in his Compositions

1. fugue
2. ensemble
3. rhythm
4. staccato
5. maestro

Challenges

Express Yourself

Write a brochure for a season of concerts or musical events for a local auditorium. Include a listing of the types of music the audience can expect to hear, as well as a brief description of the guest artists and bands. Try to convince the reader to buy tickets. After proofreading and revising your brochure, copy it neatly on a folded piece of paper. With a group, discuss the persuasiveness of your brochure and any changes that could be made to improve it.

Bonus Words: Music

percussion, octave, operetta, dulcimer, harpsichord, baritone, soprano, trombone, metronome, troubadour

Write Bonus Words to answer the questions.

Which words name instruments?

1. dulcimer
2. harpsichord
3. trombone

Which word names the eighth tone above or below another tone?

4. octave

Which word names a clockwork device?

5. metronome

Which words name or describe a singer?

6. baritone
7. soprano
8. troubadour

Which word names the group to which a drum belongs?

9. percussion

Which word names a kind of light opera?

10. operetta

116

Puzzle (Page 115) Remind students that each answer has two clues: its definition and its number of letters.

Proofreading (Page 116) Write this sentence on the board and use it to demonstrate the use of the proofreading marks in this lesson: *Although the Concirt was sold out there were empty seats in the Auditorium*

Challenges

Express Yourself (Page 116) Encourage students to think of the kinds of music they would like to hear or that their parents might like to hear. Discuss musical events that they have seen advertised locally. Tell them that they can invent guest artists and bands, or else name and describe real ones. When students have finished, you may wish to create a display of their brochures.

Bonus Words: Music (Page 116) Explain that all the Bonus Words are related to music. If available, display a dictionary of musical terms. Otherwise, use any standard dictionary to research the meaning of unfamiliar words. Encourage students to share their own musical experiences and to use the Bonus Words in oral sentences. Then have them complete the Bonus Word activity.

Bonus Word Test

1. My mother is a soprano in our local chorus.
2. The singer accompanied himself on a dulcimer.
3. A drum is a percussion instrument.
4. The queen enjoyed the songs of the troubadour.
5. Each marcher in the first row played a trombone.
6. My brother has a beautiful baritone voice.
7. My fingers can span one octave on a piano.
8. An operetta combines music and dialogue.
9. A harpsichord sounds a little like a piano.
10. The beat of the metronome helps me keep time.

Final Test

1. Listen while they play the first concerto.
2. A fugue has repetitive parts for several voices.
3. That concert pianist practices six hours a day.
4. Tap out the rhythm on the bongo drums.
5. Is a xylophone played with mallets?
6. Can a synthesizer sound like an entire orchestra?
7. Is that piece called *Rhapsody in Blue*?
8. The musical had many upbeat melodic tunes.
9. Each member of the ensemble wore black.
10. A ballerina must be strong and graceful.
11. The opera has a beautiful aria!
12. This gauge shows the number of decibels.
13. When the maestro raised his hands, we were quiet.
14. The conductor stood on the podium and bowed.
15. The music had a staccato sound, like a typewriter.
16. This auditorium holds about a thousand people.
17. For an encore, the singer sang an old favorite.
18. Here is a medley of popular Beatles' songs.
19. My neighbor plays the cello in a string quartet.
20. This television has stereophonic sound.

Lesson 29

Objective

To spell words with Spanish derivations

Pretest

1. They built the wall with adobe bricks.
2. While in Mexico, June attended a fiesta.
3. The palmetto tree cast a shadow on the lawn.
4. The leaves on the poinsettia plant are poisonous.
5. John made me a delicious tamale for lunch.
6. I went into the cabana to change my clothes.
7. Let's find a shady spot for a brief siesta.
8. Did Roger name his palomino "Goldie"?
9. The renegade jumped onto his horse.
10. Marlene wrapped beans and lettuce in a tortilla.
11. A river flowed through the canyon.
12. Have you seen Joel's pet iguana?
13. Please call me back, pronto!
14. A sombrero is a type of hat.
15. The recipe called for two teaspoons of vanilla.
16. The coyote is a member of the dog family.
17. Does a jaguar resemble a leopard?
18. The pimento is a small red pepper.
19. Cattle often stampede if they are frightened.
20. Students work in the college cafeteria.

Game Plan

Page 117

Read and discuss the Game Plan with students. For additional examples of words in the English language with Spanish roots, use *ranch, patio, mustang, barracuda, pinto, burro, burrito.* Ask students to suggest others. Stress the pronunciation/spelling "tricks" that Spanish words can create for English-speaking people, and point out that many Spanish words end with the long *e* or long *o* sound. Also point out that *pimento* is the English spelling of the Spanish word *pimiento.* Then relate the discussion of the List Words and work with students to define each one.

Warm Up

Vocabulary Development (Page 117) Before the exercise, have volunteers suggest two List Words that are members of the category *Mexican food. (tamale, tortilla)*

Dictionary Skills (Page 117) Before students begin, have a volunteer summarize the function of guide words and point out examples in a dictionary.

Practice

Word Analysis (Page 118) To extend this activity, you may wish to have students separate the words into syllables, using dictionaries to check their work.

Word Application (Page 118) Urge students to use context clues to find the List Word that best fits in each blank.

Words with Spanish Derivations — LESSON 29

Game Plan

The English language has gained many words from the Spanish language. This is particularly true of American English due to the influence of early Spanish settlements in the Southwest, and the modern influx of language and culture brought by Hispanics from Mexico, Puerto Rico, and Cuba.

The List Words are derived from Spanish words. Due to different vowel sounds, English-speaking people can find them tricky to spell. Coyote and adobe are examples of words with such "spelling tricks."

1. adobe
2. fiesta
3. palmetto
4. poinsettia
5. tamale
6. cabana
7. siesta
8. palomino
9. renegade
10. tortilla
11. canyon
12. iguana
13. pronto
14. sombrero
15. vanilla
16. coyote
17. jaguar
18. pimento
19. stampede
20. cafeteria

Warm Up

Vocabulary Development

Write the List Word that names a member of each category.

1. sweet flavors	vanilla	6. horses	palomino
2. celebrations	fiesta	7. hats	sombrero
3. building supplies	adobe	8. big cats	jaguar
4. lizards	iguana	9. flowers	poinsettia
5. restaurants	cafeteria	10. trees	palmetto

Dictionary Skills

Write the List Word that comes between each pair of dictionary guide words.

1. cab/cackle — cabana
2. pill/pine — pimento
3. tablet/top — tamale
4. pot/prune — pronto
5. clue/crayon — coyote
6. squash/steam — stampede
7. reach/repeat — renegade
8. set/sign — siesta
9. cake/coat — canyon
10. title/tune — tortilla

117

Words with Spanish Derivations — Lesson 29

Practice

Word Analysis

Write List Words under the correct categories.

Words ending with a	Words ending with e	Words ending with o
1. fiesta	9. adobe	14. palmetto
2. poinsettia	10. tamale	15. palomino
3. cabana	11. renegade	16. pronto
4. siesta	12. coyote	17. sombrero
5. tortilla	13. stampede	18. pimento
6. iguana		
7. vanilla		
8. cafeteria		

Did you know?

Siesta is a Spanish word that comes from a Latin phrase, *sexta hora*, meaning "the sixth hour" after sunrise. This is about noon, usually the hottest part of the day in Spain and many Latin American countries.

Word Application

Write the List Words to complete this letter.

Dear Miguel,

The trip was fantastic! I rode a golden palomino named Pronto. We rode through a steep, rocky canyon all day. I saw an iguana and other small lizards! We were thrilled to see a jaguar, which looked like a leopard. We ate dinner at a cafeteria in the village of Ortiz. For my first Mexican meal I had a tamale and a tortilla. Then we settled down for a siesta. It was so beautiful. See you soon.

Your friend,
Susan

118

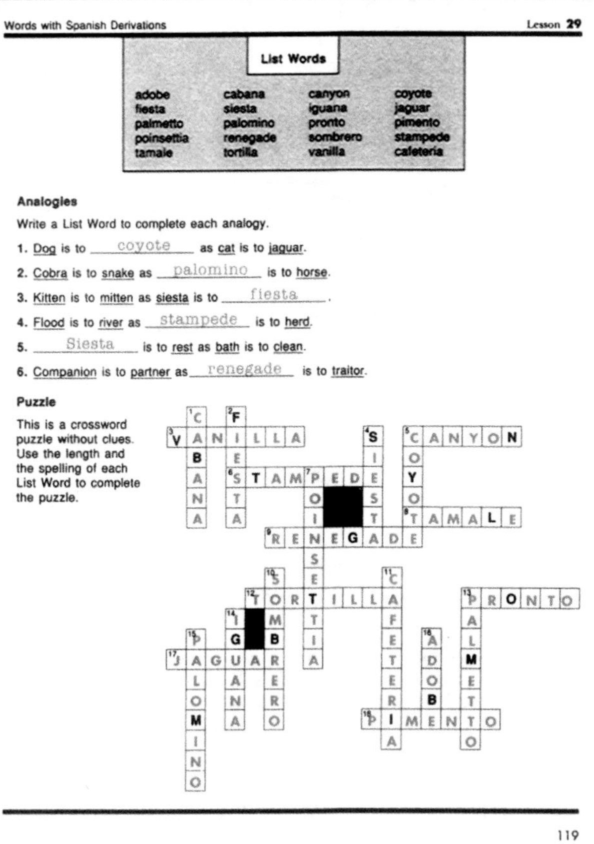

Words with Spanish Derivations Lesson **29**

List Words

adobe	cabana	canyon	coyote
fiesta	siesta	iguana	jaguar
palmetto	palomino	pronto	pimento
poinsettia	renegade	sombrero	stampede
tamale	tortilla	vanilla	cafeteria

Analogies

Write a List Word to complete each analogy.

1. Dog is to coyote as cat is to jaguar.
2. Cobra is to snake as palomino is to horse.
3. Kitten is to mitten as siesta is to fiesta.
4. Flood is to river as stampede is to herd.
5. Siesta is to rest as bath is to clean.
6. Companion is to partner as renegade is to traitor.

Puzzle

This is a crossword puzzle without clues. Use the length and the spelling of each List Word to complete the puzzle.

119

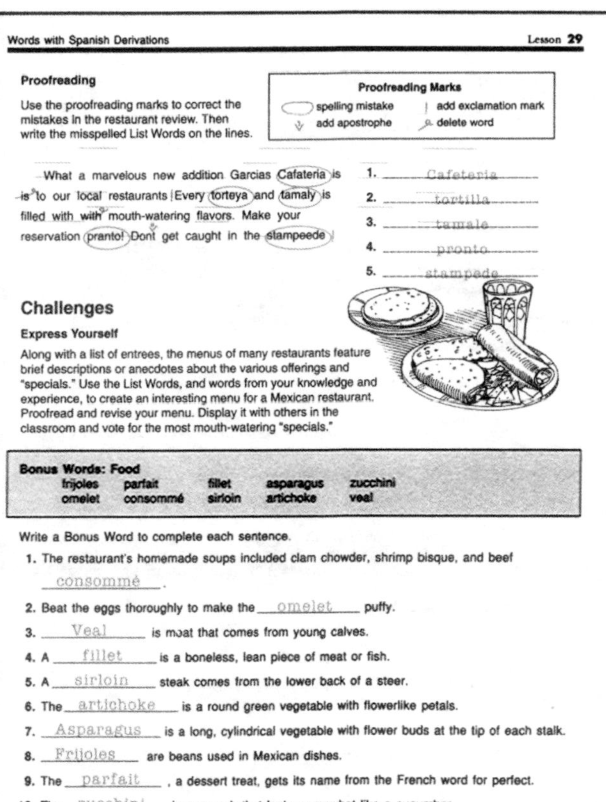

Words with Spanish Derivations Lesson **29**

Proofreading

Use the proofreading marks to correct the mistakes in the restaurant review. Then write the misspelled List Words on the lines.

Proofreading Marks
spelling mistake · add exclamation mark · add apostrophe · delete word

What a marvelous new addition Garcias Cafateria is is to our local restaurants Every torteya and tamaly is filled with with mouth-watering flavors. Make your reservation pranto! Dont get caught in the stampeede

1. Cafeteria
2. tortilla
3. tamale
4. pronto
5. stampede

Challenges

Express Yourself

Along with a list of entrees, the menus of many restaurants feature brief descriptions or anecdotes about the various offerings and "specials." Use the List Words, and words from your knowledge and experience, to create an interesting menu for a Mexican restaurant. Proofread and revise your menu. Display it with others in the classroom and vote for the most mouth-watering "specials."

Bonus Words: Food

frijoles	parfait	fillet	asparagus	zucchini
omelet	consommé	sirloin	artichoke	veal

Write a Bonus Word to complete each sentence.

1. The restaurant's homemade soups included clam chowder, shrimp bisque, and beef consommé.
2. Beat the eggs thoroughly to make the omelet puffy.
3. Veal is moat that comes from young calves.
4. A fillet is a boneless, lean piece of meat or fish.
5. A sirloin steak comes from the lower back of a steer.
6. The artichoke is a round green vegetable with flowerlike petals.
7. Asparagus is a long, cylindrical vegetable with flower buds at the tip of each stalk.
8. Frijoles are beans used in Mexican dishes.
9. The parfait, a dessert treat, gets its name from the French word for perfect.
10. The zucchini is a squash that looks somewhat like a cucumber.

120

Analogies (Page 119) To review analogies, have students select *Cuba, France,* or *Germany* to complete the analogy *English is to Great Britain as Spanish is to* ________.

Puzzle (Page 119) Urge students to count the number of spaces in each answer blank to help them to solve the puzzle. Point out that each List Word appears once.

Proofreading (Page 120) Review the use of the proofreading marks students will be using in this lesson.

Challenges

Express Yourself (Page 120) If possible, display a menu that features descriptions or anecdotes about some of the dishes. Or, work with students to write a sample description or anecdote about a special cheeseburger. Students may enjoy creating complete menu layouts with illustrations of the food or pictures of the restaurant interior. Provide time for presentation and discussion.

Bonus Words: Food (Page 120) Have students find the definitions of Bonus Words in dictionaries. Ask volunteers to use the words in oral sentences. Provide time for students to discuss their eating and cooking experiences with each food.

Bonus Word Test

1. Jules filled the omelet with mushrooms and onions.
2. Consommé is served either hot or cold.
3. Roberto ordered a sirloin steak and a salad.
4. I steamed the artichoke for forty-five minutes.
5. She served the veal with a cheese sauce.
6. This zucchini is almost as big as a baseball bat!
7. George has a large asparagus patch in his garden.
8. Al filled the tacos with frijoles and lettuce.
9. For dessert, I'll have a strawberry parfait.
10. I'd like a fillet of halibut for dinner tonight.

Final Test

1. Maria felt refreshed after her midday siesta.
2. They made baskets out of palmetto leaves.
3. I've seen snakes and lizards in that canyon.
4. John, finish your homework, pronto!
5. The palomino has a glossy golden coat.
6. Kate took a picture of a jaguar.
7. Add a teaspoon of vanilla to the cake batter.
8. The cafeteria on Elm Street serves delicious soup.
9. That stampede of horses caused a lot of dust!
10. Adobe bricks dry and harden in the sun.
11. Are the extra beach towels stored in the cabana?
12. The poinsettia was named after Joel R. Poinsett.
13. Use ground corn to make tortilla flour.
14. An iguana scurried across the big rock.
15. Is the coyote a protected animal?
16. Add two teaspoons of diced pimento to the sauce.
17. A sombrero has a broad brim to provide shade.
18. For the fiesta, we hung colored lights on the trees.
19. May I order a tamale, please?
20. The renegade horse ran away.

Lesson 30

Objective

To review spelling rules and patterns from Lessons 25–29

Game Plan

Page 121

Read and discuss the Game Plan. Reinforce by asking students to name other words to illustrate the information summarized in each of the five sections. You may wish to have students turn back to the opening pages of Lessons 25–29 to review each Game Plan separately and to apply it to its full selection of List Words.

Practice

Lesson 25 (Page 121) Have students apply the rules of the "*I* before *E*" rhyme to each List Word, telling which words follow the rule and which are exceptions. (Exceptions include *heirloom, efficient, caffeine, financier.*) Point out the additional write-on lines to students and encourage them to add two words from Lesson 25 that they found especially difficult, or select and assign certain words that seemed to be difficult for everyone. (Repeat this procedure for each lesson review that follows in the Replay.) To extend the exercise, have students create similar context-clue sentences for the additional words.

Lesson 26 (Page 122) Use the List Words to stress the similar sounds of endings *ance* and *ence,* urging students to memorize the spellings to avoid errors. Have students use the words in oral sentences to check comprehension of the definitions.

Lesson 27 (Page 122) Before the exercise, discuss these words to review the different sounds that the vowel *y* stands for: *antonym, solidify, energy, hydrogen, cymbals.*

Lesson 28 (Page 123) Before the exercise, have students turn back to the complete selection of List Words in Lesson 28. Discuss the definitions of each musical term and have students use the words in oral sentences. Point out the "spelling tricks" that occur.

Lesson 29 (Page 123) Urge students to use context clues to find the correct words. To extend, have students challenge each other with similar "wrong word" sentences, using the List Words they added to their lists.

Mixed Practice (Page 124) To extend the activity, select other words from the Replay lists and have students add them to the categories that are given or make up new categories as appropriate.

Test Yourself (Page 124) You may wish to write further test items on the board to include or to emphasize any words that students found particularly difficult.

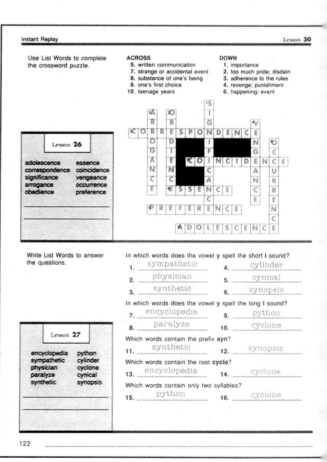

INSTANT REPLAY — LESSON **30**

Game Plan

Most words containing **ie** or **ei** follow the rules in this rhyme:

I before **E**, except after **C**,
Unless sounded like **A**, as in neighbor and weigh.

Be careful of exceptions, which include efficient and caffeine.

The endings **ance**, **ence**, and **ce** usually mean the act of. The endings **ance** and **ence** are usually added to verbs to make nouns, as in endure/endurance and prefer/preference. The ending **ce** is usually added to an adjective to form a noun, as in brilliant/brilliance. Words ending in **ance** and **ence** can be difficult to spell because the endings sound alike.

The vowel **y** can stand for the long **e** sound in truly, the long **i** sound in dry, or the short **i** sound in myth. Don't be fooled by **y** when it sounds like another vowel.

The field of music has a broad vocabulary of technical terms, such as ensemble, quartet, and staccato. Many of the words follow standard spelling patterns. Others must be memorized.

Many English words have been derived or borrowed from the Spanish language. Due to the different sounds of vowels in English and Spanish, such words as coyote and adobe contain "spelling tricks" that must be memorized.

Practice

Write a List Word to complete each sentence.

1. The president had the highest position in the hierarchy of company management.
2. Andrew Mellon was a famous American financier who amassed a fortune through shrewd investments.
3. The volcano created a fiery glow in the night sky.
4. We'll meet at a time that is convenient for both of us.
5. The lawyer appreciated the efforts of her efficient secretary.
6. The police kept the bus station under constant surveillance.
7. This ring is a valuable heirloom that I received from my grandmother.
8. Coffee and tea contain the chemical caffeine.
9. Completing a long and difficult job requires patience.
10. Toothpaste and floss are tools for dental hygiene.

Lesson 25

heirloom	convenient
efficient	financier
hierarchy	hygiene
caffeine	fiery
patience	surveillance

121

Instant Replay — Lesson **30**

Use List Words to complete the crossword puzzle.

ACROSS
5. written communication
7. strange or accidental event
8. substance of one's being
9. one's first choice
10. teenage years

DOWN
1. importance
2. too much pride; disdain
3. adherence to the rules
4. revenge; punishment
6. happening; event

Lesson 26

adolescence	essence
correspondence	coincidence
significance	vengeance
arrogance	occurrence
obedience	preference

Write List Words to answer the questions.

In which words does the vowel y spell the short i sound?

1. sympathetic 4. cylinder
2. physician 5. cynical
3. synthetic 6. synopsis

In which words does the vowel y spell the long i sound?

7. encyclopedia 9. python
8. paralyze 10. cyclone

Which words contain the prefix syn?

11. synthetic 12. synopsis

Which words contain the root **cyclo**?

13. encyclopedia 14. cyclone

Which words contain only two syllables?

15. python 16. cyclone

Lesson 27

encyclopedia	python
sympathetic	cylinder
physician	cyclone
paralyze	cynical
synthetic	synopsis

122

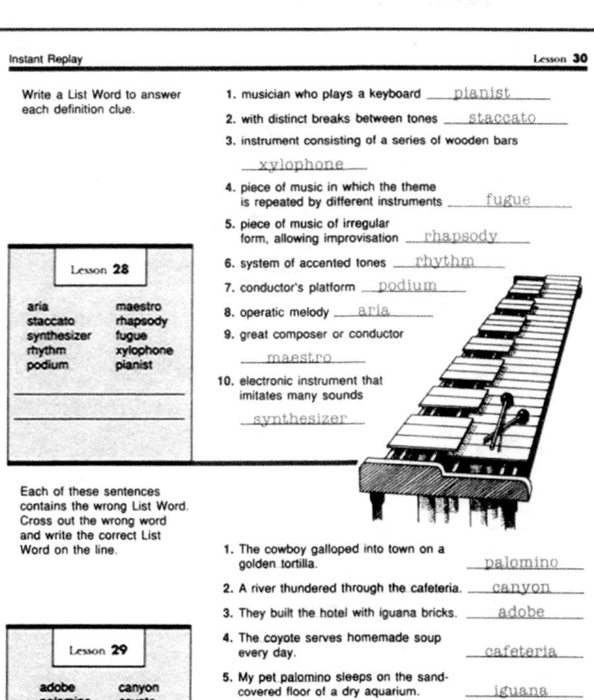
Instant Replay — Lesson 30

Write a List Word to answer each definition clue.

1. musician who plays a keyboard pianist
2. with distinct breaks between tones staccato
3. instrument consisting of a series of wooden bars xylophone
4. piece of music in which the theme is repeated by different instruments fugue
5. piece of music of irregular form, allowing improvisation rhapsody
6. system of accented tones rhythm
7. conductor's platform podium
8. operatic melody aria
9. great composer or conductor maestro
10. electronic instrument that imitates many sounds synthesizer

Lesson 28

aria	maestro
staccato	rhapsody
synthesizer	fugue
rhythm	xylophone
podium	pianist

Each of these sentences contains the wrong List Word. Cross out the wrong word and write the correct List Word on the line.

1. The cowboy galloped into town on a golden tortilla. palomino
2. A river thundered through the cafeteria. canyon
3. They built the hotel with iguana bricks. adobe
4. The coyote serves homemade soup every day. cafeteria
5. My pet palomino sleeps on the sand-covered floor of a dry aquarium. iguana
6. We enjoyed a poinsettia after lunch. siesta
7. It's hard to believe that my gentle little kitten is from the same family as a wild, snarling adobe. jaguar
8. The siesta was covered with red blossoms. poinsettia
9. Wrap the meat inside a canyon. tortilla

Lesson 29

adobe	canyon
palomino	coyote
tortilla	iguana
jaguar	siesta
poinsettia	cafeteria

123

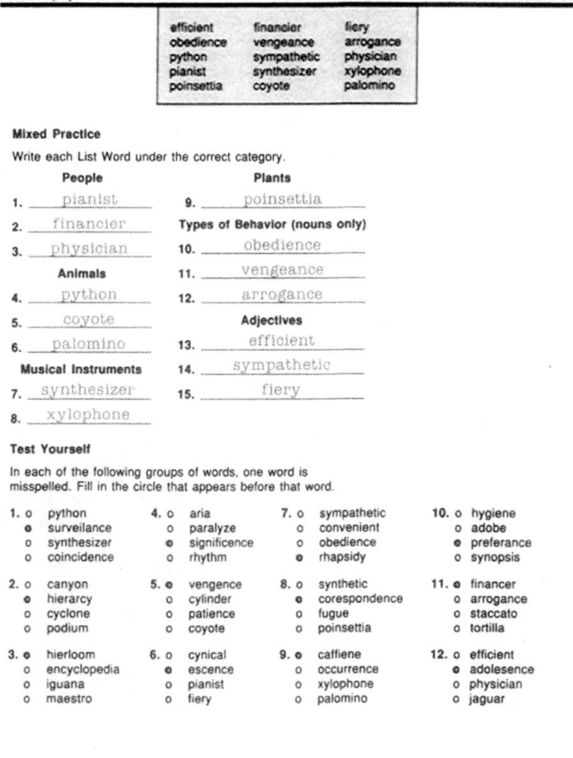
Instant Replay — Lesson 30

efficient	financier	fiery
obedience	vengeance	arrogance
python	sympathetic	physician
pianist	synthesizer	xylophone
poinsettia	coyote	palomino

Mixed Practice

Write each List Word under the correct category.

People
1. pianist
2. financier
3. physician

Animals
4. python
5. coyote
6. palomino

Musical Instruments
7. synthesizer
8. xylophone

Plants
9. poinsettia

Types of Behavior (nouns only)
10. obedience
11. vengeance
12. arrogance

Adjectives
13. efficient
14. sympathetic
15. fiery

Test Yourself

In each of the following groups of words, one word is misspelled. Fill in the circle that appears before that word.

1. ○ python ● surveilance ○ synthesizer ○ coincidence
2. ○ canyon ● hierarcy ○ cyclone ○ podium
3. ● hierloom ○ encyclopedia ○ iguana ○ maestro
4. ○ aria ○ paralyze ● significence ○ rhythm
5. ● vengence ○ cylinder ○ patience ○ coyote
6. ○ cynical ● escence ○ pianist ○ fiery
7. ○ sympathetic ○ convenient ○ obedience ● rhapsidy
8. ○ synthetic ● corespondence ○ fugue ○ poinsettia
9. ● caffiene ○ occurrence ○ xylophone ○ palomino
10. ○ hygiene ○ adobe ● preferance ○ synopsis
11. ● financer ○ arrogance ○ staccato ○ tortilla
12. ○ efficient ● adolesence ○ physician ○ jaguar

124

Final Replay Test

1. Caffeine can inhibit a person's ability to sleep.
2. The new shopping mall is at a convenient location.
3. The police put the house under surveillance.
4. A lawyer explains the significance of the evidence.
5. The family took their dog to obedience school.
6. Adolescence is a time of growth and discovery.
7. The essence of friendship is trust.
8. Did Fred check the facts in an encyclopedia?
9. Polio, an infectious disease, can paralyze a person.
10. At the zoo, Michelle was fascinated by a python.
11. Weather forecasters warned of a cyclone.
12. Helen wrote a concise synopsis of the movie.
13. The soprano sang a beautiful aria!
14. Bill plays the drums and Kei plays the synthesizer.
15. Conductor Sarah Caldwell approached the podium.
16. Was the fugue written by Bach?
17. Jim ordered a tortilla at the Mexican restaurant.
18. Roy Rogers' palomino was named Trigger.
19. Adobe bricks harden in the sun.
20. Let's meet in the cafeteria around one o'clock.
21. Ms. Wan is fifth in the company hierarchy.
22. It takes patience and practice to learn how to ski.
23. The hostess wore a fiery red dress.
24. The friends shared a correspondence for years.
25. The play relates hope, vengeance, and despair.
26. What is your preference for dinner tonight?
27. Too much power led to the emperor's arrogance.
28. Is nylon a synthetic material?
29. The song is accented by a series of staccato notes.
30. As a young composer, Mozart was a maestro.
31. The pianist played an étude by Chopin.
32. A jaguar resembles a leopard.
33. The iguana dozed on a rock in the sun.
34. It is so relaxing to take a siesta after lunch!
35. This painting is a valuable family heirloom.
36. A financier spoke to us about the stock market.
37. By coincidence, the two friends met on the train.
38. Alicia's friend was sympathetic about her mistake.
39. Does a tin can have the shape of a cylinder?
40. A cynical person is ruled by doubt and suspicion.
41. Are snare drums and cymbals rhythm instruments?
42. One of Gershwin's famous songs is a rhapsody.
43. A poinsettia may be white, pink, or red.
44. We heard a coyote howling high up in the hills.
45. I took these photographs in the canyon.
46. The occurrence of snow is very rare in Florida.
47. Becky proved herself to be an efficient sales clerk.
48. The child's favorite toy is a miniature xylophone.
49. A veterinarian is a physician who treats animals.
50. Daphne wants a career in dental hygiene.

Lesson 31

Objective

To spell words with Latin roots

Pretest

1. Do carnivorous animals eat meat?
2. A mirage is just an illusion.
3. The clown's antics in the arena were ludicrous.
4. The lawyer began to suspect that Mr. Wu was lying.
5. A versatile musician can play many instruments.
6. A rabbit can elude a fox.
7. She clung to an illusive hope of winning.
8. In retrospect, Elena understood why she failed.
9. In the midst of the tempest, the boat keeled over.
10. Both my grandparents exude youthful vitality.
11. I used extemporaneous remarks in my speech.
12. Tom is an introvert and prefers to be alone.
13. Was the lifeguard able to revive the swimmer?
14. All life on earth is temporal and will eventually end.
15. Most milk is enriched with vitamin D.
16. An extrovert is an outgoing person.
17. The inverse of upside-down is rightside-up.
18. The fireworks display was spectacular!
19. We stayed in a temporary shelter after the fire.
20. The sunset was a vivid orange-red color.

Game Plan

Page 125

Work with students to identify the Latin roots in the following words: *voracious, diversion, spectator, contemporary, vivacious, delude.* Discuss how the meaning of each word is related to the meaning of the Latin root. Then apply the discussion to the List Words. Be sure students notice the spelling patterns in *retrospect, introvert,* and *extrovert,* words that are often pronounced as if they were spelled with *a* instead of *o.*

Warm Up

Word Analysis (Page 125) Encourage students to refer to the List Words to determine the words with the same roots.

Vocabulary Development (Page 125) To review synonyms, have students identify the List Words that are synonyms for the following words: *meat-eater (carnivorous), opposite (inverse), bright (vivid).*

Practice

Word Application (Page 126) Students may wish to review the meanings of the Latin roots in the Game Plan before completing this activity.

Classification (Page 126) When students have finished the written work, encourage them to suggest other words for each series.

Latin Roots — LESSON 31

Game Plan

By recognizing Latin roots in the List Words, you can make an intelligent guess at the meaning of the words.

Latin Roots (meaning)	English Word
vor (devour, eat)	**carnivorous** (meat eater)
lud, lus (play)	**ludicrous** (ridiculous)
viv, vit (life, live)	**vitality** (full of life)
spect (see)	**spectacular** (showy)
ver (turn)	**extrovert** (out-going)
temp (time)	**temporary** (for a short time)

1. carnivorous
2. illusion
3. ludicrous
4. suspect
5. versatile
6. elude
7. illusive
8. retrospect
9. tempest
10. vitality
11. extemporaneous
12. introvert
13. revive
14. temporal
15. vitamin
16. extrovert
17. inverse
18. spectacular
19. temporary
20. vivid

Warm Up

Word Analysis

Write the List Words that have the same Latin root as the word given.

inspector 1. suspect 2. retrospect 3. spectacular

vital 4. vitality 5. revive 6. vitamin 7. vivid

devour 8. carnivorous

convert 9. versatile 10. introvert 11. extrovert 12. inverse

Vocabulary Development

Write the List Word that matches each synonym.

1. deceiving illusive
2. laughable ludicrous
3. earthly temporal
4. mirage illusion
5. storm tempest
6. escape elude
7. short-term temporary
8. unrehearsed extemporaneous

Practice

Word Application

Write List Words to answer the following questions.

Which words contain the Latin root that means to turn?
1. versatile 2. introvert 3. extrovert 4. inverse

Which words contain the Latin root that means time?
5. tempest 6. extemporaneous 7. temporal 8. temporary

Which words contain the Latin root that means to see?
9. suspect 10. retrospect 11. spectacular

Which words contain the Latin root that means to play?
12. illusion 13. ludicrous 14. elude 15. illusive

Which words contain the Latin root that means to live?
16. vitality 17. revive 18. vitamin 19. vivid

Which word contains the Latin root that means to eat?
20. carnivorous

Did you know?

The Latin word *vivere* means "to be alive or to live." The Romans used a form of the word, *viva*, as a salute, meaning "long live someone or something." *Viva* has lent its meaning to many of the words in our language. A **vitamin** is a dietary supplement that helps us live well. **Vivid** means "to be alive with color." **Revive** means "bring back to life." **Vitality** is energy and strength. Viva vitality!

Classification

Write a List Word to complete each series.

1. stupendous, astounding, spectacular
2. flexible, multi-talented, versatile
3. magician, trick, illusion
4. calorie, mineral, vitamin
5. energy, vigor, vitality
6. reverse, opposite, inverse
7. bright, colorful, vivid
8. herbivorous, omnivorous, carnivorous

Latin Roots Lesson 31

List Words

carnivorous	elude	extemporaneous	extrovert
illusion	illusive	introvert	inverse
ludicrous	retrospect	revive	spectacular
suspect	tempest	temporal	temporary
versatile	vitality	vitamin	vivid

Puzzle

Use the List Words to complete the crossword puzzle.

ACROSS
2. a violent windstorm
5. a shy inward person
8. the act of looking back
11. feeding on meat
14. to think of as guilty
15. a false idea or mistaken belief
16. having to do with everyday life; worldly; not spiritual
18. to bring back to life
19. energy or strength of mind or body

DOWN
1. done or spoken without much planning
3. an outgoing person
4. laughable; ridiculous
6. a substance needed by the body to keep healthy
7. showy; striking
9. to escape or get away by being quick
10. able to do a number of things well
12. deceiving; false, not real
13. for a short time only
15. exactly opposite
17. bright and strong

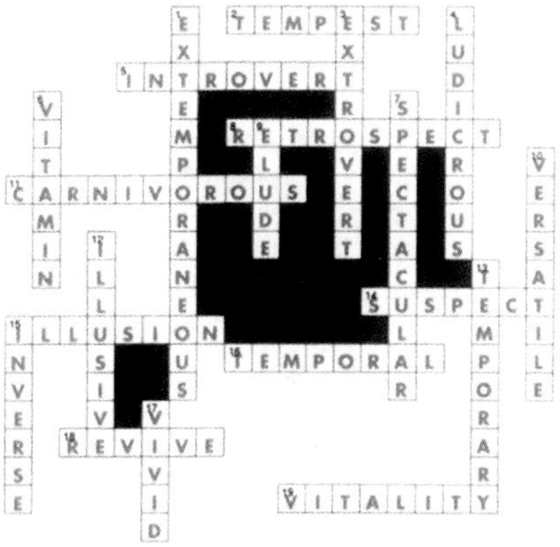

127

Latin Roots Lesson 31

Proofreading

Use the proofreading marks to correct the mistakes in the poem below. Then write the misspelled List Words on the lines.

Proofreading Marks: spelling mistake; add space; capital letter; small letter

an echo is like a sound ilushion,
which may create a little confusion.
When it bounces like a bouncing ball,
its source may eloode those Hearing its call.

now a mirage is as temperal as a Rainbow,
making far-away scenes look vivud you know.
But when trying toreach that illuzive place,
you'll see it vanish like bubbles In space.

1. illusion
2. elude
3. temporal
4. vivid
5. illusive

Challenges

Express Yourself

A **simile** compares two things using the words like or as.

The waterfall was as spectacular as fireworks.
Her vitality is like a babbling brook, forever in motion.

Write three similes. Try to include the adjectives: versatile, illusive, introverted, vivid, emaciated, earnest, and impractical. After proofreading and revising your similes, read them aloud to a group. Ask them if your comparisons make sense.

Bonus Words: Ecology

sanctuary preservation conservation chlorophyll oxidation
wildlife uninhabited photosynthesis biodegradable germinate

Write a Bonus Word to match each clue.

1. not lived in — uninhabited
2. green plant pigment — chlorophyll
3. will disintegrate — biodegradable
4. process by which a plant uses light to make food — photosynthesis
5. safe place — sanctuary
6. sprout — germinate
7. plants and animals — wildlife
8. combining of oxygen with other substances — oxidation

Write the Bonus Words that are synonyms for protection.

9. preservation 10. conservation

128

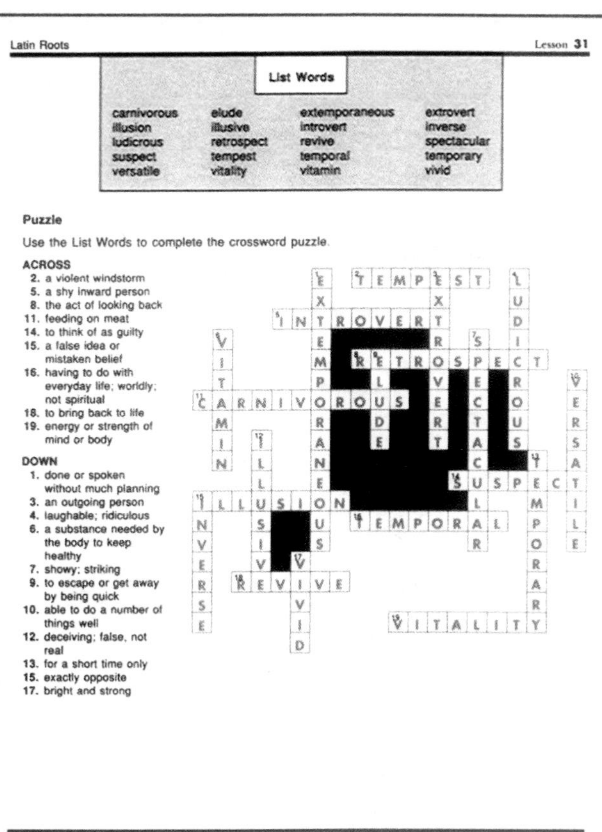

Puzzle (Page 127) Encourage students to think about the meaning of the List Words as they complete the puzzle.

Proofreading (Page 128) Write *From the empire State Building thecars looked like tinee Ants.* on the board to demonstrate the proofreading marks students will be using to correct the poem.

Challenges

Express Yourself (Page 128) Have students identify the two things being compared in each of the similes. (*waterfall, fireworks; vitality, babbling brook*) Then have students repeat orally each simile replacing *fireworks* and *babbling brook* with ideas of their own. When students have written their own similes, encourage them to share the similes with the class.

Bonus Words: Ecology (Page 128) Conduct a brief discussion on contemporary ecology issues, national and local, applying the Bonus Words to the discussion. Help students define each of the words, pointing out that *preservation* and *conservation* have similar meanings. (*keeping safe*)

Bonus Word Test

1. My parents work for the preservation of whales.
2. The state created a sanctuary for animals.
3. In photosynthesis, a plant uses light to make food.
4. Oxidation of metal causes rust.
5. The animals in the wildlife refuge are protected.
6. Chlorophyll is the green pigment in plants.
7. The seeds will germinate in several days.
8. Solar heating is a method of energy conservation.
9. Biodegradable products do not harm the environment.
10. We studied plants on the uninhabited islands.

Final Test

1. Her fame was temporal and faded quickly.
2. I have vivid memories of my vacation at the beach.
3. Exercise restored his vitality after the accident.
4. In retrospect, Franco admitted he was wrong.
5. An extemporaneous speech is unprepared.
6. What a silly, ludicrous statement he made!
7. Carnivorous animals eat meat.
8. Small details of past events elude my memory.
9. Winning the lottery is an illusive dream to people.
10. As an introvert, she keeps her feelings to herself.
11. A magician presents the illusion of magic.
12. I suspect that Cora has planned a surprise for me.
13. Joyful music will revive your low spirits.
14. Beneath her calm was a tempest ready to erupt.
15. This versatile gadget does many different things.
16. Is your job temporary or permanent?
17. The inverse of multiplication is division.
18. Fran is an extrovert and loves crowded parties.
19. The critics said his singing was spectacular.
20. Are citrus fruits a good source of vitamin C?

Lesson 32

Objective

To spell words from sports

Pretest

1. The gymnasts performed their acrobatics routine.
2. A toboggan is a long sled with a curved front end.
3. I carried my bow and arrows to the archery range.
4. The Olympics are exciting to watch!
5. The sportscaster reported the results of the game.
6. Is aerobics an exercise that benefits the heart?
7. Jim registered as a contestant in the race.
8. Sue was the top goalkeeper in the soccer league.
9. The referee blew the whistle at half time.
10. A sprinter runs short distances at top speed.
11. Do you need an agile body to be a gymnast?
12. Does the decathlon consist of ten athletic events?
13. MayLin won a gold ribbon in gymnastics.
14. The skiing conditions were great last winter.
15. The umpire called a strike.
16. Reggie broke his ankle playing football.
17. The teams will scrimmage at the end of practice.
18. A kayak is a canoe for one person.
19. Is soccer a popular sport all over the world?
20. Field hockey is played with sticks and a small ball.

Game Plan

Page 129
Have students name sports and other physical activity in which they participate regularly. Then have them name other words associated with each activity mentioned. For example, words associated with *football* might include *quarterback, penalty, Super Bowl,* etc. Point out that since sports words are used frequently in our writing and speaking vocabulary, it is important to spell them correctly. Discuss the definitions of the List Words. Emphasize the spelling patterns of the more difficult words, such as *aerobics, decathlon, gymnastics,* and *kayak.* You may wish to point out that people often confuse the spelling of *empire* and *umpire.*

Warm Up

Vocabulary Development (Page 129) Tell students to think carefully about the meanings of the List Words as they complete the activity.

Dictionary Skills (Page 129) Encourage students to pronounce each word slowly to themselves as they attempt to syllabicate the words.

Practice

Word Analysis (Page 130) Students should study the spelling patterns of the List Words on page 130 before they begin this activity.

Analogies (Page 130) To review analogies, have students identify the List Word that completes the following sentence. *Bicycle is to road as ________ is to river. (kayak)*

Words from Sports — LESSON 32

Game Plan

Sports and physical fitness have become an important part of our daily lives and language.

There are words that refer to specific sports.
soccer skiing acrobatics

There are words that refer to people in sports.
sportscaster goalkeeper

Some sports words name athletic equipment.
kayak

Some words name specific athletic events.
Olympics

All the List Words are from sports. Study the words carefully. Words like aerobics and decathlon are often misspelled.

1. acrobatics
2. toboggan
3. archery
4. Olympics
5. sportscaster
6. aerobics
7. contestant
8. goalkeeper
9. referee
10. sprinter
11. agile
12. decathlon
13. gymnastics
14. skiing
15. umpire
16. ankle
17. scrimmage
18. kayak
19. soccer
20. hockey

Warm Up

Vocabulary Development

Write the List Word that matches each definition.

1. practice play between two teams scrimmage
2. sport played on ice hockey
3. a short-distance runner sprinter
4. exercises that give the body oxygen aerobics
5. participant in athletic event contestant
6. moving with quickness and ease agile
7. a judge in a football game referee
8. a person who oversees a baseball game umpire
9. an athletic contest consisting of ten events decathlon
10. a type of canoe kayak

Dictionary Skills

Rewrite each of the following words to show how they are divided into syllables.

1. acrobatics ac ro bat ics
2. gymnastics gym nas tics
3. sportscaster sports cast er
4. Olympics O lym pics
5. goalkeeper goal keep er
6. skiing ski ing
7. soccer soc cer
8. ankle an kle
9. archery arch er y
10. toboggan to bog gan

Practice

Did you know?
Hockey probably comes from an older Dutch word meaning "hook," or "crook." Long ago the game was probably played in fields by shepherds, who used their crooks to hit a small, leather-covered ball.

Word Analysis

Write List Words to answer the following questions.

Which words end with **ics**?
1. acrobatics 2. Olympics 3. aerobics 4. gymnastics

Which words contain these double consonants?
5. mm scrimmage 6. cc soccer 7. gg toboggan

Which words contain these double vowels?
8. ii skiing 9. ee goalkeeper 10. ee referee

Which words are compound words?
11. sportscaster 12. goalkeeper

Analogies

Write a List Word to complete each analogy.

1. Nimble is to lively as agile is to flexible.
2. Five is to pentathlon as ten is to decathlon.
3. Wrist is to hand as ankle is to foot.
4. Skates are to ice as toboggan is to snow.
5. Rehearsal is to play as scrimmage is to game.
6. Musical is to musician as gymnastics is to gymnast.
7. Basket is to basketball as target is to archery.
8. Movie reviewer is to film as sportscaster is to athletic event.

Word Application

Underline the List Word in each sentence that is used incorrectly. Write the correct List Words on the lines.

1. In a scrimmage, a contestant competes in ten events. decathlon
2. Gymnastics and aerobics involve tumbling and splits. acrobatics
3. The goalkeeper sprained his ankle running to the finish line. sprinter
4. He trained to be an umpire in the youth soccer league. referee

130

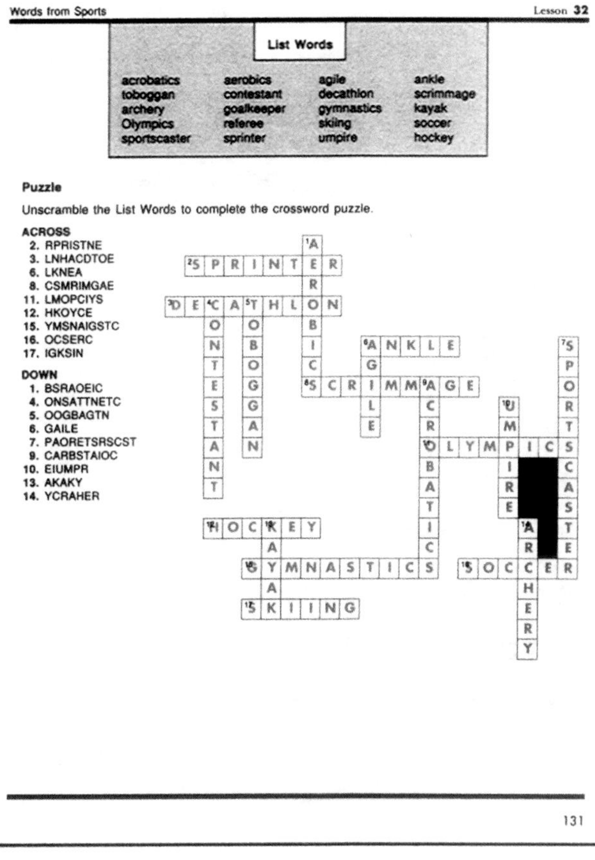
Words from Sports — Lesson **32**

List Words

acrobatics	aerobics	agile	ankle
toboggan	contestant	decathlon	scrimmage
archery	goalkeeper	gymnastics	kayak
Olympics	referee	skiing	soccer
sportscaster	sprinter	umpire	hockey

Puzzle

Unscramble the List Words to complete the crossword puzzle.

ACROSS
2. RPRISTNE
3. LNHACDTOE
6. LKNEA
8. CSMRIMGAE
11. LMOPCIYS
12. HKOYCE
15. YMSNAIGSTC
16. OCSERC
17. IGKSIN

DOWN
1. BSRAOEIC
4. ONSATTNETC
5. OOGBAGTN
6. GAILE
7. PAORETSRSCST
9. CARBSTAIOC
10. EIUMPR
13. AKAKY
14. YCRAHER

131

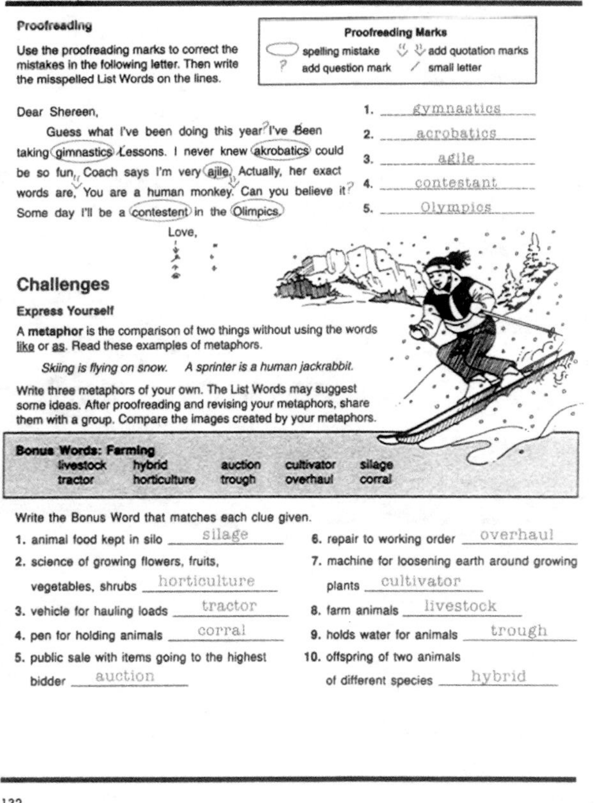
Words from Sports — Lesson **32**

Proofreading

Use the proofreading marks to correct the mistakes in the following letter. Then write the misspelled List Words on the lines.

Proofreading Marks
spelling mistake — add quotation marks — ? add question mark — / small letter

Dear Shereen,

Guess what I've been doing this year? I've Been taking gimnastics Lessons. I never knew akrobatics could be so fun. Coach says I'm very ajile. Actually, her exact words are, "You are a human monkey." Can you believe it? Some day I'll be a contestent in the Olimpics.

Love,

1. gymnastics
2. acrobatics
3. agile
4. contestant
5. Olympics

Challenges

Express Yourself

A **metaphor** is the comparison of two things without using the words like or as. Read these examples of metaphors.

Skiing is flying on snow. *A sprinter is a human jackrabbit.*

Write three metaphors of your own. The List Words may suggest some ideas. After proofreading and revising your metaphors, share them with a group. Compare the images created by your metaphors.

Bonus Words: Farming

livestock	hybrid	auction	cultivator	silage
tractor	horticulture	trough	overhaul	corral

Write the Bonus Word that matches each clue given.

1. animal food kept in silo silage
2. science of growing flowers, fruits, vegetables, shrubs horticulture
3. vehicle for hauling loads tractor
4. pen for holding animals corral
5. public sale with items going to the highest bidder auction
6. repair to working order overhaul
7. machine for loosening earth around growing plants cultivator
8. farm animals livestock
9. holds water for animals trough
10. offspring of two animals of different species hybrid

132

Word Application (Page 130) When students have completed the exercise, have volunteers read the sentences aloud, substituting their answers for the incorrect words.

Puzzle (Page 131) Students will unscramble List Words to complete the puzzle. Encourage them to refer to the words at the top of the page if they have difficulty remembering the spelling pattern of any word.

Proofreading (Page 132) Write *When are you going on Vacation asked Pat.* on the board to demonstrate the proofreading marks students will use to correct the letter.

Challenges

Express Yourself (Page 132) Elicit from students the difference between a metaphor and a simile. Then have students identify the two things being compared in each of the metaphors. (*skiing, flying on snow; sprinter, human jackrabbit*) Ask students to repeat orally each metaphor replacing *flying on snow* and *human jackrabbit* with ideas of their own. Encourage students to discuss the metaphors in small groups.

Bonus Words: Farming (Page 132) Help students define the Bonus Words. Encourage them to consult a dictionary to discover the meanings of any unfamiliar words. Students in rural areas may be familiar with these words while students in urban areas may not. You may wish to provide pictures and additional reading material on farming for these students. Help them understand the importance of farming and agriculture in our society.

Bonus Word Test

1. Mr. Smith will overhaul the damaged plow.
2. These hybrid tomatoes grow to an enormous size.
3. He'll use a cultivator to loosen the packed soil.
4. The livestock on our farm includes cattle.
5. The horses that are for sale are in the corral.
6. The pigs drank water from a wooden trough.
7. Sam towed the disabled machine with the tractor.
8. The gardener discussed the science of horticulture.
9. Mrs. West will bid on a bull at the cattle auction.
10. Silage is stored in a silo to feed animals in winter.

Final Test

1. We took a kayak expedition on the Colorado River.
2. Jeff won an ice hockey scholarship to college.
3. The team captain argued with the umpire.
4. What a great scrimmage game!
5. Each contestant in the race was issued a number.
6. Will the referee explain the rules before the game?
7. They sped down the snowy hill on the toboggan.
8. The sportscaster interviewed the winning team.
9. She was agile and climbed easily up the rope.
10. Gymnastics helps build strength and flexibility.
11. He's a sprinter and doesn't run long distances.
12. The goalkeeper made a spectacular save.
13. Competing in a decathlon requires great stamina.
14. Is Mrs. Loo the aerobics instructor at the gym?
15. Ten soccer teams competed in the state finals.
16. Her ankle ached, but she completed the marathon.
17. Ted is a member of the Junior Olympics ski team.
18. She performed acrobatics on the trampoline.
19. We spent our vacation skiing at Mount Pleasant.
20. The Swiss archery team won three gold medals.

Lesson 33

Objective

To spell words with Latin prefixes

Pretest

1. That kind of exaggeration is called hyperbole.
2. In stories, an omniscient narrator knows everything.
3. Young children are often hyperactive.
4. At beach houses, sand is an omnipresent nuisance.
5. Our multimedia advertising appeals to everyone.
6. Anna wore black slacks and a multicolored blouse.
7. The desert panorama was magnificent.
8. Greek myths show the belief in polytheism.
9. This amount of food could easily feed a multitude!
10. I have multiple sneakers, all for different sports.
11. Are tropical countries those closest to the equator?
12. The shirt looks like silk, but it's polyester.
13. Do you try to spell polysyllabic words by syllable?
14. The center is equidistant from both goal posts.
15. The practice of plural marriages is called polygamy.
16. The people believed their ruler to be omnipotent.
17. An actor can tell a story through pantomime alone.
18. At equilibrium, the scales will balance.
19. A polygon is a figure with many sides.
20. What pandemonium the apes caused at the zoo!

Game Plan

Page 133

After students have read the Game Plan, discuss the meanings of the List Words, having students consult the Game Plan to make intelligent guesses about meanings of unfamiliar words. Then elicit other words they know containing these prefixes. Analyze the spelling of each List Word and ways students might remember it.

Warm Up

Vocabulary Development (Page 133) Remind students to think carefully about the spelling of each answer word.

Dictionary Skills (Page 133) Review respelling symbols and accent marks using the word *polysyllabic/pôl´ ē si lab´ik.*

Practice

Word Analysis (Page 134) This classifying activity will help the students compare and contrast similar List Words. As an extension activity, you may wish to have students use dictionaries to research additional words beginning with a certain prefix.

Word Application (Page 134) When students have completed the exercise, have volunteers read the sentences aloud, substituting their answers for the underlined words. Discuss whether the substitutions improve the sentences.

Words with Latin Prefixes

LESSON 33

Game Plan

Many words in English have prefixes that come from Latin. An understanding of Latin prefixes can help you spell such words. Study these prefixes and their meanings.

pan, meaning all or complete, as in panorama
hyper, meaning excessive, as in hyperactive
equi, meaning equal, as in equidistant
multi, meaning many, as in multicolored
poly, meaning more than one, as in polysyllabic
omni, meaning all, as in omnipotent

1. hyperbole
2. omniscient
3. hyperactive
4. omnipresent
5. multimedia
6. multicolored
7. panorama
8. polytheism
9. multitude
10. multiple
11. equator
12. polyester
13. polysyllabic
14. equidistant
15. polygamy
16. omnipotent
17. pantomime
18. equilibrium
19. polygon
20. pandemonium

Warm Up

Vocabulary Development

Write the List Word that matches each definition.

1. an exaggeration — hyperbole
2. crowd of people — multitude
3. synthetic fiber — polyester
4. belief in more than one god — polytheism
5. all-powerful — omnipotent
6. overly active — hyperactive
7. mass confusion — pandemonium
8. more than one syllable — polysyllabic
9. all-knowing — omniscient
10. present everywhere at the same time — omnipresent
11. many-sided figure — polygon
12. an equal distance — equidistant

Dictionary Skills

Write the List Words that matches each sound-spelling.

1. (päl´ i gän´) polygon
2. (pə lig´ ə mē) polygamy
3. (mul´ tə p'l) multiple
4. (pan´ ə ram´ ə) panorama
5. (i kwāt´ ər) equator
6. (mul´ ti kul´ ərd) multicolored
7. (pan´ tə mim´) pantomime
8. (ē kwə dis´ tənt) equidistant
9. (ē kwə lib´ rē əm) equilibrium
10. (mul´ ti mē´ dē ə) multimedia

133

Words with Latin Prefixes — Lesson 33

Practice

Word Analysis

Write the List Words containing the prefixes given below.

poly

1. polytheism
2. polyester
3. polysyllabic
4. polygamy
5. polygon

multi

9. multimedia
10. multicolored
11. multitude
12. multiple

hyper

16. hyperbole
17. hyperactive

pan

6. panorama
7. pantomime
8. pandemonium

equi

13. equator
14. equidistant
15. equilibrium

omni

18. omniscient
19. omnipresent
20. omnipotent

Did you know?

Panorama was formed from two Greek words meaning "to see all" by Robert Barker about 1789 as a name for an unusual sort of picture he painted. The picture was painted on a surface that went completely around the person looking at it. From such a picture one may get the idea of a view that is open in all directions.

OMNI

Word Application

Replace the underlined word or words in each sentence with List Words. Write the List Words on the lines.

1. Some people, such as the Ancient Egyptians, believe in many gods, while others believe in one god that is everywhere and all-knowing.
   polytheism — omnipresent — omniscient
2. Todd was always an overly-active person, until the accident in which he lost his sense of balance.
   hyperactive — equilibrium
3. The many-sided figure and the sphere are the same distance from me.
   polygon — equidistant
4. Sandy described the riot as mass confusion, but she always leans toward exaggeration.
   pandemonium — hyperbole
5. A large group of people, ready for the parade, assembled under the many-colored banner.
   multitude — multicolored

134

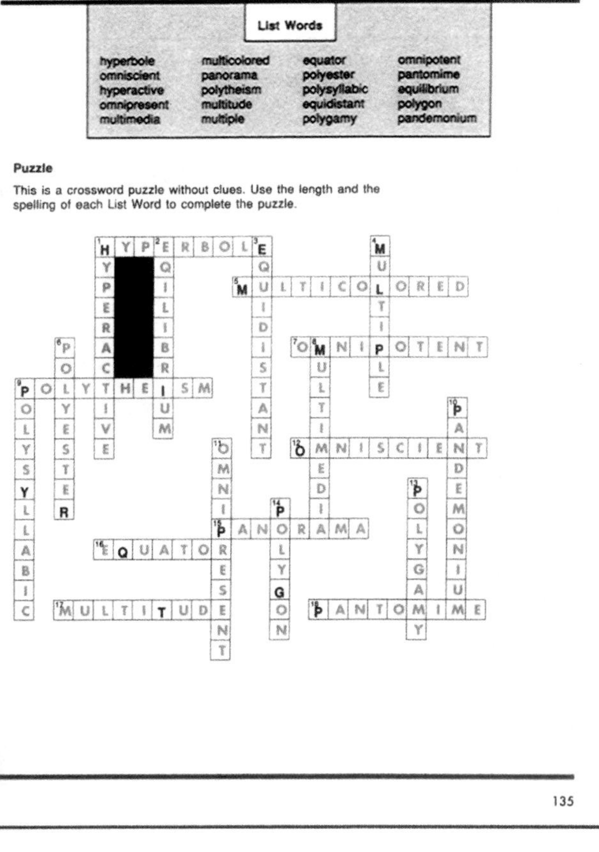

Words with Latin Prefixes — Lesson 33

List Words

hyperbole	multicolored	equator	omnipotent
omniscient	panorama	polyester	pantomime
hyperactive	polytheism	polysyllabic	equilibrium
omnipresent	multitude	equidistant	polygon
multimedia	multiple	polygamy	pandemonium

Puzzle

This is a crossword puzzle without clues. Use the length and the spelling of each List Word to complete the puzzle.

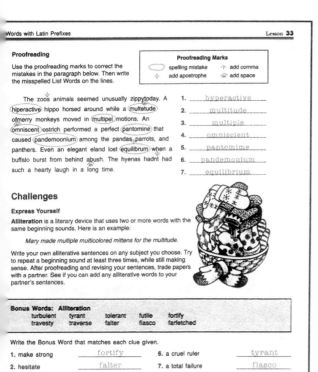

135

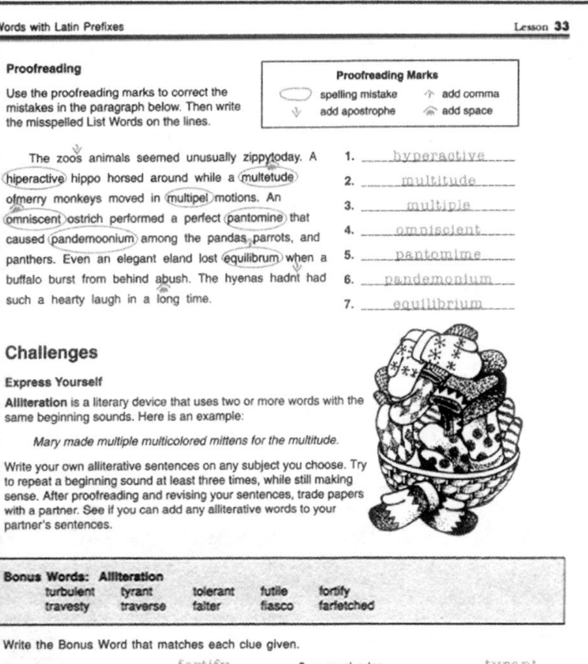

Words with Latin Prefixes — Lesson 33

Proofreading

Use the proofreading marks to correct the mistakes in the paragraph below. Then write the misspelled List Words on the lines.

Proofreading Marks: spelling mistake; add comma; add apostrophe; add space

The zoos animals seemed unusually zippytoday. A hiperactive hippo horsed around while a multetude ofmerry monkeys moved in multipel motions. An omniscent ostrich performed a perfect pantomine that caused pandemoonium among the pandas parrots, and panthers. Even an elegant eland lost equilibrum when a buffalo burst from behind abush. The hyenas hadnt had such a hearty laugh in a long time.

1. hyperactive
2. multitude
3. multiple
4. omniscient
5. pantomime
6. pandemonium
7. equilibrium

Challenges

Express Yourself

Alliteration is a literary device that uses two or more words with the same beginning sounds. Here is an example:

Mary made multiple multicolored mittens for the multitude.

Write your own alliterative sentences on any subject you choose. Try to repeat a beginning sound at least three times, while still making sense. After proofreading and revising your sentences, trade papers with a partner. See if you can add any alliterative words to your partner's sentences.

Bonus Words: Alliteration

turbulent, tyrant, tolerant, futile, fortify, travesty, traverse, falter, fiasco, farfetched

Write the Bonus Word that matches each clue given.

1. make strong — fortify
2. hesitate — falter
3. stirred up — turbulent
4. strained; improbable — farfetched
5. grotesque imitation — travesty
6. a cruel ruler — tyrant
7. a total failure — fiasco
8. go across — traverse
9. hopeless or ineffective — futile
10. easygoing; unprejudiced — tolerant

136

Puzzle (Page 135) Review the students' strategies for solving crossword puzzles without clues. Then have them complete the puzzle independently.

Proofreading (Page 136) Review the proofreading marks students will use in this lesson. Then remind them how each mark is used.

Challenges

Express Yourself (Page 136) Point out to students that many tongue-twisters use alliteration, such as "She sells sea shells by the sea shore." Encourage students to be playful with language and to think of alliterative word combinations. As a group, you may wish to generate lists of words starting with certain letters. Then have students write their sentences.

Bonus Words: Alliteration (Page 136) Point out that the Bonus Words in this lesson are related by sound, not topic. Through discussion and dictionary use, help students understand the words' meanings. If possible, find and display examples of alliteration from literature or poetry. Then have students complete the Bonus Word activity.

Bonus Word Test

1. The manufacturers fortify milk with vitamin D.
2. The engine started to falter, but then ran smoothly.
3. The turbulent water foamed over the rocks.
4. During the revolution, the tyrant was overthrown.
5. That news story was a travesty of television news.
6. Your idea sounds far-fetched, but it just might work.
7. I don't want my name associated with this fiasco!
8. It snowed, so we can traverse the slopes on skis.
9. Our efforts to keep dry were futile, so we got wet.
10. Some people are more tolerant of cold than others.

Final Test

1. Sasha's bed is covered with a multicolored quilt.
2. What a beautiful panorama I saw from the window!
3. Their polytheism was expressed in their art.
4. Today you have a multitude of decisions to make.
5. The shop has multiple cages, each filled with birds.
6. Very young children think parents are omnipotent.
7. In charades, you pantomime different actions.
8. Can an ear infection affect a person's equilibrium?
9. Each figure is a polygon, except the circle.
10. The cat at the dog show caused pandemonium.
11. Do tall tales use hyperbole for a humorous effect?
12. Ron was unaware, not omniscient of the situation.
13. When I'm tired, other people seem hyperactive.
14. At the shore, dampness is an omnipresent force.
15. A multimedia show was planned for the event.
16. In this country, polygamy is against the law.
17. Let's meet at a place equidistant from our homes.
18. She has a polysyllabic name—Saltinstall.
19. I rarely have to iron this polyester shirt.
20. The equator divides the earth into equal halves.

Lesson 34

Objective

To spell compound words and hyphenated words

Pretest

1. Throughout her life, she worked to fight poverty.
2. The handlebars on Diane's new bike are too low.
3. His motorcycle is at the automotive repair shop.
4. That absent-minded boy always forgets things!
5. There are twenty-nine students in our math class.
6. The astronauts climbed aboard the spacecraft.
7. Did the police question the eyewitness?
8. I was able to buy the car after much self-sacrifice.
9. The captain was looking for able-bodied sailors.
10. Jesse is a part-time employee at the factory.
11. On hot days, we enjoy our air-conditioned house.
12. We tasted the purple grapes from the vineyard.
13. Ann keeps her recipes in a loose-leaf binder.
14. Lia won the race by two-thousandths of a second.
15. The quarterback threw a touchdown pass.
16. A bookkeeper keeps a company's financial records.
17. Does a copyright protect work from being copied?
18. Is this film strip from the audio-visual department?
19. The answer to the problem is nine-hundredths.
20. Three-fourths of the class went on the field trip.

Game Plan

Page 137

To reinforce the Game Plan, say the following words and have students consult a dictionary to determine which words are compounds and which are hyphenates: *self-control, pothole, outspoken, stagestruck.* Then have students identify the two words that form each compound word and hyphenated word in the List Words. Point out that most numbers between twenty-one and ninety-nine are hyphenated. Review the syllabication rule, by calling on volunteers to write a List Word on the board, placing a dot between syllables.

Warm Up

Vocabulary Development (Page 137) Remind students that a word that requires a hyphen is misspelled if the hyphen is omitted just as if a letter were eliminated.

Dictionary Skills (Page 137) If there is sufficient time when students complete the activity, have them look in the dictionary to find the sound spellings for additional List Words.

Practice

Word Application (Page 138) When students have finished the exercise, they may enjoy making up riddle questions of their own for the List Words *vineyard, eyewitness, three-fourths, quarterback,* and then exchanging them with a partner.

Analogies (Page 138) To review analogies, have students identify the List Word that completes the following sentence. *Heated is to winter as ________ is to summer. (air-conditioned)*

Compound Words and Hyphenates

LESSON **34**

Game Plan

A **compound word** is a combination of two or more words.
space + craft = spacecraft
A compound word may have a hyphen between the words.
loose-leaf
Many number words are also spelled with a hyphen.
twenty-nine

Warm Up

1. throughout
2. handlebars
3. motorcycle
4. absent-minded
5. twenty-nine
6. spacecraft
7. eyewitness
8. self-sacrifice
9. able-bodied
10. part-time
11. air-conditioned
12. vineyard
13. loose-leaf
14. two-thousandths
15. quarterback
16. bookkeeper
17. copyright
18. audio-visual
19. nine-hundredths
20. three-fourths

Vocabulary Development

Match the words in columns A and B to form List Words.

	A	B	
1.	able	cycle	able-bodied
2.	space	leaf	spacecraft
3.	self	conditioned	self-sacrifice
4.	motor	out	motorcycle
5.	copy	fourths	copyright
6.	loose	witness	loose-leaf
7.	air	bodied	air-conditioned
8.	through	sacrifice	throughout
9.	eye	right	eyewitness
10.	three	craft	three-fourths

Dictionary Skills

Write the List Word that matches each sound-spelling.

1. (han´ d' l bärz) handlebars
2. (kwôr´ tər bak) quarterback
3. (book´ kēp´ ər) bookkeeper
4. (ab´ s'nt mīn´ did) absent-minded
5. (nīn hun´ dridths) nine-hundredths
6. (to͞o tho͞u´ z' ndths) two-thousandths
7. (ô´ dē ō vizh´ o͞o wəl) audio-visual
8. (pärt´ tīm) part-time
9. (twen´ te nīn) twenty-nine
10. (vin´ yərd) vineyard

137

Compound Words and Hyphenates — Lesson **34**

Practice

Word Application

Write List Words to answer the following questions.

1. What do you call someone who is always forgetting things? absent-minded
2. What do you call someone who is in good health? able-bodied
3. What is a two-wheeled motor vehicle? motorcycle
4. What is another name for a rocket? spacecraft
5. What protects someone from stealing a story? copyright
6. What kind of place keeps you cool in the summer? air-conditioned
7. What is another name for an accountant? bookkeeper
8. What do you call paper that fits in a three-ring binder? loose-leaf
9. What do you call it when you deprive yourself of something? self-sacrifice
10. What kind of job would you have if you worked only ten hours weekly? part-time

What word numbers do these numerals represent?

11. .09 nine-hundredths
12. 3/4 three-fourths
13. 29 twenty-nine
14. .002 two-thousandths

Analogies

Write a List Word to complete each analogy.

1. Pitcher is to baseball, as quarterback is to football.
2. Steering wheel is to car, as handlebars are to bicycle.
3. Sailor is to ship, as astronaut is to spacecraft.
4. Grapes are to vineyard, as vegetables are to farm.

Did you know?

On a football team, the **quarterback** is the player who calls the plays and receives the ball when it is snapped back by the center. The name most likely comes from the early days of football. The quarterback was one of four players that formed a backfield formation called the power T.

138

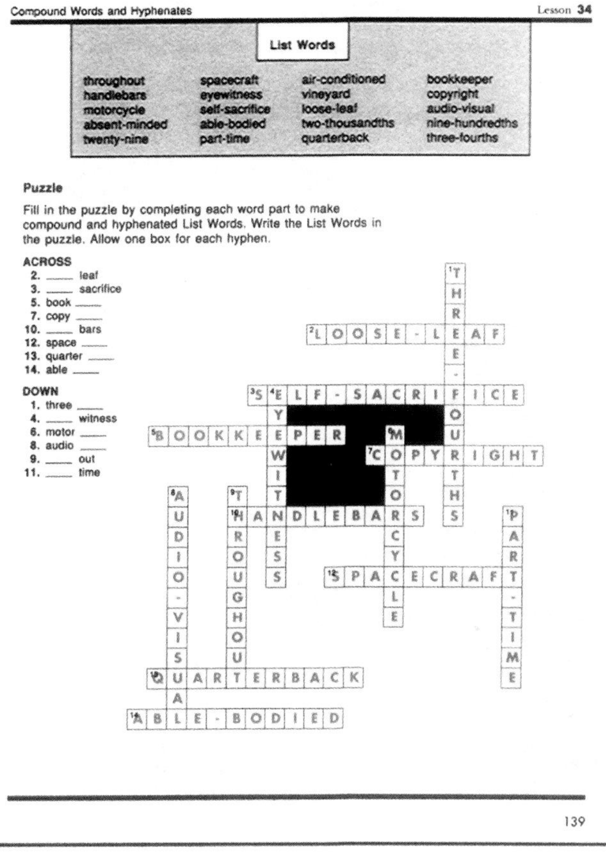

Compound Words and Hyphenates — Lesson **34**

List Words

throughout, handlebars, motorcycle, absent-minded, twenty-nine, spacecraft, eyewitness, self-sacrifice, able-bodied, part-time, air-conditioned, vineyard, loose-leaf, two-thousandths, quarterback, bookkeeper, copyright, audio-visual, nine-hundredths, three-fourths

Puzzle

Fill in the puzzle by completing each word part to make compound and hyphenated List Words. Write the List Words in the puzzle. Allow one box for each hyphen.

ACROSS
2. ____ leaf
3. ____ sacrifice
5. book ____
7. copy ____
10. ____ bars
12. space ____
13. quarter ____
14. able ____

DOWN
1. three ____
4. ____ witness
6. motor ____
8. audio ____
9. ____ out
11. ____ time

139

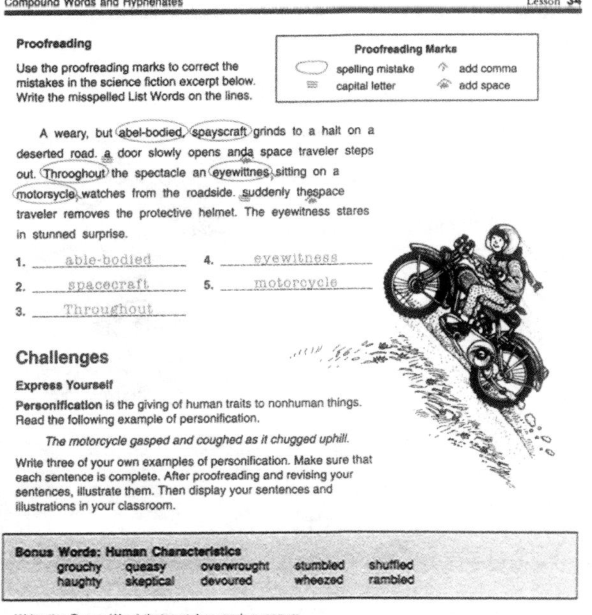

Compound Words and Hyphenates — Lesson **34**

Proofreading

Use the proofreading marks to correct the mistakes in the science fiction excerpt below. Write the misspelled List Words on the lines.

Proofreading Marks: spelling mistake; capital letter; add comma; add space

A weary, but abel-bodied, spayscraft grinds to a halt on a deserted road. a door slowly opens anda space traveler steps out. Throoghout the spectacle an eyewittnes, sitting on a motorsycle, watches from the roadside. suddenly thespace traveler removes the protective helmet. The eyewitness stares in stunned surprise.

1. able-bodied
2. spacecraft
3. Throughout
4. eyewitness
5. motorcycle

Challenges

Express Yourself

Personification is the giving of human traits to nonhuman things. Read the following example of personification.

The motorcycle gasped and coughed as it chugged uphill.

Write three of your own examples of personification. Make sure that each sentence is complete. After proofreading and revising your sentences, illustrate them. Then display your sentences and illustrations in your classroom.

Bonus Words: Human Characteristics

grouchy, queasy, overwrought, stumbled, shuffled, haughty, skeptical, devoured, wheezed, rambled

Write the Bonus Word that matches each synonym.

1. nervous — overwrought
2. grumpy — grouchy
3. doubtful — skeptical
4. arrogant — haughty
5. dragged — shuffled
6. tripped — stumbled
7. gasped — wheezed
8. ate — devoured
9. nauseous — queasy
10. roamed — rambled

140

Puzzle (Page 139) Emphasize to students that if a word has a hyphen they are to write a hyphen in a box. To be sure students understand, complete item 2 across with them.

Proofreading (Page 140) Write *We goto New york next week said Maria.* on the board to show the proofreading marks students will use to correct the excerpt.

Challenges

Express Yourself (Page 140) Ask students to name the object that is being personified and what human traits are attributed to it. (*motorcycle: gasped, coughed*) Then have students suggest different objects that they might like to write about. List the suggestions on the board and have the class think of human traits that might be applied to these objects. Encourage students to use these ideas as they write.

Bonus Words: Human Characteristics (Page 140) Ask students to define the Bonus Words and have them consult a dictionary to discover the meanings of any unfamiliar words. Encourage volunteers to use each word in an oral sentence that clearly demonstrates the meaning of the word. You may wish to have students use one or more of these words to write a brief character sketch of a real or fictional person.

Bonus Word Test

1. The man rambled around the country for years.
2. My stomach was queasy after the rough ferry ride.
3. Leon was so hungry he quickly devoured the steak.
4. Al has a grouchy voice, but he's really very pleasant.
5. She wheezed and coughed because of her allergies.
6. Pam was skeptical about what she read in the paper.
7. The elderly man shuffled up the hall in his slippers.
8. In a haughty tone, he ordered me to move his bags.
9. The actress stumbled onto the stage and fell.
10. Mom was overwrought with worry when I was late.

Final Test

1. The light flashed in two-thousandths of a second.
2. That motorcycle has a powerful engine!
3. Ella used audio-visual aids in her science project.
4. Was he an eyewitness to the first space launch?
5. Cassie gripped the handlebars of her new bike.
6. It was chilly in the air-conditioned theater.
7. The spacecraft orbited the moon for three days.
8. Tanya bought loose-leaf paper for her notebook.
9. The inn's bookkeeper totaled the day's receipts.
10. These grapes were grown in Granddad's vineyard.
11. Through self-sacrifice, she succeeded.
12. Juan has a part-time job two days a week.
13. The absent-minded woman lost her keys again.
14. Is the copyright date on our encyclopedia 1992?
15. Len did the job in three-fourths the normal time.
16. The news spread quickly throughout the school.
17. We need able-bodied people to move the piano.
18. Add three-hundredths to nine-hundredths.
19. The quarterback is going for the touchdown!
20. Maria earned twenty-nine dollars mowing lawns.

Lesson 35

Objective

To spell words that do not follow spelling rules

Pretest

1. The continuous rain was beneficial to the crops.
2. Did they eliminate two of the contestants?
3. We had numerous complaints about the service.
4. Which restaurant serves the best Chinese food?
5. Folk tales were passed down in an oral tradition.
6. A hypocrite says one thing and means another.
7. The price of this dress is extravagant!
8. He has the privilege of leading the holiday parade.
9. Ron's new bike is similar to the one Will has.
10. Vi has a tremendous ability to learn new things.
11. Such harsh criticism of the book was unexpected.
12. Lying in bed late on Saturday mornings is a luxury.
13. Mrs. Lopez is a prominent official in the town.
14. Mieko signed her letter, "Sincerely yours."
15. The boys took sailing lessons at the yacht club.
16. The school board sets the educational standards.
17. Joan of Arc was a martyr who died for her beliefs.
18. We will probably go to the beach for our vacation.
19. Stacy is not susceptible to the influence of others.
20. Did the suddenness of the storm surprise you?

Game Plan

Page 141

Discuss the Game Plan and stress that there are some words to which no handy spelling rules apply. Point out that the pronunciation of these hurdle words gives little assistance in spelling them. The spelling patterns of these words must be studied and practiced. Then discuss the spelling patterns of the List Words, helping students recognize the special spelling problems of each word.

Warm Up

Vocabulary Development (Page 141) When students finish the exercise, you may wish to have them find antonyms for as many of the words in the activity as possible.

Dictionary Skills (Page 141) Before students begin the activity, you may wish to have them consult the pronunciation key at the beginning of their dictionaries to help them understand and review diacritical marks.

Practice

Word Analysis (Page 142) Remind students that repeating the word to themselves may not help them recall what letters are missing. Encourage them to refer to the List Words on page 143 if they are doubtful about the spelling of any word.

Word Application (Page 142) Have a volunteer explain the directions. If necessary, elicit from students the answers to the first item to be sure they understand the process.

Hurdle Words

LESSON 35

Game Plan

Some words are difficult to spell because they don't follow the usual spelling rules. The best way to become familiar with these hurdle words is to study, memorize, and practice using them.

Hurdle Word	"Trick"	Hurdle Word	"Trick"
debtor	silent b	**jealousy**	ea = /e/, ou = /ə/
matinee	ee = /ā/	**mayonnaise**	o = /ə/; double n
calendar	ar = /ər/	**synonym**	y = /i/, o = /ə/

1. beneficial
2. eliminate
3. numerous
4. restaurant
5. tradition
6. hypocrite
7. extravagant
8. privilege
9. similar
10. tremendous
11. criticism
12. luxury
13. prominent
14. sincerely
15. yacht
16. educational
17. martyr
18. probably
19. susceptible
20. suddenness

Warm Up

Vocabulary Development

Write the List Word from column B that matches the synonym in column A.

A		B
1. inclined	susceptible	suddenness
2. favorable	beneficial	numerous
3. informative	educational	criticism
4. remove	eliminate	restaurant
5. many	numerous	eliminate
6. eatery	restaurant	extravagant
7. review	criticism	prominent
8. outstanding	prominent	educational
9. lavish	extravagant	susceptible
10. abruptness	suddenness	beneficial

Dictionary Skills

Write the List Word that matches each sound-spelling.

1. (luk′ shə rē)	luxury	6. (sim′ ə lər)	similar
2. (trə dish′ ən)	tradition	7. (sin sir′ lē)	sincerely
3. (priv′ lij)	privilege	8. (yät)	yacht
4. (hip′ ə krit)	hypocrite	9. (märt′ tər)	martyr
5. (tri men′ dəs)	tremendous	10. (präb′ ə blē)	probably

141

Hurdle Words — Lesson 35

Practice

Word Analysis

Fill in the missing letters to form List Words. Then write the words on the line.

1. trem _e_ nd _o_ _u_ s — tremendous
2. m _a_ rt _y_ r — martyr
3. ben _e_ fic _i_ al — beneficial
4. prob _a_ _b_ ly — probably
5. educat _i_ _o_ n _a_ l — educational
6. sin _c_ er _e_ ly — sincerely
7. su _d_ _d_ e _n_ _n_ e _s_ _s_ — suddenness
8. h _y_ p _o_ _c_ rite — hypocrite
9. crit _i_ ci _s_ _m_ — criticism
10. su _s_ _c_ ept _i_ ble — susceptible
11. _e_ lim _i_ nate — eliminate
12. ya _c_ _h_ t — yacht
13. prom _i_ n _e_ nt — prominent
14. rest _a_ _u_ r _a_ nt — restaurant
15. priv _i_ l _e_ _g_ e — privilege

Did you know?

Restaurant comes from the French word meaning "restore." When we go to a restaurant to eat, we hope to have our strength and energy restored.

Word Application

Replace the underlined words in each sentence with List Words and write them on the lines.

1. There have been many occasions on which important people have visited the monument.
   numerous — prominent
2. It is a high honor to share the custom of Thanksgiving with such kind people.
   privilege — tradition
3. Lack of funds will help to do away with all of the unnecessary frills that we once enjoyed.
   eliminate — extravagant
4. The quickness of the storm caught the captain of the large boat off guard.
   suddenness — yacht
5. Ruby's eatery is comparable to those found along major highways throughout the country.
   restaurant — similar

142

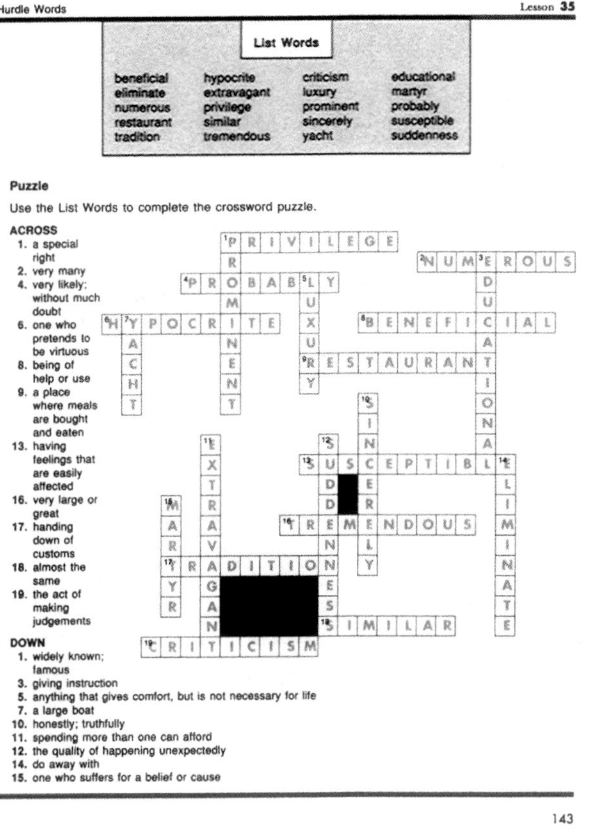

Hurdle Words — Lesson **35**

List Words

beneficial	hypocrite	criticism	educational
eliminate	extravagant	luxury	martyr
numerous	privilege	prominent	probably
restaurant	similar	sincerely	susceptible
tradition	tremendous	yacht	suddenness

Puzzle

Use the List Words to complete the crossword puzzle.

ACROSS

1. a special right
2. very many
4. very likely; without much doubt
6. one who pretends to be virtuous
8. being of help or use
9. a place where meals are bought and eaten
13. having feelings that are easily affected
16. very large or great
17. handing down of customs
18. almost the same
19. the act of making judgements

DOWN

1. widely known; famous
3. giving instruction
5. anything that gives comfort, but is not necessary for life
7. a large boat
10. honestly; truthfully
11. spending more than one can afford
12. the quality of happening unexpectedly
14. do away with
15. one who suffers for a belief or cause

143

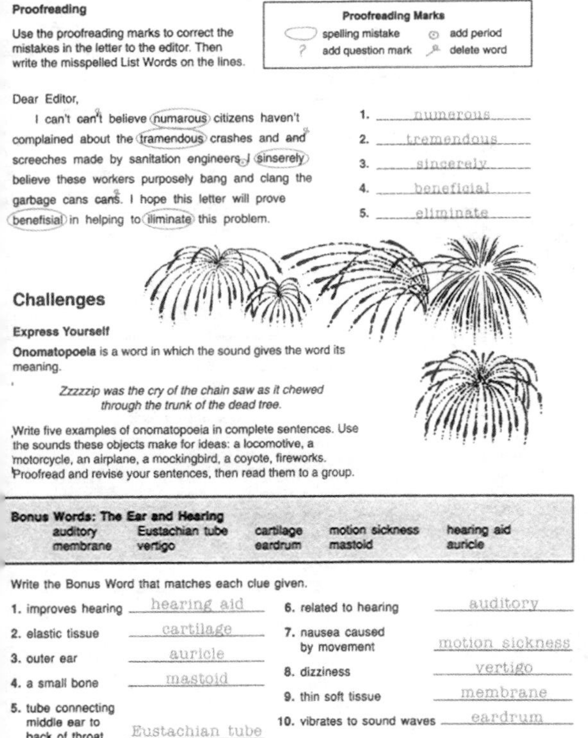

Hurdle Words — Lesson **35**

Proofreading

Use the proofreading marks to correct the mistakes in the letter to the editor. Then write the misspelled List Words on the lines.

Proofreading Marks
spelling mistake · add period · add question mark · delete word

Dear Editor,

I can't can't believe numarous citizens haven't complained about the tramendous crashes and and screeches made by sanitation engineers I sinserely believe these workers purposely bang and clang the garbage cans cans. I hope this letter will prove benefisial in helping to iliminate this problem.

1. numerous
2. tremendous
3. sincerely
4. beneficial
5. eliminate

Challenges

Express Yourself

Onomatopoeia is a word in which the sound gives the word its meaning.

Zzzzzip was the cry of the chain saw as it chewed through the trunk of the dead tree.

Write five examples of onomatopoeia in complete sentences. Use the sounds these objects make for ideas: a locomotive, a motorcycle, an airplane, a mockingbird, a coyote, fireworks. Proofread and revise your sentences, then read them to a group.

Bonus Words: The Ear and Hearing
auditory, Eustachian tube, cartilage, motion sickness, hearing aid, membrane, vertigo, eardrum, mastoid, auricle

Write the Bonus Word that matches each clue given.

1. improves hearing — hearing aid
2. elastic tissue — cartilage
3. outer ear — auricle
4. a small bone — mastoid
5. tube connecting middle ear to back of throat — Eustachian tube
6. related to hearing — auditory
7. nausea caused by movement — motion sickness
8. dizziness — vertigo
9. thin soft tissue — membrane
10. vibrates to sound waves — eardrum

44

Puzzle (Page 143) Remind students to use capital letters and to print clearly and neatly as they fill in the puzzle.

Proofreading (Page 144) Write *What does the word word "buzz" remind you of asked Leah.* on the board and demonstrate the proofreading marks in this lesson.

Challenges

Express Yourself (Page 144) Before discussing onomatopoeia, point out the special spelling problems in the difficult hurdle word *onomatopoeia.* Then have students identify the example of onomatopoeia in the sentence. (*zzzzip*) Before they begin to write, encourage students to make a list of three sounds for each of the items mentioned. Have students read their sentences, using good oral expression.

Bonus Words: The Ear and Hearing (Page 144) Discus the human ear and apply the Bonus Words to the discussion. Encourage students to consult a dictionary or encyclopedia to discover the meanings of any unfamiliar words. If possible provide a diagram or model of the human ear and have students point out the auditory canal, eardrum or tympanic membrane, mastoid, Eustachian tube, and auricle.

Bonus Word Test

1. The fleshy outer ear consists of skin and cartilage.
2. The auricle, or outer ear, collects sound waves.
3. The eardrum is the tympanic membrane.
4. Sound waves cause the eardrum to vibrate.
5. Sound travels from the auditory canal to the inner ear.
6. Air gets to the inner ear through the Eustachian tube.
7. The mastoid is the bony area of the middle ear.
8. An ear infection may cause vertigo, or dizziness.
9. A hearing aid is a device that improves hearing.
10. Motion sickness may result from inner-ear problems.

Final Test

1. Lionel's baby is susceptible to ear infections.
2. It's tradition to eat turkey on Thanksgiving.
3. Daily exercise is beneficial to your health.
4. What a privilege it would be to meet them!
5. There are educational programs on television.
6. He is sincerely sorry that he broke the window.
7. The princess sailed into the harbor on her yacht.
8. The suddenness of his actions startled us.
9. A beaver has prominent teeth.
10. Did the girls buy similar dresses for the prom?
11. I'd be a hypocrite if I said I liked that hat.
12. Stricter state laws will eliminate litter on the roads.
13. The car was much too extravagant for his budget.
14. We probably won't be late if we leave now.
15. The tremendous crash of thunder scared me.
16. Debra ate dinner at the new Mexican restaurant.
17. A martyr sacrifices his or her life for a cause.
18. The editor explained her criticism of my story.
19. We saw numerous animals at the wildlife preserve.
20. They won a trip to a luxury hotel in Hawaii.

Lesson 36

Objective

To review spelling patterns of words from Lessons 31–35

Game Plan

Page 145

Tell students that in this lesson they will review the skills and spelling words they studied in Lessons 31–35. You may wish to have students refer to previous Game Plans to review Latin roots and Latin prefixes, words from sports, compound words, and hurdle words.

Practice

Lesson 31 (Page 145) To review the Latin roots *vor, lud, lus, viv, spect, ver, temp,* write on the board: *suspect, elude, vitality, introvert, temporal.* Then have students identify the Latin roots in the List Words. Point out the additional write-on lines to students and encourage them to add two words from Lesson 31 that they found especially difficult, or select and assign certain words that seemed to be difficult for everyone. (Repeat this procedure for each lesson review that follows in the Replay.)

Lesson 32 (Page 146) Ask students what *archery, sprinter, hockey, goalkeeper* have in common. (*They are sports words.*) Elicit that the List Words are words from sports and discuss their meanings.

Lesson 33 (Page 146) Discuss the meanings of Latin prefixes in these words: *hyperactive, multiple, polytheism, omnipresent, pandemonium, equidistant.* Then have students identify the prefixes in the List Words. Be sure students understand that the first part of each sentence contains a clue to the missing List Word.

Lesson 34 (Page 147) Have students come to the board and draw a line between the two words that make up each of these compound words. *handlebars, motorcycle, self-sacrifice, quarterback, able-bodied.* Then have students identify the words that make up each of the compound List Words. You may wish to do the first item of the activity with students, helping them recognize that *twenty* and *nine* make up the compound word *twenty-nine.*

Lesson 35 (Page 147) Ask students to spell these words: *eliminate, prominent, educational, suddenness.* Remind students that these words are examples of hurdle words with unexpected spellings that don't follow specific rules. Then discuss the spellings of the List Words. Elicit from students that they must unscramble List Words to complete the puzzle.

Mixed Practice (Page 148) You may wish to do the first item of the activity with students, helping them select *absent-minded, omniscient referee* as the answer.

Test Yourself (Page 148) Encourage students to review the List Words one last time before completing the activity.

INSTANT REPLAY — LESSON **36**

Game Plan

There are many ways to determine the meaning of an unfamiliar word.

Recognizing and understanding Latin roots and Latin prefixes in unfamiliar words can help you spell and understand these words.

Some Latin roots and their meanings include **ver** (turn) as in extrovert (outgoing) and **viv, vit** (live) as in revive (return to life).

Some Latin prefixes include **pan** (all) as in panorama (sweeping view) and **multi** (many) as in multicolored (many colors).

Some English words are associated with one specific topic. These words are from sports.

acrobatics umpire scrimmage

There are numerous spelling rules that will help you figure out how to spell a difficult word.

When you spell a compound word, think about the way the individual words that make up the compound word are spelled. Some compound words are spelled with a hyphen dividing the two words.

throughout two-thousandths

Remember to divide compound words into syllables between the words that form the compound word.

book/keeper

Some words do not follow ordinary spelling rules. Memorize and practice spelling tricky hurdle words.

numerous martyr similar

Practice

Write List Words to answer the questions.

Which List Words contain the Latin root **temp** that means time?

1. tempest 3. temporary
2. extemporaneous

Which List Word contains the Latin root **vor** that means eat?

4. carnivorous

Which List Word contains the Latin root **spect** that means see?

5. spectacular

Which List Words contain the Latin roots **viv** or **vit** that mean life?

6. vitamin 7. vivid

Which List Words contain the Latin roots **lus** or **lud** that mean play?

8. illusion 9. ludicrous

Which List Word contains the Latin root **ver** that means turn?

10. versatile

Lesson **31**

vivid	extemporaneous
illusion	vitamin
ludicrous	spectacular
versatile	temporary
tempest	carnivorous

145

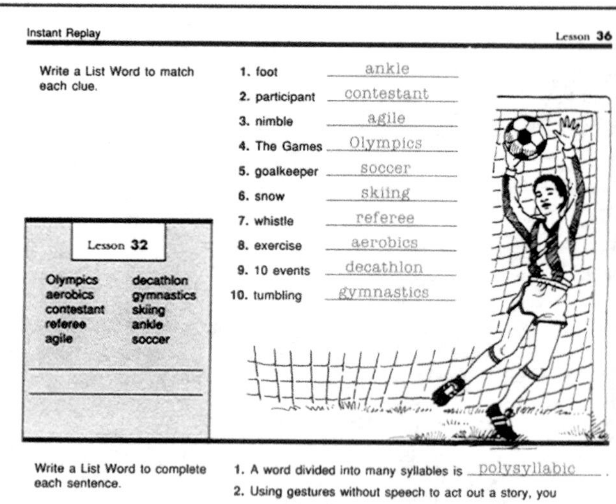

Instant Replay — Lesson **36**

Write a List Word to match each clue.

1. foot ankle
2. participant contestant
3. nimble agile
4. The Games Olympics
5. goalkeeper soccer
6. snow skiing
7. whistle referee
8. exercise aerobics
9. 10 events decathlon
10. tumbling gymnastics

Lesson **32**

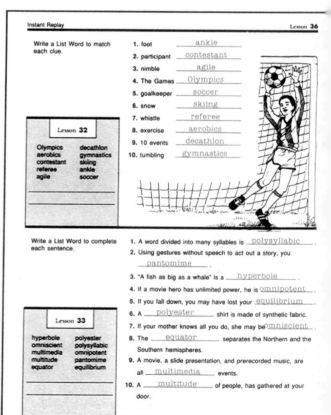

Olympics	decathlon
aerobics	gymnastics
contestant	skiing
referee	ankle
agile	soccer

Write a List Word to complete each sentence.

1. A word divided into many syllables is polysyllabic.
2. Using gestures without speech to act out a story, you pantomime.
3. "A fish as big as a whale" is a hyperbole.
4. If a movie hero has unlimited power, he is omnipotent.
5. If you fall down, you may have lost your equilibrium.
6. A polyester shirt is made of synthetic fabric.
7. If your mother knows all you do, she may be omniscient.
8. The equator separates the Northern and the Southern hemispheres.
9. A movie, a slide presentation, and prerecorded music, are all multimedia events.
10. A multitude of people, has gathered at your door.

Lesson **33**

hyperbole	polyester
omniscient	polysyllabic
multimedia	omnipotent
multitude	pantomime
equator	equilibrium

146

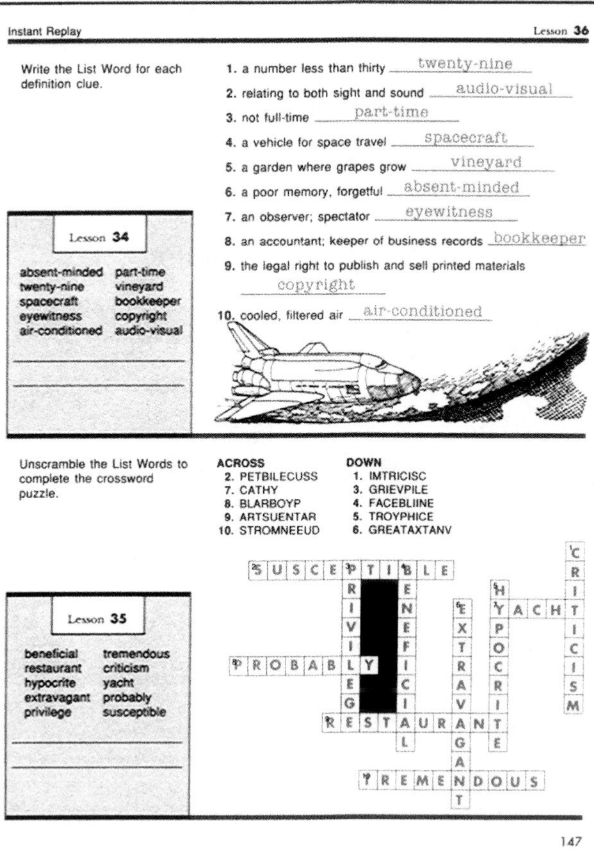

Instant Replay — Lesson 36

Write the List Word for each definition clue.

1. a number less than thirty twenty-nine
2. relating to both sight and sound audio-visual
3. not full-time part-time
4. a vehicle for space travel spacecraft
5. a garden where grapes grow vineyard
6. a poor memory, forgetful absent-minded
7. an observer; spectator eyewitness
8. an accountant; keeper of business records bookkeeper
9. the legal right to publish and sell printed materials copyright
10. cooled, filtered air air-conditioned

Lesson 34

absent-minded, part-time, twenty-nine, vineyard, spacecraft, bookkeeper, eyewitness, copyright, air-conditioned, audio-visual

Unscramble the List Words to complete the crossword puzzle.

ACROSS
2. PETBILECUSS
7. CATHY
8. BLARBOYP
9. ARTSUENTAR
10. STROMNEEUD

DOWN
1. IMTRICISC
3. GRIEVPILE
4. FACEBLIINE
5. TROYPHICE
6. GREATAXTANV

Lesson 35

beneficial, tremendous, restaurant, criticism, hypocrite, yacht, extravagant, probably, privilege, susceptible

147

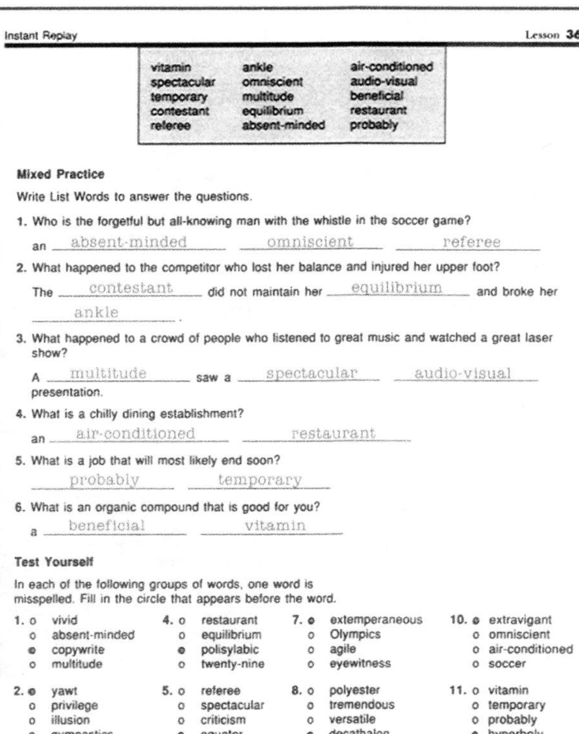

Instant Replay — Lesson 36

vitamin, ankle, air-conditioned, spectacular, omniscient, audio-visual, temporary, multitude, beneficial, contestant, equilibrium, restaurant, referee, absent-minded, probably

Mixed Practice

Write List Words to answer the questions.

1. Who is the forgetful but all-knowing man with the whistle in the soccer game?
   an absent-minded omniscient referee
2. What happened to the competitor who lost her balance and injured her upper foot?
   The contestant did not maintain her equilibrium and broke her ankle.
3. What happened to a crowd of people who listened to great music and watched a great laser show?
   A multitude saw a spectacular audio-visual presentation.
4. What is a chilly dining establishment?
   an air-conditioned restaurant
5. What is a job that will most likely end soon?
   probably temporary
6. What is an organic compound that is good for you?
   a beneficial vitamin

Test Yourself

In each of the following groups of words, one word is misspelled. Fill in the circle that appears before the word.

1. o vivid o absent-minded ● copywrite o multitude
2. ● yawt o privilege o illusion o gymnastics
3. ● parttime o pantomime o susceptible o beneficial
4. o restaurant o equilibrium ● polisylabic o twenty-nine
5. o referee o spectacular o criticism ● equater
6. o omnipotent ● vinyard o skiing o tempest
7. ● extemperaneous o Olympics o agile o eyewitness
8. o polyester o tremendous o versatile ● decathalon
9. ● airobics o spacecraft o multimedia o hypocrite
10. ● extravigant o omniscient o air-conditioned o soccer
11. o vitamin o temporary o probably ● hyperboly
12. ● bookeeper o ankle o carnivorous o ludicrous

148

Final Replay Test

1. Bears eat meat, which means they're carnivorous.
2. They ordered tickets for the Olympics.
3. I used hyperbole when I said I could eat a horse.
4. Dan is so absent-minded; he loses his keys!
5. A week relaxing will be beneficial to your health.
6. The magician's trick was an illusion.
7. The aerobics instructor demonstrated the exercise.
8. Our omniscient teacher is aware of everything.
9. Are there twenty-nine students in Ms. Woo's class?
10. Randy got a job as a waiter in a restaurant.
11. The comedian wore a ludicrous, fruit-covered hat.
12. Amir was the first contestant in the diving event.
13. The multimedia music and laser show was fun.
14. The spacecraft landed after a month in space.
15. A hypocrite will not give you a sincere opinion.
16. Alexa is a versatile athlete who plays many sports.
17. The coach and referee argued about the penalty.
18. The king waved to the multitude from the balcony.
19. The eyewitness told the police what happened.
20. The silk blouse was an extravagant purchase.
21. Torrential rain accompanied the violent tempest.
22. The agile athlete moved quickly.
23. Is the United States north of the equator?
24. Is Tammy a part-time or full-time worker?
25. It was a privilege to shake the President's hand.
26. Her extemporaneous speech was dynamic.
27. Bruce Jenner won the Olympic decathlon in 1976.
28. The t-shirt is made from cotton and polyester.
29. We rode in an air-conditioned bus.
30. What a tremendous noise the explosion made!
31. His disease was caused by a lack of vitamin B.
32. The gymnastics competition was held in our gym.
33. *Onomatopoeia* is a polysyllabic word.
34. The smell of ripe grapes permeated the vineyard.
35. Her severe criticism of my song hurt my feelings.
36. Look at that spectacular double rainbow!
37. Tim went cross-country skiing in Maine last winter.
38. Ancient Greeks believed the gods were omnipotent.
39. Dad works as a bookkeeper.
40. The luxury yacht has five bedrooms.
41. Her job is temporary and will end soon.
42. Donna taped her ankle before she played soccer.
43. He acted out a pantomime of a monkey in a cage.
44. Pablo will apply for a copyright of his play.
45. You probably don't remember, but we've met.
46. Alma uses startling, vivid colors in her paintings.
47. Most soccer balls are black and white.
48. Her equilibrium was disturbed by the flight.
49. I returned the film to the audio-visual room.
50. The old dog is weak and susceptible to disease.

Lesson 6

abdomen
amateur
allegiance
actual
bachelor
advancement
alien
anniversary
association
approximately
exaggerate
recollection
sterilize
lenient
embarrass
tedious
medium
estimate
hostess
environment
cinnamon
circular
prohibit
isolate
illustration

testimony
capacity
bulletin
villain
peninsula
microphone
competition
complicated
opponent
anticipation
patriotic
continuous
commercial
conclusion
ominous
amusement
circumference
culture
industrious
linoleum
unity
premium
smudge
subtle
vacuum

Instant Replay Word List

Lesson 12

appendage
appendix
apparatus
appropriate
appraise
assault
appreciation
apprentice
assurance
apparel
accelerate
accurate
acquire
attraction
attitude
accent
affix
accomplice
accommodate
accustomed
complexion
expression
occasion
suspicion
civilization

recitation
lotion
proportion
revolution
occupation
boulevard
camouflage
courteous
lacquer
pursuit
lieutenant
gourmet
chauffeur
expertise
silhouette
affliction
fractured
historical
construction
persistent
tactful
distract
dictator
impact
minister

Lesson 18

conscientious
confidential
harmonious
influential
unconscious
spacious
infectious
initial
financial
provincial
academically
drastically
economic
incidentally
systematic
mutual
annual
gradual
ideally
comically
commission
fluctuate
influence
intermission
omission
fluent
manual
manipulate
fluoride
inanimate
responsible
consumable
legible
permissible
available
quotable
charitable
pitiable
reliable
attainable
calendar
fragile
league
phenomenon
synonym
essential
gauge
neutral
sergeant
valise

Lesson 24

dialect
foliage
aerial
horizontal
hurricane
reservoir
fertile
irrigate
plateau
vicinity
analyze
diagram
frequency
specific
contour
epidemic
bacteria
crucial
evolution
sociology
symmetrical
minimum
trapezoid
denominator
protractor
equation
variable
diagonal
isosceles
vertical
aggressor
legislature
propaganda
alliance
nuclear
rebellion
ghetto
recession
inaugurate
referendum
calculator
repossess
authorize
executive
salary
collateral
signature
bureau
remittance
statistics

Lesson 30

heirloom
efficient
hierarchy
caffeine
patience
convenient
financier
hygiene
fiery
surveillance
adolescence
correspondence
significance
arrogance
obedience
essence
coincidence
vengeance
occurrence
preference
encyclopedia
sympathetic
physician
paralyze
synthetic

python
cylinder
cyclone
cynical
synopsis
aria
staccato
synthesizer
rhythm
podium
maestro
rhapsody
fugue
xylophone
pianist
adobe
palomino
tortilla
jaguar
poinsettia
canyon
coyote
iguana
siesta
cafeteria

Instant Replay Word List

Lesson 36

vivid
illusion
ludicrous
versatile
tempest
extemporaneous
vitamin
spectacular
temporary
carnivorous
Olympics
aerobics
contestant
referee
agile
decathlon
gymnastics
skiing
ankle
soccer
hyperbole
omniscient
multimedia
multitude
equator

polyester
polysyllabic
omnipotent
pantomime
equilibrium
absent-minded
twenty-nine
spacecraft
eyewitness
air-conditioned
part-time
vineyard
bookkeeper
copyright
audio-visual
beneficial
restaurant
hypocrite
extravagant
privilege
tremendous
criticism
yacht
probably
susceptible

Instant Replay Test

Side A

Read each set of words. Fill in the circle next to the word that is spelled correctly.

1. ⓐ envirement ⓑ enviroment ⓒ enviremint ⓓ environment
2. ⓐ onimous ⓑ omminous ⓒ ominus ⓓ ominous
3. ⓐ allegience ⓑ allegance ⓒ allegiance ⓓ alegiance
4. ⓐ cinamon ⓑ cinnamon ⓒ cinnoman ⓓ cinnamen
5. ⓐ commercial ⓑ comercial ⓒ comertial ⓓ commertial
6. ⓐ cuntinuos ⓑ continuos ⓒ continous ⓓ continuous
7. ⓐ tedious ⓑ tideous ⓒ tedeous ⓓ tidious
8. ⓐ abdoman ⓑ abdomen ⓒ abdemen ⓓ abdamen
9. ⓐ circumfrance ⓑ circumference ⓒ circumferance ⓓ circumfrence
10. ⓐ ilustration ⓑ illustrateion ⓒ illustration ⓓ illustrasion
11. ⓐ exxagerate ⓑ exaggarate ⓒ exaggerrate ⓓ exaggerate
12. ⓐ testemony ⓑ testimoney ⓒ testimony ⓓ testamoney
13. ⓐ amateur ⓑ ammature ⓒ amachure ⓓ amatuer

Name ______________________________

LESSON 6

Instant Replay Test

Side B

Read each set of words. Fill in the circle next to the word that is spelled correctly.

14. ⓐ villen ⓑ villan ⓒ villian ⓓ villain
15. ⓐ linoluem ⓑ linoleum ⓒ linolleum ⓓ linnoleum
16. ⓐ anniversary ⓑ anniversery ⓒ aniversary ⓓ aniversery
17. ⓐ embarass ⓑ emberass ⓒ embarrass ⓓ embarras
18. ⓐ opponant ⓑ oponent ⓒ oponant ⓓ opponent
19. ⓐ premium ⓑ primiem ⓒ premiem ⓓ premuim
20. ⓐ peninsula ⓑ penensula ⓒ peninsulla ⓓ penninsula
21. ⓐ vacume ⓑ vacuem ⓒ vaccum ⓓ vacuum
22. ⓐ linient ⓑ leniant ⓒ lenient ⓓ leaniant
23. ⓐ subtle ⓑ sudtle ⓒ suddle ⓓ subtel
24. ⓐ approximately ⓑ aproximatly ⓒ aproximately ⓓ approximatly
25. ⓐ competetion ⓑ compitition ⓒ competition ⓓ compettition

 Name ______________________

Instant Replay Test

LESSON **12**

Side A

Read each set of phrases. Fill in the circle next to the phrase with an underlined word that is spelled correctly.

1. ⓐ his tactful manner ⓑ your tackful comment ⓒ that tacktful statement ⓓ her tactfull criticism
2. ⓐ his lengthy recitetation ⓑ her public recitasion ⓒ your monotonous resitasion ⓓ a dramatic recitation
3. ⓐ this commercial bulevard ⓑ the tree-lined boulavard ⓒ densely populated boulevard ⓓ that residential bolevard
4. ⓐ weight-lifting apparatus ⓑ the gymnastics aparratus ⓒ safety aparrattus ⓓ firefighting apparratus
5. ⓐ the famous expresion ⓑ a witty expreshion ⓒ that humorous expression ⓓ a quotable expretion
6. ⓐ the previous dicktator ⓑ the despised dicktater ⓒ the amiable dictater ⓓ the country's dictator
7. ⓐ the aproppriate answer ⓑ an approppriate response ⓒ apropriate attire ⓓ an appropriate amount
8. ⓐ an ambitious persuit ⓑ in dedicated pursuit ⓒ in persuite of happiness ⓓ in pursuite of criminals
9. ⓐ his dark complexion ⓑ her fair cumplection ⓒ her freckled complection ⓓ his clear cumplexion
10. ⓐ that courtous student ⓑ his curteous disposition ⓒ the courteous diplomat ⓓ a corteous pilot
11. ⓐ the decorated lieutenant ⓑ a female leutenant ⓒ a first lieutenent ⓓ the commanding liutenant
12. ⓐ apreciation and gratitude ⓑ with sincere appretiation ⓒ apretiation and thoughtfulness ⓓ with genuine appreciation
13. ⓐ to acommodate your idea ⓑ to accomadate patients ⓒ to accommodate guests ⓓ to acomodate the crowd

Name ______________________________

Instant Replay Test

Side B

Read each set of phrases. Fill in the circle next to the phrase with an underlined word that is spelled correctly.

14. ⓐ your positive atitude
ⓑ a negative attitude
ⓒ this poor attittude
ⓓ his healthy atittude

15. ⓐ a likable shauffeur
ⓑ hired a shofer
ⓒ the family chauffer
ⓓ an experienced chauffeur

16. ⓐ this church's minaster
ⓑ the compassionate minister
ⓒ the sympathetic minisster
ⓓ a female minnister

17. ⓐ the blacksmith's apprentice
ⓑ an electrician's apprentiss
ⓒ that mason's aprentiss
ⓓ a carpentry aprentice

18. ⓐ her lifelong ocuppation
ⓑ an unusual occupation
ⓒ this lucrative ocuppasion
ⓓ a demanding occupasion

19. ⓐ to affix the label
ⓑ to affixe with glue
ⓒ will afixe his signature
ⓓ to afix the sticker

20. ⓐ this hystorical city
ⓑ historicle fiction
ⓒ an historical event
ⓓ hystoricle diaries

21. ⓐ that criminal's acompplice
ⓑ the smuggler's accompliss
ⓒ this alleged acompliss
ⓓ the thief's accomplice

22. ⓐ a special occassion
ⓑ a memorable ocassion
ⓒ this joyous ocasion
ⓓ a festive occasion

23. ⓐ informal apparel
ⓑ sleep aparrel
ⓒ formal apparrel
ⓓ traditional apparell

24. ⓐ a fracksured thumb
ⓑ her fractured ankle
ⓒ the frackture bone
ⓓ his fracturred toe

25. ⓐ acquire a taste
ⓑ acquir a phone
ⓒ aquire his degree
ⓓ acquier knowledge

 Name ____________________

Instant Replay Test

Side A

LESSON 18

Read each sentence and set of words. Fill in the circle next to the word that is spelled correctly to complete the sentence.

1. This famous artist prefers to paint ____ objects.
   ⓐ inannimate ⓒ inaminate
   ⓑ inanimate ⓓ inanimmate

2. Food and water are ____ for human survival.
   ⓐ essencial ⓒ esencial
   ⓑ esential ⓓ essential

3. The ____ office could accommodate both physicians' practices.
   ⓐ spacious ⓒ spacous
   ⓑ spatious ⓓ spatous

4. The entire cast is ____ for the production's tremendous success.
   ⓐ responsible ⓒ risponsible
   ⓑ risponsable ⓓ responsable

5. A ____ was formed to investigate the alleged corruption.
   ⓐ comission ⓒ commision
   ⓑ commition ⓓ commission

6. The subway provides a ____ source of public transportation.
   ⓐ relyable ⓒ reliable
   ⓑ relyible ⓓ relible

7. The performers changed their costumes during the play's ____.
   ⓐ intermision ⓒ intermission
   ⓑ intramission ⓓ intamission

8. ____ correspondence is filed in a locked cabinet.
   ⓐ Confadential ⓒ Confadencial
   ⓑ Confidential ⓓ Confidencial

9. The prime minister's major concern is ____ stability.
   ⓐ econnomic ⓒ economic
   ⓑ ecanomic ⓓ ecconomic

10. The man was ____ after the accident.
    ⓐ unconscious ⓒ unconcience
    ⓑ unconscius ⓓ unconscience

Name ______________________________

Instant Replay Test

Side B

Read each sentence and set of words. Fill in the circle next to the word that is spelled correctly to complete the sentence.

11. The newlyweds consulted a ____ advisor for investment advice.
    - (a) finantiel
    - (b) financial
    - (c) finantial
    - (d) finnancial

12. Using a ____ contributes to good time management.
    - (a) calender
    - (b) calander
    - (c) calandar
    - (d) calendar

13. Outerwear was ____ reduced during the winter clearance sale.
    - (a) drastically
    - (b) drasticly
    - (c) drasticaly
    - (d) drasticcly

14. The all-star ____ includes the best male and female players.
    - (a) leag
    - (b) leuge
    - (c) league
    - (d) leage

15. The elderly man was commended for his numerous ____ acts.
    - (a) charitabal
    - (b) charitible
    - (c) charatible
    - (d) charitable

16. Attendance at the ____ realtor's convention was larger than expected.
    - (a) anuall
    - (b) anual
    - (c) annule
    - (d) annual

17. The town committee voted to put ____ in the water.
    - (a) floride
    - (b) floruide
    - (c) fluoride
    - (d) flouride

18. My cousin is a ____ in the army.
    - (a) sargent
    - (b) sargeant
    - (c) seargeant
    - (d) sergeant

19. Food is a ____ commodity.
    - (a) consumable
    - (b) consumeable
    - (c) connsumable
    - (d) consumabel

20. I ____ saw Mark at the meeting.
    - (a) insidentally
    - (b) incidentaly
    - (c) insidentally
    - (d) incidentally

Name ______________________________

Instant Replay Test

Side A

LESSON **24**

Read each set of words. Fill in the circle next to the word that is spelled wrong.

1. ⓐ proppaganda ⓑ epitome ⓒ camouflage ⓓ signature
2. ⓐ sphere ⓑ isthmus ⓒ verticle ⓓ dialect
3. ⓐ reservor ⓑ executive ⓒ adhesive ⓓ communism
4. ⓐ theorem ⓑ allience ⓒ bayou ⓓ bureau
5. ⓐ statistics ⓑ isoseles ⓒ vacate ⓓ calculator
6. ⓐ referendum ⓑ facsimile ⓒ furtile ⓓ strategic
7. ⓐ foliage ⓑ delegate ⓒ ghettoe ⓓ merchandise
8. ⓐ symetrical ⓑ lesion ⓒ rebellion ⓓ resources
9. ⓐ nuclear ⓑ chaplain ⓒ bristle ⓓ irigate
10. ⓐ stethoscope ⓑ legislature ⓒ affection ⓓ reccession
11. ⓐ manuscript ⓑ diagonal ⓒ presistent ⓓ denominater
12. ⓐ tremor ⓑ huricane ⓒ barrier ⓓ plateau
13. ⓐ photogenic ⓑ inaugurrate ⓒ affirm ⓓ aggressor

ame ____

Instant Replay Test

Side B

Read each set of words. Fill in the circle next to the word that is spelled wrong.

14. ⓐ collateral ⓑ specific ⓒ trapazoid ⓓ ambitious

15. ⓐ horizontle ⓑ inequality ⓒ tangerine ⓓ protractor

16. ⓐ vicinity ⓑ armistice ⓒ historical ⓓ reposess

17. ⓐ policy ⓑ analize ⓒ intelligible ⓓ accomplice

18. ⓐ jealousy ⓑ crutial ⓒ frequency ⓓ ferocious

19. ⓐ variable ⓑ debtor ⓒ impartial ⓓ colatteral

20. ⓐ diegram ⓑ lullaby ⓒ appendage ⓓ minimum

21. ⓐ sociology ⓑ substantial ⓒ evelution ⓓ compatible

22. ⓐ animosity ⓑ heroically ⓒ remitance ⓓ epidemic

23. ⓐ emphatic ⓑ prolific ⓒ salery ⓓ progressive

24. ⓐ appetizer ⓑ dividend ⓒ bacteria ⓓ contuor

25. ⓐ muscular ⓑ autherize ⓒ equation ⓓ gradual

Name ______________________________

Instant Replay Test

Side A

Read each set of phrases. Fill in the circle next to the phrase with an underlined word spelled wrong.

1. (a) an official signature
   (b) appease the crowd
   (c) the correspondance course
   (d) a gracious hostess
2. (a) the composer's rhapsody
   (b) a regional dialect
   (c) the mistaken notion
   (d) an accomplished peanist
3. (a) that palamino mare
   (b) recorded statistics
   (c) had tremendous appeal
   (d) an efficient cashier
4. (a) these staccato notes
   (b) fertile soil
   (c) difficulty with digestion
   (d) a bright red pointsettia
5. (a) the respected maistro
   (b) colorful foliage
   (c) the synthesizer keyboard
   (d) unanimous approval
6. (a) a varied assortment
   (b) that symmetrical design
   (c) rythym and blues
   (d) filled to capacity
7. (a) the architect's protractor
   (b) a complicated sequence
   (c) an afternoon seista
   (d) the convicted assassin
8. (a) the deepest canyen
   (b) nuclear energy
   (c) a patriotic gesture
   (d) in total cooperation
9. (a) hierarchy of authority
   (b) your color perference
   (c) his sociology class
   (d) her bridal boutique
10. (a) the conductor's podeum
    (b) a conscientious lawyer
    (c) a brief synopsis
    (d) to applaud enthusiastically
11. (a) the cyclone damage
    (b) a spacious apartment
    (c) an electrical appliance
    (d) this torteya batter
12. (a) vengance and greed
    (b) a commemorative affair
    (c) effects of caffeine
    (d) sterilize the equipment
13. (a) cone or cylinder
    (b) a chronic affliction
    (c) a melodious arria
    (d) estimate the cost

ame ______________________________

LESSON 30

Instant Replay Test

Side B

Read each set of phrases. Fill in the circle next to the phrase with an underlined word spelled wrong.

14. ⓐ that moisturizing lotion
    ⓑ the synical comedian
    ⓒ an unconscious victim
    ⓓ this harmonious fugue

15. ⓐ a monthly occurrence
    ⓑ our initial meeting
    ⓒ of equal proportion
    ⓓ arogance and conceit

16. ⓐ self-service cafeteria
    ⓑ a conveniant location
    ⓒ an unfounded suspicion
    ⓓ injure or paralyze

17. ⓐ this knowledgeable financier
    ⓑ her musical expertise
    ⓒ that howling coyote
    ⓓ a giant pythonn

18. ⓐ an incredible coincidence
    ⓑ of adobe construction
    ⓒ resistant to change
    ⓓ under police surveilance

19. ⓐ of major signifacance
    ⓑ hunger and fatigue
    ⓒ this Braille encyclopedia
    ⓓ an infectious disease

20. ⓐ a simpathetic listener
    ⓑ the responsible chaperone
    ⓒ influential politicians
    ⓓ a systematic method

21. ⓐ an unresolved conflict
    ⓑ conscientious dental hygene
    ⓒ comically resolved
    ⓓ the leaping jaguar

22. ⓐ entering adolescence
    ⓑ manual operation
    ⓒ a comfortable cushion
    ⓓ pacience and tolerance

23. ⓐ his fluoride treatment
    ⓑ repossess the house
    ⓒ the amicable phisician
    ⓓ lacquer application

24. ⓐ a cherished airloom
    ⓑ obedience and respect
    ⓒ their daily routine
    ⓓ a fiery display

25. ⓐ legible handwriting
    ⓑ of synthetec material
    ⓒ essence of life
    ⓓ this majestic view

 Name ______________________________

Instant Replay Test

Side A

Read each set of words. Fill in the circle next to the word that is spelled wrong.

1. ⓐ versatile ⓑ Fahrenheit ⓒ motorcycle ⓓ decathalon
2. ⓐ multimedia ⓑ peasant ⓒ audiovisual ⓓ ferocious
3. ⓐ ambulance ⓑ beneficial ⓒ toboggan ⓓ equillibrium
4. ⓐ carniverous ⓑ loose-leaf ⓒ currency ⓓ absent-minded
5. ⓐ probabley ⓑ basis ⓒ Olympics ⓓ besiege
6. ⓐ mythical ⓑ soccor ⓒ umpire ⓓ spacecraft
7. ⓐ encore ⓑ privelege ⓒ hyperactive ⓓ multitude
8. ⓐ tempest ⓑ quarterback ⓒ pantamime ⓓ medium
9. ⓐ referree ⓑ martyr ⓒ agile ⓓ occurrence
10. ⓐ tremendous ⓑ vitality ⓒ pyramid ⓓ bookeeper
11. ⓐ pandemonium ⓑ equator ⓒ scrimmage ⓓ polysylabic
12. ⓐ dictator ⓑ vinyard ⓒ educational ⓓ extemporaneous
13. ⓐ able-bodied ⓑ extravagent ⓒ gymnastics ⓓ bulletin

ame ______________________________

Instant Replay Test

Side B

Read each set of words. Fill in the circle next to the word that is spelled wrong.

14. ⓐ criticism ⓑ introvert ⓒ silhouette ⓓ hypacrite

15. ⓐ precipitation ⓑ vivvid ⓒ equidistant ⓓ vitamin

16. ⓐ polyester ⓑ luxury ⓒ contestent ⓓ copious

17. ⓐ part-time ⓑ civilization ⓒ eye-witness ⓓ elude

18. ⓐ omnicient ⓑ retrospect ⓒ hockey ⓓ skiing

19. ⓐ microscopic ⓑ matinee ⓒ yacht ⓓ temporery

20. ⓐ copyright ⓑ airobics ⓒ polytheism ⓓ eliminated

21. ⓐ liquefy ⓑ ludicrus ⓒ serum ⓓ susceptible

22. ⓐ restaraunt ⓑ appropriate ⓒ temporal ⓓ ankle

23. ⓐ hyperbolee ⓑ influenza ⓒ panorama ⓓ spectacular

24. ⓐ air-conditioned ⓑ numerous ⓒ twentynine ⓓ communicable

25. ⓐ omnipotent ⓑ accord ⓒ illussion ⓓ congruent

Name ______________________________

Instant Replay Tests

ANSWER KEY

Lesson 6

1. d
2. d
3. c
4. b
5. a
6. d
7. a
8. b
9. b
10. c
11. d
12. c
13. a
14. d
15. b
16. a
17. c
18. d
19. a
20. a
21. d
22. c
23. a
24. a
25. c

Lesson 12

1. a
2. d
3. c
4. a
5. c
6. d
7. d
8. b
9. a
10. c
11. a
12. d
13. c
14. b
15. d
16. b
17. a
18. b
19. a
20. c
21. d
22. d
23. a
24. b
25. a

Lesson 18

1. b
2. d
3. a
4. a
5. d
6. c
7. c
8. b
9. c
10. a
11. b
12. d
13. a
14. c
15. d
16. d
17. c
18. d
19. a
20. d

Lesson 24

1. a
2. c
3. a
4. b
5. b
6. c
7. c
8. a
9. d
10. d
11. d
12. b
13. b
14. c
15. a
16. d
17. b
18. b
19. d
20. a
21. c
22. c
23. c
24. d
25. b

Lesson 30

1. c
2. d
3. a
4. d
5. a
6. c
7. c
8. a
9. b
10. a
11. d
12. a
13. c
14. b
15. d
16. b
17. d
18. d
19. a
20. a
21. b
22. d
23. c
24. a
25. b

Lesson 36

1. d
2. c
3. d
4. a
5. a
6. b
7. b
8. c
9. a
10. d
11. d
12. b
13. b
14. d
15. b
16. c
17. c
18. a
19. d
20. b
21. b
22. a
23. a
24. c
25. c

List Words

WORD	LESSON
abdomen	1
able-bodied	34
absent-minded	34
absolute	21
academically	14
accelerate	8
accent	8
access	8
accommodate	8
accompany	8
accomplice	8
accord	8
accurate	8
accustomed	8
acquire	8
acre	19
acrobatics	32
actual	1
adhesive	1
administration	23
adobe	29
adolescence	26
advancement	1
aerial	19
aerobics	32
affair	8
affection	9
affirm	8
affix	8
affliction	11
affront	8
aggressor	22
agile	32
air-conditioned	34
alfalfa	1
alien	1
align	3
allegiance	1
alliance	22
amateur	1
ambitious	13
ambulance	26
amiable	16
amusement	5
analyze	20
animation	15
animosity	15
ankle	32
anniversary	1
annual	14
anticipation	4
antonym	27
apparatus	7
apparel	7
appeal	7
appease	7
appendage	7
appendix	7
appetizer	7
applaud	7
appliance	7
appraise	7
appreciation	7
apprentice	7
appropriate	7
approval	7
approximately	1
archaeology	20
archery	32
arctic	17
aria	28
armistice	22
armory	4
arrogance	26
arsenal	22
assassin	7
assault	7
assert	7
asset	7
association	1
assortment	7
assurance	7
astronomy	1
attaché	8
attachment	8
attainable	16
attentive	8
attire	3
attitude	8
attraction	8
attribute	5
attune	8
audio-visual	34
auditorium	28
authorize	23
available	16
axis	19
bachelor	1
bacteria	20
ballerina	28
barrier	3
basically	14
basis	1
bayou	19
beige	25
beneficial	35
besiege	25
betray	2
billion	23
blockade	4
bookkeeper	34
boulevard	10
boutique	10
brilliance	26
bristle	3
bulletin	3
bureau	23
burial	13
cabana	29
cafeteria	29
caffeine	25
calculator	23
calendar	17
calorie	10
camouflage	10
campus	5
canyon	29
capacity	3
capitalist	22
carnivorous	31
caucus	22
ceremonial	13
certification	23
chaperone	10
chaplain	10
characteristics	20
charitable	16
chauffeur	10
cinnamon	3
circular	3
circumference	5
civilization	9
classic	14
clearance	26
cockpit	4
coincidence	26
collapse	17
collateral	23
comically	14
commence	26
commercial	4
commission	15
communicable	16
communism	22
compact	11
compass	20
compatible	16
competition	4
complexion	9
complicated	4
concerto	28
conclusion	4
confidential	13
conflict	11
congruent	21
conscientious	13
consist	11
constrict	11
construction	11
consumable	16
contestant	32
continent	4
continuous	4
contour	20
contract	11
convenient	25
conviction	9
cooperation	9
copious	4
copyright	34
correspondence	26
courteous	10
coyote	29
criticism	35
crucial	20
crystals	27
culture	5
curable	16
currency	23
cushion	9
cycle	20
cyclone	27
cylinder	27
cymbals	27
cynical	27
debtor	17
decathlon	32
decibels	28
defiance	26
delegate	2
denominator	21
desist	11
despise	2
devotion	9
diagonal	21
diagram	20
dialect	19
diameter	1
dictator	11
diction	11
digestion	9
disposable	16
distract	11
district	11
dividend	23
donor	4
dramatic	14
drastically	14
ecological	19
economic	14
educational	35
efficient	25
elegance	26
eliminate	35
elude	31
emancipate	15
embarrass	2
embassy	2
emission	15
emphatic	14
encore	28
encyclopedia	27
endeavor	17
endurance	26
ensemble	28
environment	2
epidemic	20
epitome	2
equation	21
equator	33
equidistant	33
equilateral	21
equilibrium	33
erode	2
essence	26
essential	17
estimate	2
ethnic	19
evidence	26
evolution	20
exaggerate	2
executive	23
expedition	19
expertise	10
expression	9
extemporaneous	31

List Words

WORD	LESSON
extravagant	35
extrovert	31
eyewitness	34
fabric	1
facsimile	20
Fahrenheit	25
fatigue	10
ferocious	13
fertile	19
fiend	25
fiery	25
fiesta	29
financial	13
financier	25
fluctuate	15
fluent	15
fluid	15
fluoride	15
foliage	19
fractured	11
fragile	17
frantically	14
frequency	20
frontier	25
fugue	28
gauge	17
geranium	5
ghetto	22
glorious	13
goalkeeper	32
gourmet	10
gracious	13
gradual	14
grieve	25
gymnastics	32
habitable	16
handlebars	34
harmonious	13
heinous	25
heirloom	25
heroically	14
hiccups	3
hierarchy	25
historical	11
hockey	32
horizontal	19
hostess	2
hurricane	19
hydrogen	27
hygiene	25
hyperactive	33
hyperbole	33
hypocrite	35
ideally	14
idle	3
ignorance	3
iguana	29
illusion	31
illusive	31
illustration	3
impact	11
impartial	13
inanimate	15
inaugurate	22
incidentally	14
industrious	5
inequality	21
infectious	13
influence	15
influential	13
influenza	15
initial	13
insurance	3
intelligible	16
intention	9
interest	23
intermission	15
introvert	31
inverse	31
invoice	23
involve	3
irrigate	19
isolate	3
isosceles	21
isthmus	19
italics	23
jaguar	29
jealousy	17
justify	23
kayak	32
lacquer	10
league	17
leeway	2
legible	16
legislature	22
lenient	2
lesion	9
lieutenant	10
linoleum	5
liquefy	20
livable	16
loose-leaf	34
lotion	9
ludicrous	31
lullaby	5
luxury	35
maestro	28
majestic	10
mandate	15
maneuver	17
manicure	5
manipulate	15
manual	15
manuscript	1
martial	13
martyr	35
masquerade	10
material	13
matinee	17
mayonnaise	17
medium	2
medley	28
melodic	28
merchandise	23
meridian	19
meteorite	17
microphone	4
microscopic	14
minimum	21
minister	11
motorcycle	34
multicolored	33
multimedia	33
multiple	33
multitude	33
muscular	5
mutual	14
mythical	27
nasal	17
neutral	17
nine-hundredths	34
notable	16
notion	9
nuclear	22
numerous	35
obedience	26
oblique	21
obtuse	21
occasion	9
occupation	9
occurrence	26
Olympics	32
ominous	4
omission	15
omnipotent	33
omnipresent	33
omniscient	33
opponent	4
orchid	3
oxygen	27
palmetto	29
palomino	29
pandemonium	33
panorama	33
pantomime	33
paralyze	27
part-time	34
passport	10
patience	25
patriotic	4
peasant	22
peninsula	3
performance	26
permissible	16
persistent	11
phenomenon	17
photogenic	4
physician	27
pianist	28
pier	25
pimento	29
pitiable	16
plateau	19
podium	28
poinsettia	29
policy	4
polyester	33
polygamy	33
polygon	33
polysyllabic	33
polytheism	33
portable	16
precipitation	19
preference	26
premium	5
privilege	35
probably	35
prohibit	3
prohibition	22
prolific	14
prominent	35
pronto	29
propaganda	22
proportion	9
prospector	4
protractor	21
provincial	13
pursuit	10
pyramid	27
python	27
quarterback	34
quartet	28
quotable	16
rebellion	22
receipt	25
recession	22
recitation	9
recollection	2
referee	32
referendum	22
reliable	16
remittance	23
renegade	29
repossess	23
reprieve	25
reservoir	19
residence	26
resistant	11
resources	19
responsible	16
restaurant	35
restrict	11
retrospect	31
revive	31
revolution	9
rhapsody	28
rhythm	28
routine	10
sacred	2
salary	23
scrimmage	32
self-sacrifice	34
senior	2
sergeant	17
serum	5
siesta	29
signature	23
significance	26
silhouette	10
similar	35
sincerely	35
skew	21
skiing	32
slogan	4
smudge	5
soccer	32

List Words

WORD	LESSON
socialist	22
sociology	20
solidify	27
sombrero	29
spacecraft	34
spacious	13
spatial	20
specific	20
spectacular	31
sphere	21
sportscaster	32
sprinter	32
staccato	28
stampede	29
statistics	23
stereophonic	28
sterilize	2
stethoscope	20
strategic	22
submission	15
substance	5
substantial	14

WORD	LESSON
subtle	5
suddenness	35
suite	10
surveillance	25
susceptible	35
suspect	31
suspenders	5
suspicion	9
symbolic	27
symmetrical	21
sympathetic	27
synonym	17
synopsis	27
synthesizer	28
synthetic	27
systematic	14
tactful	11
tamale	29
tangent	21
tangerine	1
tedious	2
tempest	31

WORD	LESSON
temporal	31
temporary	31
tenacious	13
tension	9
testify	2
testimony	3
theorem	21
three-fourths	34
throughout	34
toboggan	32
tortilla	29
toxic	20
tradition	35
tragic	14
traitor	22
transmission	15
transparency	1
trapezoid	21
tremendous	35
tremor	20
twenty-nine	34
two-thousandths	34

WORD	LESSON
typical	27
umpire	32
unanimous	15
unconscious	13
unity	5
uranium	5
vacate	1
vacuum	5
valise	17
vanilla	29
variable	21
vengeance	26
versatile	31
vertical	21
vicinity	19
villain	3
vineyard	34
vitality	31
vitamin	31
vivid	31
xylophone	28
yacht	35

Bonus Words

WORD	LESSON
absurdity	5
acclamation	4
accountable	15
accusation	11
aerospace	9
Afghanistan	19
amendment	2
analogy	16
analysis	23
anecdote	5
application	17
arbitrate	2
Argentina	19
artichoke	29
asparagus	29
aspiration	17
assailant	11
assembly	2
astute	8
auction	32
audible	21
auditory	35
auricle	35
authentic	4
awareness	20
ballad	3
baritone	28
Beirut	26
Belgium	19
beverage	1
biodegradable	31
blacksmith	22
blanch	1
booster	9
boudoir	10

WORD	LESSON
breeding	25
broadcast	21
Buenos Aires	26
buffet	1
Cairo	26
capsule	9
carburetor	14
cartilage	35
casserole	1
chassis	14
chlorophyll	31
chromosome	25
chronicle	21
coalition	2
colloquial	13
commentator	21
computation	7
consecutive	7
conservation	31
conservative	2
consolation	15
consommé	29
conversion	27
corral	32
couplet	3
crankshaft	14
cue	21
cultivator	32
cursor	27
data processing	27
decimal	16
determined	17
development	23
devise	23
devoured	34

WORD	LESSON
dexterous	8
diplomatic	2
disposition	11
dissatisfied	15
distributor	14
documentation	27
dominant	25
Dublin	26
dulcimer	28
eardrum	35
ecosystem	20
egregious	13
elliptical	7
emit	20
endorsement	4
epaulet	10
epic	3
equivalent	16
erroneous	15
espionage	10
Ethiopia	19
Eustachian tube	35
exhibition	4
exonerate	11
experiment	23
exponent	16
factor	16
falter	33
familial	13
farcical	5
farfetched	33
fastidious	8
federal	2
felony	11
fiasco	33

WORD	LESSON
fillet	29
folklore	22
formula	23
fortify	33
fractions	16
frijoles	29
frustration	15
furious	13
futile	33
garnish	1
gazette	21
generate	23
generator	14
genes	25
genetics	25
genteel	8
germinate	31
graphic	27
gravitation	9
gregarious	5
grouchy	34
gullible	8
haiku	3
harpsichord	28
haughty	34
hazardous	20
hearing aid	35
heroine	22
hilarity	5
honesty	15
horticulture	32
humble	13
hybrid	32
hypotenuse	7
imagery	3

Bonus Words

WORD	LESSON
impertinent	8
impetuous	8
inherited	25
insight	23
inspection	20
integer	7
integrity	15
interpret	16
interview	17
inventive	23
irony	5
jester	22
jurisdiction	11
knave	22
laboratory	23
larceny	11
Libya	19
limerick	3
livestock	32
lobbyist	2
lucid	13
luncheon	1
lyrical	3
management	27
marinate	1
marquee	10
mastoid	35
membrane	35
menagerie	10
merchant	22
message	4
metronome	28
microwave	1
mode	7
modem	27
motion sickness	35
mutation	25
narrative	3
New Delhi	26
newscast	21
Nicaragua	19
noxious	20
obligation	15
obnoxious	8
octave	28
odometer	14
offspring	25
omelet	29
operetta	28
opportunity	17
originate	23
Oslo	26
Ottawa	26
overhaul	32
overwrought	34
oxidation	31
ozone	20
parfait	29
percussion	28
perishable	1
personable	8
Philadelphia	26
Philippines	19
photosynthesis	31
pirouette	10
piston	14
placard	4
pollutant	20
potpourri	10
precarious	13
prediction	16
preservation	31
princess	22
printout	27
probability	16
probation	11
proficient	17
promenade	10
promote	4
propellant	9
proponent	2
publicity	21
pun	5
purchase	4
quadrant	16
quaint	13
qualifications	17
queasy	34
radiator	14
radioactive	20
ragout	10
rambled	34
ratio	7
recessive	25
reciprocal	7
reentry	9
references	17
reimburse	4
remunerate	15
rendezvous	9
request	15
resignation	17
resumé	17
rhyme	3
sanctuary	31
sarcastic	5
satire	5
Seoul	26
servant	22
shuffled	34
silage	32
sirloin	29
skeptical	34
slapstick	5
soldier	22
sonnet	3
soprano	28
sovereign	2
speedometer	14
square root	7
squeamish	8
statute	11
storage	27
structured	27
stumbled	34
Switzerland	19
Sydney	26
tabloid	21
televise	21
Thailand	19
throttle	14
thrust	9
tolerant	33
tractor	32
trait	25
trajectory	9
traverse	33
travesty	33
trombone	28
troubadour	28
trough	32
turbulent	33
tyrant	33
uninhabited	31
utensils	1
veal	29
velocity	9
Venezuela	19
vertices	7
vertigo	35
vicarious	13
vicious	13
vignette	10
volatile	20
voucher	4
waiver	11
wheezed	34
wildlife	31
wizard	22
zucchini	29

Group Practice

Crossword Relay First draw a large grid on the board. Then divide the class into several teams. Teams compete against each other to form separate crossword puzzles on the board. Individuals on each team take turns racing against members of the other teams to join list words until all possibilities have been exhausted. A list word may appear on each crossword puzzle only once. The winning team is the team whose crossword puzzle contains the greatest number of correctly spelled list words or the team who finishes first.

Proofreading Relay Write two columns of misspelled list words on the board. Although the errors can differ, be sure that each list has the same number of errors. Divide the class into two teams and assign each team to a different column. Teams then compete against each other to correct their assigned lists by team members taking turns erasing and replacing an appropriate letter. Each member may correct only one letter per turn. The team that is first to correct its entire word list wins.

Detective Call on a student to be a detective. The detective must choose a spelling word from the list and think of a structural clue, definition, or synonym that will help classmates identify it. The detective then states the clue using the format, "I spy a word that…" Students are called on to guess and spell the mystery word. Whoever answers correctly gets to take a turn being the detective.

Spelling Tic-Tac-Toe Draw a tic-tac-toe square on the board. Divide the class into *X* and *O* teams. Take turns dictating spelling words to members of each team. If the word is spelled correctly, allow the team member to place an *X* or *O* on the square. The first team to place three *X's* or *O's* in a row wins.

Words of Fortune Have students put their heads down while you write a spelling word on the board in large letters. Then cover each letter with a sheet of sturdy paper. The paper can be fastened to the board with a magnet. Call on a student to guess any letter of the alphabet they think may be hidden. If that particular letter is hidden, then reveal the letter in every place where it appears in the word by removing the paper.

The student continues to guess letters until an incorrect guess is made or the word is revealed. In the event that an incorrect guess is made, a different student continues the game. Continue the game until every list word has been hidden and then revealed.

Applied Spelling

Journal Allow time each day for students to write into a journal. A spiral bound notebook can be used for this purpose. Encourage students to express their feelings about events that are happening in their lives at home or at school. Or they could write about what their plans are for the day. To get them started, you may have to provide starter phrases. Allow them to use "invented" spelling for words they can't spell.

You may wish to collect the journals periodically to write comments that echo what the student has written. For example, a student's entry might read, "I'm hape I gt to plae bazball todae." The teacher's response could be, "Baseball is my favorite game, too. I'd be happy to watch you play baseball." This method allows students to learn correct spelling and sentence structure without emphasizing their errors in a negative way.

Letter to the Teacher On a regular basis, have students each write a note to the teacher. At first the teacher may have to suggest topics or provide a starter sentence. It may be possible to suggest a topic that includes words from the spelling list. The teacher should write a response at the bottom of each letter that provides the student with a model of any spelling or sentence structure that apparently needs improvement.

Daily Edit Each day, provide a brief writing sample on the board that contains errors in spelling, capitalization, or punctuation. Have students rewrite the sample correctly. Provide time later in the day to have the class correct the errors on the board while students self-correct their work.

Word Locker Have students use a stenographer's notebook or staple together pages of the reproducible **Word Locker** (provided on page 111 in the teacher's edition) to keep a record of words they encounter difficulty spelling. Tabs could be added to some of the pages to separate the notebook into sections for each letter of the alphabet. Encourage students to use a dictionary or ask the teacher to help them spell the words with which they are having trouble. Periodically, allow the students to work in pairs to test each other on a set of words taken from their personal word list.

Acrostic Poems Have students write a word from the spelling list vertically. Then instruct them to join a word horizontally to each letter of the list word. The horizontal words must begin with the letters in the list word. They also should be words that describe or relate feelings about the list word. Encourage students to refer to a dictionary for help in finding appropriate words. Here is a sample acrostic poem:

Zebras
Otters
Ostriches

Nursery Rhyme Exchange Provide students with copies of a familiar nursery rhyme. Discuss how some of the words can be exchanged for other words that have similar meanings. Ask the students to rewrite the nursery rhyme exchanging some of the words. You may want to encourage the students to try this technique with nursery rhymes of their choice. Be sure to give students the opportunity to read their rhymes to the class.

Level G
Student Record Chart

Name ____________________________________

			Pretest	Final Test	BonusTest
Lesson	1	Vowel **a**			
Lesson	2	Vowel **e**			
Lesson	3	Vowel **i**			
Lesson	4	Vowel **o**			
Lesson	5	Vowel **u**			
Lesson	6	Instant Replay	■		■
Lesson	7	Words Beginning with **ap, as**			
Lesson	8	Prefixes **ac, af, at**			
Lesson	9	Words Ending with **ion**			
Lesson	10	Words with French Derivations			
Lesson	11	Latin Roots			
Lesson	12	Instant Replay	■		■
Lesson	13	Endings **ial, ious**			
Lesson	14	Endings **al, ally, ic, ically, ly**			
Lesson	15	Latin Roots			
Lesson	16	Endings **able, ible**			
Lesson	17	Hurdle Words			
Lesson	18	Instant Replay	■		■
Lesson	19	Words from Geography			
Lesson	20	Words from Science			
Lesson	21	Words from Math			
Lesson	22	Words from History			
Lesson	23	Words from Business			
Lesson	24	Instant Replay	■		■
Lesson	25	Words with **ei** and **ie**			
Lesson	26	Endings **ance, ence, ce**			
Lesson	27	**y** as a Vowel			
Lesson	28	Words from Music			
Lesson	29	Words with Spanish Derivations			
Lesson	30	Instant Replay	■		■
Lesson	31	Latin Roots			
Lesson	32	Words from Sports			
Lesson	33	Words with Latin Prefixes			
Lesson	34	Compound Words and Hyphenates			
Lesson	35	Hurdle Words			
Lesson	36	Instant Replay	■		■

Lesson	6	12	18	24	30	36
Standardized Instant Replay Test						